# A PLURALIST THEORY OF AGE DISCRIMINATION

This book provides a comprehensive theory of age discrimination that can guide the direct and indirect age discrimination provisions of the Equality Act 2010. The Act holds that unequal treatment on the grounds of age, and measures that are on their face age-neutral but have the effect of disadvantaging particular age groups, are lawful only if the treatment can be shown either to be a 'proportionate means of achieving a legitimate aim' or if the treatment fits into a specifically prescribed exception. In this way, the proportionality test distinguishes justified and unjustified age-differential treatment with only the former legally permissible.

This book outlines and defends a pluralist theory of age discrimination that assists in making the distinction between justified and unjustified age-differential treatment. The theory identifies the principles that explain when and why age-differential treatment wrongs people and the principles that can justify this treatment. It is a pluralist theory because it recognises that age-differential treatment can wrong people for a number of different, overlapping reasons, and these different reasons should inform how we apply age discrimination law. The pluralist approach to age discrimination theory can improve legal reasoning in age discrimination cases by articulating the relevant principles and competing interests that are at stake in age discrimination claims.

In constructing the theory, the book adopts the reflective equilibrium method. This requires that we examine our initial moral beliefs about age discrimination by seeking coherence with beliefs we have about similar moral and philosophical issues and revising the initial beliefs as a result of challenges to them. In applying this method, the book identifies the following five principles to form a pluralist theory of age discrimination: equality of opportunity, social equality, respect, autonomy and efficiency.

# A Pluralist Theory of Age Discrimination

Stuart Goosey

•HART•
OXFORD • LONDON • NEW YORK • NEW DELHI • SYDNEY

HART PUBLISHING

Bloomsbury Publishing Plc

Kemp House, Chawley Park, Cumnor Hill, Oxford, OX2 9PH, UK

1385 Broadway, New York, NY 10018, USA



First published in Great Britain 2020



A catalogue record for this book is available from the British Library.

Library of Congress Cataloging-in-Publication data

Names: Goosey, Stuart, author.

Title: A pluralist theory of age discrimination / Stuart Goosey.

Description: Oxford, UK ; New York, NY : Hart Publishing, an imprint of Bloomsbury Publishing, 2020. | Includes bibliographical references and index.

Identifiers: LCCN 2020038507 (print) | LCCN 2020038508 (ebook) | ISBN 9781509933761 (hardback) | ISBN 9781509944071 (paperback) | ISBN 9781509933778 (Epub) | ISBN 9781509933785 (pdf)

Subjects: LCSH: Age discrimination—Law and legislation. | Equality before the law. | Ageism.

Classification: LCC K3242 .G66 2020 (print) | LCC K3242 (ebook) | DDC 342.08/77—dc23

LC record available at https://lccn.loc.gov/2020038507

LC ebook record available at https://lccn.loc.gov/2020038508

ISBN: HB: 978-1-50993-376-1
ePDF: 978-1-50993-378-5
ePub: 978-1-50993-377-8

Typeset by Compuscript Ltd, Shannon

# ACKNOWLEDGEMENTS

This book develops and revises my PhD manuscript. I would like to thank Lizzie Barmes, Kate Malleson and Richard Ashcroft for their advice, guidance and support in supervising my PhD project. I would also like to thank my PhD examiners, Jo Wolff and Colm O'Cinneide, for their detailed and thoughtful comments on the manuscript. This book responds to their comments, and, consequently, this book's argument is more thorough and robust than the original PhD manuscript.

I developed the idea for a research project on age discrimination law after attending Sandra Fredman and Tarunabh Khaitan's seminars on comparative equality law at the University of Oxford, which included discussions on why people tend to have different moral intuitions about the wrongness of age discrimination vis-à-vis race discrimination and sex discrimination.

I also offer special thanks to Aaron Baker, who, after meeting me for the first time at Durham Law School, read my PhD manuscript and encouraged me to submit a book proposal on the topic to Hart Publishing. Thanks to the Durham Law School students who participated in my seminars on age discrimination law, where many of the ideas in this book were discussed and debated.

My good friend, Samuel Brewer, and my partner, Danyu Tong, have offered a great deal of support to me, including offering encouragement and engaging in discussions on this book's themes.

Finally, thanks to London North Eastern Railway. I had written much of this book in the 'quiet' carriages of their trains and I used their free Wi-Fi to conduct research for this book.

Chapters five and seven of this book contain material from my earlier publication 'Is Age Discrimination a Less Serious Form of Discrimination' (2019) 39 *Legal Studies* 533. This material is reprinted with permission from © Cambridge University Press.

# CONTENTS

# TABLE OF CASES

**United Kingdom**

**United States**

# TABLE OF LEGISLATION

# 1

# Introduction

The economic and social issues raised by age and ageing have become increasingly prominent in the UK. As the UK faces an ageing population, there is much debate and concern about what impact this will have on welfare costs, economic growth and opportunities for the young.[1] This has led to questions about how to fairly distribute resources across different generations.[2] At the same time, the gradual incorporation of anti-discrimination policies into mainstream political discourse has led policymakers to grapple with the question of age discrimination.

Legal interventions concerning age were once generally limited to setting minimum age limits for activities such as marriage, leaving education, paid employment, consuming alcohol and driving, and for establishing rules concerning retirement. However, increasingly there is a recognition that the law should engage with promoting fairness between age groups, most recently in the Equality Act 2010, which prohibits age discrimination in access to employment, training and education; membership of associations and clubs; and provision of goods and services.[3]

Despite this legal intervention, there is relatively little commentary on the rationales for age discrimination law, and much of the literature on the topic is dismissive of age discrimination as a problem requiring a legal solution.[4]

Applying age discrimination laws, however, requires careful thought about when and why age-differential treatment is wrong and when and why it is justified. This is because the Equality Act 2010 provides that age-differential treatment is subject to a proportionality test, which provides that less favourable treatment on the grounds of age (which engages the direct age discrimination provisions) and measures that are age-neutral but have the effect of disadvantaging particular

[1] D Bloom, D Canning and G Fink, 'Implications of Population Ageing for Economic Growth' (2010) 26 *Oxford Review of Economic Policy* 583.

[2] See D Willetts, *The Pinch: How the Baby Boomers Took Their Children's Future-and Why They Should Give it Back* (Atlantic Books, 2011).

[3] Equality Act 2010, pts 3, 6 and 7.

[4] R Posner, *Aging and Old Age* (University of Chicago Press, 1995) 204 argued that age discrimination is not a real problem and that the concept only exists in the minds of 'some radical egalitarians' who 'see discrimination everywhere'. For an argument that age discrimination should not be banned because it does not reach the level of seriousness of race or sex discrimination, see S Issacharoff and EW Harris, 'Is Age Discrimination Really Age Discrimination: The ADEA's Unnatural Solution' (1997) 72 *New York University Law Review* 780.

age groups (which engages the indirect age discrimination provisions) are justified and lawful only if the treatment is a 'proportionate means of achieving a legitimate aim'[5] or if the treatment fits into a specifically prescribed exception to the prohibition on age-differential treatment.[6]

Measures are only proportionate when they pursue a legitimate aim, are necessary to achieve that aim and do not impose burdens or cause harms to other legitimate interests that outweigh the objectives achieved.[7] This proportionality assessment requires courts and tribunals (and anyone else seeking to determine the lawfulness of treatment subject to the proportionality test) to engage with and choose between competing moral interests and principles at stake.[8] In other words, the proportionality test distinguishes between justified age-differential treatment, which is lawful, from unjustified age-differential treatment, which is unlawful. To make this distinction, courts and tribunals should engage with theoretical questions about the principles that determine when it is unjustified to treat people less favourably on the grounds of age and when it is unjustified to disadvantage particular age groups.

The aim of this book is to construct a comprehensive theory of age discrimination that can support this process. This theory consists of a framework of principles that assist in determining whether an impugned measure pursues a legitimate aim and whether such a measure adopts an appropriate balance between the competing interests at stake. I construct this theory of age discrimination by outlining substantive anti-discrimination and equality principles that both fit and justify our moral intuitions about different forms of discrimination and inequality. I then verify the extent to which these principles explain age discrimination and, in doing so, form a theory of age discrimination that can distinguish justified from unjustified age-differential treatment. This book has both a theoretical and a legal purpose. It aims to clarify age discrimination as a moral problem and to use this work to create a moral framework that can assist in applying age discrimination law.

I argue that in applying this theory of age discrimination, courts and tribunals should also be aware of the need to follow legal precedent and to show deference to the original decision-maker where the original decision-maker is better placed to determine proportionality.[9]

[5] Equality Act 2010, ss 13 and 19 hold that impugned treatment does not constitute unlawful age discrimination if the treatment is a 'proportionate means of achieving a legitimate aim'.

[6] Notable exceptions include measures that constitute occupational requirements (Equality Act 2010, sch 9, pt 1) and measures that aim at alleviating disadvantage for particular age groups (Equality Act 2010, ss 158 and 159). Chapter 2 details a large number of other exceptions.

[7] In *Seldon v Clarkson, Wright and Jakes* [2012] UKSC 16, [2012] ICR 716 [50], the Supreme Court held this is the appropriate test for proportionality assessments in age discrimination cases.

[8] Chapter 2 defends this argument in detail.

[9] Chapter 7 details why and when it is appropriate for the courts and tribunals to defer to the original decision-maker.

# I. Age as a Protected Characteristic

The Equality Act 2010 prohibits discrimination on the grounds of nine protected characteristics: age; disability; gender reassignment; marriage and civil partnership; pregnancy and maternity; race; religion or belief; sex; and sexual orientation.[10] This book focuses on one of the nine, age. There are a number of reasons for this focus. First, age discrimination is an under-theorised area. There is detailed theoretical work on discrimination law in the literature,[11] but relatively little application of these ideas to the topic of age discrimination.[12] There is an important opportunity to consider the extensive philosophical literature on the morality of discrimination and to determine the implications this has for applying age discrimination laws. The UK case law has not to date provided a rigorous account of the morality of age discrimination when applying age discrimination laws, which furthers the importance of this book's project.[13]

Secondly, there is increasing political focus on the fairest way to balance the interests of different age groups, including the recent establishment of political think tanks focused on intergenerational fairness[14] and increasing focus of parliamentary debates and reports on the topic,[15] and therefore there is an important opportunity for this book to make a significant contribution to this debate by offering a principled framework for balancing the interests at stake in age and ageing issues.

Thirdly, it is important to focus on age as a protected characteristic because the age provisions of the Equality Act 2010 have a different legal framework to the provisions relating to other protected characteristics, which requires that we focus on age discrimination as a separate topic. For example, the Equality Act 2010 provides that direct age-differential treatment is lawful and justified when it is a 'proportionate means of achieving a legitimate aim' while unequal treatment on the grounds of other protected characteristics, including race and sex, is lawful in much more restricted circumstances,[16] including when the treatment is a genuine occupational requirement or if the treatment fits in the positive action criteria.[17] These different legal frameworks imply that something is different about age that warrants this different legal structure. The theory of age discrimination outlined

[10] Equality Act 2010, s 4.

[11] Notable examples include T Khaitan, *A Theory of Discrimination Law* (Oxford University Press, 2015); I Solanke, *Discrimination as Stigma: A Theory of Anti-Discrimination Law* (Bloomsbury, 2017).

[12] A prominent work on the morality of age discrimination is M Sargeant, *Age Discrimination in Employment* (Routledge, 2016).

[13] This is illustrated in ch 2 of this book.

[14] Examples include the Intergenerational Foundation and the work on intergenerational fairness by the Resolution Foundation.

[15] See Intergenerational Fairness and Provision Committee, *Tackling Intergenerational Unfairness* (HL 2017–19, 329).

[16] Equality Act 2010, ss 13 and 19.

[17] Equality Act 2010, sch 9, ss 158 and 159.

in this book has an important role to verify whether and, if so, why age discrimination is different, and to explain the impact this should have for applying age discrimination law.[18]

## II. The Value of a Theory of Age Discrimination

There are a number of benefits to constructing a theory of discrimination to guide age discrimination law. Most notably, it can improve legal reasoning in age discrimination disputes by articulating the relevant principles and competing interests at stake. Without a comprehensive theory of age discrimination, it is easy for courts and tribunals to overlook important moral considerations or to make assumptions about other forms of discrimination and apply those assumptions to age issues.

A theory of age discrimination can ensure courts and tribunals have a greater grasp of the moral issues of age discrimination by offering a framework to approach these issues. Age discrimination is morally complex. There are many age issues that provoke controversial and difficult moral dilemmas. For example, there are questions about whether it is it justified to help the disadvantaged young if this means diverting resources away from older people; questions about when is it justified to use age distinctions to further business interests; or questions relating to distribution of healthcare, for example, whether the state should use age to distribute healthcare if this is more efficient than other methods. It is difficult to find satisfactory answers to these dilemmas without a theory of age discrimination. Furthermore, it is improbable that a court or tribunal will be able to consider all the interests and moral requirements at stake without some guidance.

The pluralist theory of age discrimination also provides for greater transparency in legal judgments by requiring courts and tribunals to articulate all the relevant principles that are at stake in a case and to require courts and tribunals to make judgments founded on sound principles. This enhances accountability by ensuring that it is possible to criticise the legal reasoning.[19] As I explain in chapter two, the courts and tribunals have been approaching age discrimination cases without a comprehensive theory of age discrimination, and therefore the reasons and principles for deciding cases have remained opaque and difficult to critique.[20]

The pluralist theory of age discrimination can also help non-lawyers determine whether measures are justified and therefore lawful. For example, employers can use the theory to consider whether their recruitment practices and redundancy policies can be justified. In addition, employees can use the theory to help determine whether their employer's actions are justified and lawful.

[18] See S Goosey, 'Is Age Discrimination a Less Serious Form of Discrimination?' (2019) 39 *Legal Studies* 533.

[19] For an account of the value of judicial accountability, see D Shapiro, 'In Defense of Judicial Candor' (1987) 100 *Harvard Law Review* 731.

[20] Chapter 2 of this book details the opaqueness of the reasoning in the age discrimination case law.

Furthermore, the theory of age discrimination can enhance the legitimacy of age discrimination law by ensuring that courts and tribunals can apply the law in a way that is sensitive to principles of justice.[21] Law is inherently an act of coercion. To have moral legitimacy, the law must justify this coercion. We can promote the legitimacy of the law by ensuring that those enforcing the law are guided by principles that justify reasons for having the law in question. The pluralist theory of age discrimination can do this by directing courts and tribunals to apply age discrimination law in a way that supports the point of having age discrimination law.[22]

## III. Rejecting Unitary Theories of Discrimination

In constructing a theory capable of guiding age discrimination law, we must identify the justifying aims of this law. In other words, we must identify when and why discrimination wrongs people and the principles that explain how the law can address these wrongs.

Academics have argued for various principles that explain the justifying reasons for discrimination law.[23] A common approach has been to provide a norm that can work to explain all the reasons why we have such a law. There is no consensus, however, on which norm should prevail as a foundation of discrimination law and some theorists have doubted that a single norm can provide a complete explanation.[24]

The literature on the subject has advanced a number of principles, including equality, autonomy and respect, that individually provide a foundation for explaining how and why discrimination wrongs people and therefore can explain the justifying purpose of discrimination law. On the equality account, for example, Segall has argued that discrimination wrongs people when it places the discriminatee at a disadvantage because of a trait that a person should not be held responsible for.[25] Discrimination law, on this account, has a justifying aim of promoting equality of opportunity. Another account holds that discrimination is wrong when it

[21] M Daneker, 'Moral Reasoning and the Quest for Legitimacy' (1993) 4 *American University Law Review* 49.

[22] The theory of discrimination operates in a similar way to Ronald Dworkin's theory of adjudication: see R Dworkin, *Taking Rights Seriously* (Harvard University Press, 1977). At 165, Dworkin argued that 'judges should decide hard cases by interpreting the political structure of their community in the following, perhaps special way: by trying to find the best justification they can find, in principles of political morality, for the structure as a whole, from the most profound constitutional rules and arrangements to the details of, for example, the private law of tort or contract'. To ensure the legitimacy of age discrimination law, judges should postulate a principled purpose or point to the legislation in deciding cases.

[23] See Khaitan (n 11) and Solanke (n 11).

[24] For a detailed argument that there is no single foundation for discrimination law, see P Shin, 'Is There a Unitary Concept of Discrimination?' in D Hellman and S Moreau (eds), *Philosophical Foundations of Discrimination Law* (Oxford University Press, 2013).

[25] S Segall, 'What's So Bad about Discrimination?' (2012) 24 *Utilitas* 82.

has the effect of harming the capacity of people to live autonomous lives. Khaitan, for example, has argued that discrimination law is primarily concerned not with equality, but with attempting to create valuable opportunities for disadvantaged social groups.[26] The respect account holds that discrimination is wrong when it demeans people. Discrimination demeans when it has the effect of conveying that certain people have a diminished social and moral worth.[27]

These accounts each provide insight into the wrong of discrimination, but, as I demonstrate in chapter four, no single principle can explain every case of wrongful discrimination in the remit of discrimination law. Some forms of wrongful discrimination do not create inequality of opportunity, some forms do not harm autonomy and some forms do not disrespect people. Instead, we should adopt a pluralist account of age discrimination that accepts that there are a number of different, sometimes conflicting, principles that must be used together to explain the concept.[28]

## IV. Towards a Pluralist Theory of Age Discrimination

I present five principles in this book that distinguish justified from unjustified age-differential treatment. These principles can assist in determining the proportionality of measures that engage the direct and indirect age discrimination provisions. I arrive at these five substantive principles by identifying the different ways discrimination wrongs people and apply these principles to age discrimination to determine whether they provide a comprehensive account of age discrimination. This pluralist account, I argue, is necessary to capture the complexity and richness of age discrimination as a concept and to explain our intuitions about different forms of age discrimination.

The principles of my theory of age discrimination include equality of opportunity, social equality, respect, autonomy and efficiency. Equality of opportunity requires an equal distribution of benefits and burdens over a complete life except insofar as an individual is personally responsible for their unequal position.[29] This principle can justify some forms of age-based distinctions. Age distinctions promote equality of opportunity when they are stable over time and apply

[26] Khaitan (n 11).

[27] See D Hellman, *When Is Discrimination Wrong?* (Harvard University Press, 2008).

[28] For notable pluralist accounts of the wrong of discrimination, see R Segev, 'Making Sense of Discrimination' (2014) 27 *Ratio Juris* 47; Shin (n 24); S Fredman, *Discrimination Law*, 2nd edn (Oxford University Press, 2011).

[29] This equality of opportunity principle reflects luck egalitarianism, including Dworkin's theory that people should begin with equal resources but can end up with unequal economic benefits because of personal choices. R Dworkin, 'What is Equality? Part 1: Equality of Resources' (1981) 10 *Philosophy and Public Affairs* 185; R Dworkin, 'What is Equality? Part 2: Equality of Welfare' (1981) 10 *Philosophy and Public Affairs* 283.

uniformly to all people as they reach the age subject to the age-based distinction. For example, policies such as flu vaccines for people over 65 years of age ensures that each person will benefit from the resource provided they live to 65 years of age.

Social equality requires individuals to be capable of participating equally in social, economic and political life.[30] Less favourable treatment on the grounds of age and age-neutral measures that disadvantage particular age groups can violate social equality by creating conditions that undermine individuals' status as equals in society. An example I discuss is a mandatory retirement age that can lock older people out of the labour market. Social equality can also justify some age distinctions, including positive action that aims to promote social inclusion of disadvantaged age groups.

The principle of autonomy requires conditions where people have control over their lives.[31] Age discrimination can undermine autonomy by diminishing choice over a person's lifetime. An example is older people internalising the message that they are less useful and productive than other age groups and must leave the labour force when they may prefer to carry on. The principle of respect recognises the harm of denying access to goods when that denial expresses that some age groups are less entitled to proper treatment.[32] On this account, age-differential treatment can harm people by communicating the message that particular age groups have a diminished moral or social worth. The principle of efficiency explains that it is possible to justify age-differential treatment if the treatment efficiently promotes valuable social goods.[33] Age distinctions can be efficient because age can be an accurate proxy for some attributes. Using age as a proxy for these traits is less costly than assessing each person individually for them. Age distinctions can also be efficient by forcing people to sequence and order their lives chronologically. This can force people to undertake tasks at a time of life when there is the greatest benefit to the individual and wider society.

These principles should figure in the different stages of the proportionality test to determine whether a measure furthers a legitimate aim, is necessary to achieve that aim and does not impose burdens or cause harms to other legitimate interests that outweigh the aims achieved. Importantly, however, I argue that courts and tribunals should apply the pluralist theory of age discrimination alongside considerations about whether judges are in an appropriate position to substitute their view on the morality of the action for that of the original decision-maker. In other words, I argue that judges must consider both substantive reasons for deciding a case (and this includes the moral principles of the pluralist theory of age

[30] D Miller, 'What Kind of Equality Should the Left Pursue?' in J Franklin (ed), *Equality* (Institute for Public Policy Research, 1997) 83.

[31] J Gardner, 'On the Ground of Her Sex(uality)' (1998) 18 *OJLS* 167.

[32] B Eidelson, *Discrimination and Disrespect* (Oxford University Press, 2015).

[33] A Gosseries, 'What Makes Age Discrimination Special? A Philosophical Look at the ECJ Case Law' (2014) 43 *Netherlands Journal of Legal Philosophy* 59.

discrimination) and the appropriateness of applying this reasoning to decide a case given any possible institutional limitations of the judicial process.[34] Deference can be appropriate at the necessity stage and the final balancing stage of the proportionality test. The court or tribunal must make a judgment concerning whether the original decision-maker has more expertise to determine whether a measure is necessary to achieve a legitimate aim and whether the original decision-maker is in a better position to weigh up competing interests in a justifiable way. If the courts or tribunals have reason to think that a party to the case is more likely to get these considerations right, then there is a strong reason to defer to that party.[35]

The level of deference depends on the severity of a violation of the interests of the person subject to the impugned treatment. For example, the greater a measure contributes to oppressive relations, expresses contempt or violates autonomy, the greater the need to scrutinise the decision-maker's treatment. This means that institutional questions about the extent judges should defer to the primary decision-maker depend in part on the extent of harm against an individual's interests. Where the extent of violation of interests is low, then institutional considerations and deference towards the primary decision-maker should play a more prominent role. But when there is a clear and substantial violation of an individual's equality interests (say, by the measure negatively stereotyping a person), this may outweigh concerns about institutional limitations of the judicial process. In such situations, the balance may favour judicial intervention and intense scrutiny of the measures on the substantive principles.

Importantly, judges should decide consistently with previous cases that have relevantly similar facts. This has implications for applying the pluralist theory of discrimination. Precedent might conflict with the framework of principles I defend in this book. In these circumstances, it follows from the purpose of my book (which is concerned with recommending an appropriate method of applying age discrimination law) that I recommend the framework of principles should prevail in circumstances where courts are capable of overturning precedent.

## V. The Scope of this Book

The principles identified in this book work in relation to the full scope of the direct and indirect age discrimination provisions, including those relating to employment, training and education; membership of associations and clubs; and provision of goods and services. This book, however, does not concern the harassment and victimisation provisions of the Equality Act 2010. Harassment and victimisation

[34] For the argument that judges should consider both the substantive reasons for a decision and the institutional limitations of the judicial process, see A Kavanagh, 'Judicial Restraint in the Pursuit of Justice' (2010) 60 *University of Toronto law Journal* 23.

[35] Chapter 7 details the appropriate deference factors.

are different concepts from direct and indirect age discrimination, and are not the focus of my inquiry.[36]

This book relates to the legal concept of discrimination provided in the Equality Act 2010 rather than the colloquial understanding of the term. This is because the book offers a theory that should guide age discrimination law rather than constituting a theoretical work on the concept of discrimination. In ordinary language, discrimination relates to the intentional and wrongful use of a trait to impose a disadvantage, for example, racism.[37] The legal concept of discrimination, in contrast, includes conduct that does not reflect an intention to disadvantage or cause harm to others. It includes actions that are age-neutral that have the effect of disadvantaging people of a particular chronological age.[38] The discrimination concept in the Equality Act 2010, therefore, is not directly related to fault. As a result, the Act labels as discrimination a much wider range of actions than the colloquial understanding of discrimination. I focus my analysis on core elements of UK age discrimination law rather than trying to capture a universal concept of discrimination.[39]

Furthermore, this book does not concern whether or not age discrimination is an area in which the law should intervene, even though it is a vital question. Instead, this work starts from the assumption that the law, for better or worse, will continue to play a part in regulating social and economic relations around age and that legal intervention in this area is likely to increase. If it does, we need to base that legal intervention on a sound moral framework. The aim of this work is to contribute to this project.

Although the book relates to UK discrimination law, the arguments and conclusions made are likely to have relevance in other jurisdictions.[40] Age discrimination law varies between jurisdictions, but many states have age discrimination laws similar to that of the UK and similar justifying aims, including the EU Member States, South Africa, Canada and the USA. EU Member States, for example, are each required to have age discrimination laws in accordance with the Employment Equality Framework Directive 200/78/EC (Framework Directive). States that have

[36] Nonetheless, the pluralist theory of age discrimination might cover moral principles that can work for the harassment and victimisation provisions, although this would need independent verification. The Equality Act 2010 defines harassment as 'unwanted conduct related to a relevant protected characteristic' which 'has the purpose or effect of violating [the victim's] dignity, or creating an intimidating, hostile, degrading, humiliating or offensive environment for [the victim]'. The principle of respect – which holds that a wrong occurs when someone engages in demeaning conduct towards others – is likely to be useful for illuminating when an action creates an 'intimidating, hostile, degrading, humiliating or offensive environment'.

[37] For a discussion of the different meanings of discrimination, see A Altman, 'Discrimination' in E Zalta (ed), *The Stanford Encyclopedia of Philosophy*, Winter 2016 edn https://plato.stanford.edu/archives/win2016/entries/discrimination/.

[38] Equality Act 2010, s 19.

[39] For an explanation of the meaning of discrimination as a concept see ch 1 of Eidelson (n 32).

[40] I discuss this in more detail in the conclusion to this book.

age discrimination laws also tend to share certain normative assumptions, for example, a commitment to equality. Given the similar aims and normative foundations of age discrimination laws in a range of jurisdictions, the pluralist theory of age discrimination may (although probably subject to adaptation) work as a guide in these states.

Although this book concerns UK discrimination law, it cannot be isolated from EU law. EU law obligates the UK to implement age discrimination laws to further the aims of the Framework Directive. While the UK remains a member of the EU, decisions of the CJEU are binding on the UK courts to ensure that the UK does not undermine the aims of the Framework Directive. However, the UK national courts will not be under an obligation to follow the case law of the CJEU that is decided after the UK leaves the EU.[41]

This book outlines key CJEU and UK case law that illustrates key features of the age discrimination duties under EU and UK law but focuses on five UK age discrimination cases to illustrate the difference a theory of age discrimination can make to deciding age discrimination cases. These cases cover retirement ages,[42] redundancy pay,[43] cost savings as a reason for age-differential treatment,[44] direct age discrimination[45] and indirect age discrimination.[46] The decision to focus on a relatively small number of cases is to allow for an in-depth analysis and a clear communication of the philosophical ideas on age discrimination developed in this book. An outline and critique of a large number of cases across the EU and UK, I had considered, would complicate the presentation of the ideas and shift the focus of this book to a more doctrinal work rather than the philosophical work I intend the book to be. There is published work with overviews of the development of the CJEU case law on age discrimination, so I do not aim to replicate this detail here.[47]

## VI. Possible Objections to Courts and Tribunals Using a Theory of Age Discrimination in Adjudication

This book argues that courts and tribunals should engage in moral reasoning about age discrimination by weighing and choosing between different interests and moral considerations to decide age discrimination cases. Some may object

[41] Chapter 2 details the possible implications of the UK's exit from the EU on age discrimination law.

[42] *Seldon v Clarkson, Wright and Jakes* [2012] UKSC 16, [2012] ICR 716.

[43] *Lockwood v Department of Work & Pensions & Anor* [2013] EWCA Civ 1195, [2014] 1 All ER 250.

[44] *Woodcock v Cumbria Primary Care Trust* [2012].

[45] *Seldon v Clarkson, Wright and Jakes* [2012] UKSC 16, [2012] ICR 716.

[46] *Homer v Chief Constable of West Yorkshire Police* [2012] UKSC 15, [2012] ICR 704.

[47] For an overview of the CJEU jurisprudence on age discrimination, see C O'Cinneide, 'Age Discrimination and the European Court of Justice: EU Equality Law Comes of Age' (2009) 2 *Revue des affaires europeennes* 253.

to this argument. For example, Richard Posner argues that moral reasoning is something judges, for the most part, should eschew.[48] Posner attacks moralising in legal judgments because judges are not moral philosophers. Judges, Posner argues, should be willing to defer to democratic institutions on moral questions.

In reply to Posner, democratic institutions can and do pass legislation that can direct judges to engage in moral reasoning. This means legislation gives judges the responsibility and legitimacy to engage directly with moral problems. For example, I argue in this book that the Equality Act 2010 directs judges to engage in moral reasoning by requiring them to assess whether impugned measures are a proportionate means of achieving a legitimate aim. One of the features of the proportionality test is that it directs judges to assess the weights of the competing principles.[49] When courts and tribunals must decide whether age distinctions or measures causing disadvantage to certain age groups are justified under the Equality Act 2010, they must consider what equality requires and whether the requirements of equality trump other values that may be advanced by the measures.

A further objection to judges engaging with moral reasoning is the argument that they are not free to do so because the doctrine of precedent requires that they defer to findings in cases with similar facts. However, this process still constitutes moral reasoning because judging relative similarity is also a moral judgement.[50] For example, to compare and contrast cases requires finding principles to determine whether cases are in fact morally alike. And applying precedent is to defer to the moral reasoning of another court in undertaking the proportionality assessment.

Even taking a legal positivist stance (the position that rejects any dependence of the existence of law on its merits),[51] we can still accept that the law can, in certain instances, like the age discrimination provisions of the Equality Act 2010, direct courts and tribunals to switch to a role of making moral judgements to determine legality.[52] When a law instructs judges to reason morally, the courts and tribunals have a legal duty to do so. The Equality Act 2010 is a statute that determines legal validity by moral criteria by directing courts and tribunals to consider a range of moral questions (eg do the measures pursue a legitimate aim? Is it necessary to achieve that aim? Does the measure impose burdens or cause harms to other legitimate interests that outweigh the aims achieved?).

[48] R Posner, *The Problematics of Moral and Legal Theory* (Harvard University Press, 2009).

[49] K Möller, 'Proportionality: Challenging the Critics' (2012) 10 *International Journal of Constitutional Law* 709.

[50] J Waldron, 'Judges as Moral Reasoners' (2009) 7 *International Journal of Constitutional Law* 2.

[51] J Gardner, 'Legal Positivism: 5 ½ Myths' (2001) 46 *American Journal of Jurisprudence* 199.

[52] HLA Hart has argued that 'The law of every modern state shows at a thousand points the influence of both the accepted social morality and wider social ideals … In some systems, as in the United States, the ultimate criteria of legal validity explicitly incorporate principles of justice or substantive moral values': HLA Hart, *The Concept of Law*, 2nd edn (Clarendon Press, 1994) 203–04.

# VII. The Reflective Equilibrium Method

To construct a theory of age discrimination capable of guiding age discrimination law, I adopt the reflective equilibrium method.[53] Reflective equilibrium is a method that requires that we start from our intuitions about the morality of a situation and, on reflecting on the plausibility of the intuitions in light of other beliefs that we hold, are open to revising those beliefs. The reflection process requires taking everything relevant into account about age discrimination (all the principles that can explain why it is a moral problem and all the theories relating to the phenomena of age and ageing) and seeks to form a set of beliefs that are coherent and stable.[54] This method tests the plausibility of moral principles by evaluating whether the principles fit and explain our moral judgements.

There are two major versions of reflective equilibrium: narrow reflective equilibrium and wide reflective equilibrium. I argue that narrow reflective equilibrium is a good starting point for ensuring our beliefs are coherent, but it is too limited to provide justification for using particular principles. Instead, I adopt a 'wide' version of reflective equilibrium, which, in addition to building coherence between moral beliefs, provides justification for principles by requiring that those beliefs are consistent with background theories – for example, theories of the nature of age and ageing.

## A. Narrow Reflective Equilibrium

Reflective equilibrium starts with moral intuitions about a scenario.[55] The next stage is to find principles that can account for the intuitions. The third stage is to reach narrow reflective equilibrium by seeking coherence between the set of moral beliefs we hold and the principles that account for those judgements. If we find principles conflict with our moral judgements, then we should try to create coherence by revising either the principles or the moral beliefs until we have a coherent set of beliefs and principles.

[53] John Rawls uses the reflective equilibrium method in his theory of justice. For principles of justice to be justified, Rawls has argued that they must cohere with our considered judgements in reflective equilibrium. Principles of justice, according to Rawls, should be determined by what we will agree upon in a hypothetical social contract where we agree on principles without knowledge of our social position. These principles in the social contract, however, must be in reflective equilibrium with the rest of our beliefs about justice. J Rawls, *A Theory of Justice* (Harvard University Press, 2009).

[54] Norman Daniels offers the most detailed account of the reflective equilibrium method. See N Daniels, 'Wide Reflective Equilibrium and Theory Acceptance in Ethics' (1979) 76 *Journal of Philosophy* 256.

[55] Intuition are moral beliefs formed before any reflection on whether those beliefs are true or false. J Pust, 'Intuition' in E Zalta (ed), *The Stanford Encyclopedia of Philosophy*, Spring 2016 edn https://plato.stanford.edu/archives/spr2016/entries/intuition/.

## B. An Example of Narrow Reflective Equilibrium

We can start with the moral intuition that it is wrong to deny a person a job because of their race. The next step is to provide a moral principle to explain this intuition – for example, the principle that it is wrong to deny opportunities because of immutable traits. At first, we may believe this to be an appropriate principle to explain the wrongness of race discrimination, since race is an immutable trait.[56] But on testing this principle against our other moral intuitions, we will find that it fails to account for our beliefs regarding discrimination. It is often justifiable to treat people differently because of immutable traits.[57] For example, we would consider it justifiable to deny a blind person a driver's licence. Additionally, many forms of wrongful discrimination concern mutable traits, for example, discrimination on the grounds of religion.

To find equilibrium, we may start to consider the quality of traits that we believe can be the subject of wrongful discrimination. We may consider that there has been a historical practice of discriminating against race as a way to signify that some people have a diminished moral status. As a result, race discrimination may have taken on the meaning of an expression of the inferiority of particular groups. We could suggest a further moral principle, namely that discrimination manifests an attitude that members of certain races are morally inferior to members of other races.[58] Then we can move on to see if this principle coheres with our other intuitions about discrimination. We keep doing this until we have a stable set of principles and then we have reached a narrow reflective equilibrium.

## C. Wide Reflective Equilibrium

The problem for narrow reflective equilibrium is that people may start with different moral intuitions and therefore find after the reflective equilibrium process that they have reached different results from others. From the narrow reflective equilibrium approach, there would be no way to determine which person has reached the correct judgement.[59] To overcome this problem, we should adopt a wider version of reflective equilibrium.

Wide reflective equilibrium requires that we consider anything that might have an impact on our moral beliefs, and requires adjusting our beliefs to cohere with

[56] Note, however, that there is a consensus among scientists that we can only explain race classification by culture, not biology. It may, therefore, be inaccurate to describe race as immutable. For example, people with a white mother and a black father would be labelled coloured in apartheid South Africa but would be labelled black in the USA. Race is not always a fixed characteristic.

[57] B Boxill, *Blacks and Social Justice*, revised edn (Rowman & Littlefield, 1992) 12–17.

[58] This principle reflects Deborah Hellman's theory of discrimination in *When is Discrimination Wrong?* (n 27).

[59] R Brandt, 'The Science of Man and Wide Reflective Equilibrium' (1990) 100 *Ethics* 259 argued that constructing a coherent set of beliefs does not mean that these beliefs are justified. Coherent fictions, he argues, are still fictions.

factual issues and background theories, including theories about personhood and the nature of morality.[60] The importance of adopting wide reflective equilibrium is that the adoption of a plausible background theory may force us to revise our initial moral judgements. For example, to determine the morality of abortion, we must consider not only our immediate intuitions and their coherence to other beliefs we hold, but also the background theory of personhood. Since persons have the right to life, we need to consider if a foetus constitutes a person. If we understand that personhood requires sentience, then abortion is permissible in the early stages of pregnancy when a foetus does not have sentience and therefore lacks the right to life generated by personhood. In this way, the background theory of personhood generates a philosophical argument that supports moral principles that are in coherence with our moral judgements, and this, in turn, should increase the support for the moral conclusion that abortion in the early stages of pregnancy is morally justified.

To construct a theory of age discrimination, we need a background theory on the meaning of age in society. We can construct such a theory by looking at the science concerning ageing and the meaning of age in society. This empirical data can provide important facts that are relevant in forming moral judgements.[61]

A background theory of age may force us to revise our beliefs about the wrongness of age discrimination.[62] Norman Daniels gives the example of an initial moral judgement that age distinctions in healthcare are wrong because they create inequality in accessing valuable resources.[63] Daniels then highlights that a background theory of age reveals that we all gradually age and this can lead to the realisation that age distinctions in healthcare do not create inequality in access if we apply age distinctions over complete lifespans. Age distinctions favouring older people will lead to a detriment for young people, but as young people age they will benefit from the age distinction. This forces us to discard the moral principle that age distinctions in healthcare are wrong because they lead to inequality in access to resources.

## D. Reasons for Adopting the Wide Reflective Equilibrium Method

I adopt the wide reflective equilibrium method in constructing a theory of age discrimination because it is the method best directed to providing answers to moral questions. This is because alternative methods must either

> abandon reflection entirely, direct the inquirer to reflect, but to do so incompletely (that is, to leave certain beliefs, principles, theories, or what have you out of account), or

[60] Daniels (n 54) developed this wide version of reflective equilibrium in response to the criticisms of narrow reflective equilibrium.

[61] Chapter 5 of this book formulates a background theory of age and ageing to find a wide reflective equilibrium.

[62] Daniels (n 54).

[63] Norman Daniels, 'Reflective Equilibrium' in E Zalta (ed), *The Stanford Encyclopedia of Philosophy*, Fall 2018 edn http://plato. stanford. edu/archives/sum2003/entries/reflective-equilibrium.

not allow the results of the inquirer's reflections to determine what the inquirer goes on to believe.[64]

Wide reflective equilibrium, in contrast, subjects moral beliefs to detailed reflection and ensures coherence with background theories.

Wide reflective equilibrium can also increase the credibility of our moral beliefs by incorporating the intuitions of other thinkers. For example, Ghislaine van Thiel offers a version of reflective equilibrium that requires reflecting upon the beliefs of people who work within a moral practice and who, therefore, possess a specific form of moral wisdom gained from working in that practice.[65] For example, in constructing a theory of age discrimination, we should consider and reflect on the moral beliefs of people who have experience working on issues relating to age discrimination. If we incorporate their moral intuitions into our moral reasoning, we are more likely to arrive at judgements that grasp their moral experience and therefore reach the right answers to problems.

I adopt this approach by considering the moral beliefs of people in the practice of thinking and suggesting solutions to age discrimination. For example, in chapters three, four and five, I reflect on the moral judgements of academics on equality and discrimination. In chapter six, I consider the moral beliefs of governments that have been responsible for introducing age discrimination law. In chapter seven, I consider the moral beliefs of judges responsible for deciding age discrimination cases. In chapter eight, I 'test' the theory of age discrimination against a case study of healthcare rationing. I scrutinise these different moral beliefs and only retain those that I consider to have sufficient justificatory power.

## VIII. Criticism of Reflective Equilibrium

To demonstrate that the reflective equilibrium method is the best method for finding principles to guide age discrimination law, it is important to deal with some important criticisms of the method. The strongest criticism is that reflective equilibrium fails to produce justified moral beliefs because it relies on unreliable intuitions. Peter Singer, for example, has argued that our moral intuitions are the by-products of evolution and therefore track the 'gene survival norm'.[66]

[64] M DePaul and W Ramsey, *Rethinking Intuition: The Psychology of Intuition and its Role in Philosophical Inquiry* (Rowman & Littlefield, 1998) 301.

[65] This method is called normative empirical reflective equilibrium (NE-RE). See G van Thiel and J van Delden, 'Reflective Equilibrium as a Normative Empirical Model' (2010) 17 *Ethical Perspectives* 183.

[66] Peter Singer discusses evidence from neuroimaging that reveals that our intuitions are deep and immediate emotional reactions and therefore likely to be shaped by evolutionary forces: P Singer, 'Ethics and Intuitions' (2005) 9 *Journal of Ethics* 331.

This means, Singer argues, that our moral intuitions reflect norms that help us survive rather than reflecting moral truth.[67]

In answer to Singer's argument, we can acknowledge that the gene survival norm influences the content of our moral intuitions, but we can deny that this means that we cannot have confidence in the truth of the outcomes of the reflective equilibrium method. Reflective equilibrium requires that we arrive at beliefs by intelligent reflection on the reasons why a particular action is wrong. We should not, according to wide reflective equilibrium, uncritically accept that our intuitions represent moral truth. We must always be open to revising our beliefs if reason dictates this.[68] For example, we may start with the intuition that age discrimination is less serious than race discrimination, but if, on reflection, we find that the principles that explain why we consider race discrimination wrong also applies to some instances of age discrimination, then the reflective process of reflective equilibrium requires that we revise our initial moral intuition that age discrimination is always less serious than race discrimination.

Another argument against reflective equilibrium is that it cannot provide an objectively truthful answer to moral problems because different people adopting wide reflective equilibrium based on their personal intuitions will reach different conclusions.[69] Reflective equilibrium, according to this argument, is simply shuffling personal beliefs.[70]

My adoption of van Thiel's version of reflective equilibrium seeks to avoid this charge of relativism by ensuring I consider the intuitions and beliefs of a range of people who have moral experience with discrimination issues, including academics, legislators and judges.[71] This ensures that the outcome of the reflective equilibrium method is a process of incorporating and evaluating beliefs from a range of sources rather than shuffling personal intuitions. While this does not create certainty about the moral judgements, since beliefs can always be subject to revision after further critical reflection, the reflective equilibrium process can help to persuade by demonstrating that the results of reflective equilibrium are convincing because they cohere with a person's moral judgements about similar or analogous issues.[72] In other words, reflective equilibrium identifies moral principles and judgements people generally share about discrimination and equality, and are endorsed in academic literature and case law as a way to illustrate that

[67] Singer uses this argument to attack reflective equilibrium as a guide for finding moral truth. However, some academics go further and argue that the evolutionary origins of morality mean that there can be no moral knowledge. See R Joyce, *The Evolution of Morality* (MIT Press, 2006).

[68] See Thomas Nagel's argument in *Mortal Questions* (Cambridge University Press, 1979) 142 that we are capable of autonomous thought that can release us from evolutionary constraints.

[69] Fred D'Agostino, 'Relativism and Reflective Equilibrium' (1998) 71 *The Monist* 420.

[70] Richard Brandt has argued that simply making 'coherent' a set of beliefs does not make those beliefs justified: R Brandt, *A Theory of the Good and the Right* (Oxford University Press, 1979).

[71] van Thiel and van Delden (n 65).

[72] See W van der Burg and T van Willigenburg (eds), *Reflective Equilibrium: Essays in Honour of Robert Heeger*, vol 2 (Springer Science & Business Media, 2012) 5.

holding these beliefs requires endorsing the content of the pluralist theory of age discrimination outlined in this book, which can then be used as a guide for age discrimination law to decide cases.

## IX. The Limitations of Reflective Equilibrium

A limitation of the reflective equilibrium method is its difficulty in selecting between conflicting and incommensurable values.[73] John Finnis describes the problem of incommensurability as follows:

> There are many basic forms of human good, all equally or incommensurably basic and none reducible to any or all of the others; none of them is attainable by any one choice or finite set of choices; to commit oneself to one course of action, project, commitment, even life-plan, is to turn one's back on perhaps countless other opportunities of worthwhile action, project, commitment, life …[74]

Values are incommensurable when they cannot be measured in terms of a single value, for example, when values conflict and pull in different directions without there being a common metric to determine which values should prevail.

Incommensurability of values is a problem for applying age discrimination law because the Equality Act 2010 has a proportionality test that requires 'balancing' values in order to determine the legality of any impugned treatment. If values are plural and incommensurable (as I defend in the context of discrimination in chapter four), then there is difficulty determining which value should prevail in any given case. To illustrate the incommensurability values, we can consider an employer dismissing older employees who command higher salaries and justifying this on the grounds that it improves the *efficiency* of the business by cutting costs. If a court or tribunal rules that it was disproportionate and unlawful for the employer to dismiss the older workers, then this will help remove the discriminatory impact of the policy that undermines the *autonomy* of the older workers. However, this decision could then lead to the employer becoming less efficient, possibly resulting in lower productivity and lower wages. The value of autonomy and efficiency in this scenario can pull in different directions because a decision favouring one principle can undermine the other. This raises the issue of what to do with the efficiency principle if this should not prevail in this scenario. We could reject the efficiency principle from our considerations of proportionality in age discrimination claims, but this could conflict with the intuition that efficiency is

[73] For classic texts arguing for value pluralism, see I Berlin, 'Two Concepts of Liberty' in *Four Essays on Liberty* (Oxford University Press, 1969); J Finnis, *Natural Law and Natural Rights* (Clarendon Press, 1980); B Williams, *Moral Luck* (Cambridge University Press, 1981) 71–82; J Raz, *The Morality of Freedom* (Clarendon Press, 1986).

[74] J Finnis, *Fundamentals of Ethics* (Georgetown University Press, 1983) 66–67.

an important principle to bear on the case even if it is not always prioritised in the resulting decision.

The pluralist theory of age discrimination outlined in this book argues that a range of principles, including efficiency, equality of opportunity, social equality, autonomy and respect, should be considered in determining whether impugned age-differential treatment is justified. Reflective equilibrium requires that we are guided by principles that cohere with our moral judgements and intuitions, and I argue here that the principles of the pluralist theory of age discrimination cohere with our moral judgements and intuition on the morality of age discrimination and therefore are essential in determining the outcome of age discrimination cases.[75] However, the reflective equilibrium process does not itself decide which principles should prevail over others to determine the appropriate outcome in age discrimination cases because the principles of the pluralist theory of age discrimination do not themselves support a particular form of balancing or weighing for deciding which one should prevail.

The reflective equilibrium process in this book works to decide cases and therefore decide between potentially conflicting principles by requiring that decisions are made from the 'broadest evidence and critical scrutiny',[76] including reflection on a range of intuitions relating to discrimination, principles and background theories of age and ageing, and testing these ideas against concrete case scenarios. Reflective equilibrium ensures deliberation on all the relevant arguments that bear on a case, and a decision must be made on which of these arguments remains the most compelling, all things considered.

## X. The Structure of this Book

This book also illustrates how a theory of age discrimination can decide age discrimination cases and how it can decide the justifiability of policies such as the Quality-Adjusted Life Year (QALY) healthcare rationing method in the UK.

Further to this, in chapter two, I explain the meaning of direct and indirect age discrimination under the Equality Act 2010 and the exceptions and defences to claims under these provisions, including positive action, genuine occupational requirements and proportionality. I argue that determining the legality of measures that engage the direct and indirect age discrimination provisions require that we consider the moral principles and competing interests at stake and choose whether, on the balance of reasons, the principles require holding that the measure is proportionate and therefore lawful. This analysis reveals the need for a theory

[75] The principles operate prima facie. For a detailed account of the idea of prima facie principles, see D Ross and WD Ross, *The Right and the Good* (Oxford University Press, 2002).

[76] N Daniels, *Justice and Justification: Reflective Equilibrium in Theory and Practice* (Cambridge University Press, 1996) 2–3.

of age discrimination to undertake the proportionality test in a way that is transparent about the competing moral interests at stake. The UK courts and tribunals have failed to approach cases with a comprehensive theory of age discrimination to date.

In chapter three, I move on to the process of constructing a theory of age discrimination that should guide age discrimination law. Age discrimination is a concept linked to equality. The Equality Act 2010 identifies the features of age discrimination as including less favourable treatment on the grounds of age and disadvantage to particular age groups. Therefore, discrimination under the Equality Act 2010 is concerned with actions that place people in a worse position than others. Given the connection between the legal definition of age discrimination and inequality, it is important to identify equality principles that can explain when and why it is wrong for some to be worse off than others in order to determine when and why age-differential treatment is unjustified. Further to this, I identify the principles of equality of opportunity and social equality.

In identifying these principles, I compare equality of opportunity, which holds that it is wrong for someone to be worse off when they are not directly responsible for their condition of being worse off, with equality of outcome, which requires equal distribution of resources regardless of individual behaviour. I find that equality of opportunity fits better with our intuitions because a background theory of personal responsibility coheres with this principle. Equality of outcome, in contrast, is implausible because it requires significant invasions into people's free choices undermining personal responsibility.

There are, however, limitations to equality of opportunity as an explanation for when and why it is wrong for some to be worse off than others. Equality of opportunity can produce inequalities in social status – a result that follows from some citizens being more productive than others – to the extent that some social groups can be in a position of dominance over others. To explain our intuition that it is wrong for a society to permit the domination of some groups of people over other groups, I appeal to the principle of social equality, which requires conditions in which people can participate in democratic society as equals.

Finally, I argue that we should understand equality as the aim to secure equal opportunities to experience the constitutive components of a flourishing life. Rather than selecting one value to equalise, I argue that egalitarians ought to be concerned with creating equal opportunities to experience a range of intrinsic goods, including welfare, autonomy, health and education.

In chapter four, I move on to assess the principles that explain when and why discrimination wrongs people. This creates a groundwork theory of discrimination that I use to later verify when and why age-differential treatment wrongs people. I argue that the equality of opportunity principle identified in chapter three explains that discrimination is wrong when it imposes disadvantages on the grounds of traits that people should not be held responsible for, including characteristics such as sex, race and religious status. The social equality principle explains that discrimination wrongs people when it contributes to oppressive social relations.

I also argue that autonomy as a principle can explain the wrong of discrimination. Each of these accounts explains the wrong of discrimination in the consequences of the action – its effects on distribution and social relations. However, we can also identify the wrong of discrimination in the message conveyed. The principle of respect explains that disadvantaging on the grounds of social-group membership can convey a message that the discriminatee has a diminished moral or social worth. There are, however, cases of discrimination that the respect account is unable to explain.

I argue that there is no distinctive wrong of discrimination, but instead there are a number of explanations for the wrong of discrimination depending on the particular circumstances. A pluralist account of discrimination that includes equality of opportunity, social equality, autonomy and respect is more plausible than an attempt to define the wrong of discrimination by reference to one principle.

In chapter five, I begin constructing the theory of age discrimination by verifying whether the principles identified in chapters three and four explain when and why age-differential treatment is wrong. I argue that the principles of equality of opportunity, social equality, autonomy and respect can explain age discrimination as a concept (including explaining when less favourable treatment on the grounds of age and measures that disadvantage particular age groups can be justified or unjustified). However, I also consider the principle of efficiency as an important part of a theory of age discrimination because it explains the potential benefits of age distinctions that can justify the treatment.

I consider a background theory of age and ageing, and its meaning as a concept. I examine how this theory supports moral principles and, in turn, our moral intuitions. Age is both a biological and a sociological concept connected to the passing of time. Age is correlated to physical, emotional and intellectual changes. The connection between age and other traits, such as intellectual and physical ability, means we can use age classifications as useful proxies for these traits. By using age as a reliable proxy, we can maximise efficiency in pursuing a number of social goods.

Further, age distinctions can be a useful way of sequencing people's lives chronologically, for example, being involved with education in youth, productive work in adulthood and retirement in older age. This forces people to sequence their lives to undertake certain tasks at a time of life when there is the greatest benefit to the individual and society. However, there are many age distinctions that wrong individuals by violating equality of opportunity, social equality, autonomy and respect. Chapter five concludes with a groundwork theory of age discrimination. In the rest of the book, I consider revising the theory in light of the government rationales for age discrimination law, the approaches to age discrimination law in UK case law and, finally, how the theory works against age-based healthcare rationing in the UK. In chapter six, I consider the case for and against courts and tribunals using the legislative history of age discrimination law as an aid in determining whether age-differential treatment is justified or unjustified. I argue that there are a number of problems with relying on legislative history in this context, and that courts and tribunals should not defer to the judgments in these sources.

Chapter six then moves on to consider whether the pluralist theory of age discrimination should incorporate the approaches to age discrimination found in the legislative history of age discrimination law. This process furthers my method of reflective equilibrium, which requires assessing moral beliefs from a range of sources to gain knowledge from people with direct experience of confronting the problem of age discrimination.

The consultation documents on the introduction of age discrimination law outline two major rationales (found in different consultation documents written by different governments) for age discrimination law: the promotion of efficiency and tackling unfair treatment on the grounds of age. I consider and reject the government's view that age-differential treatment is wrong because it inhibits efficiency. The efficiency account of the wrongness of age discrimination is problematic because it can lead to the view that age discrimination is justified so long as it does not harm efficiency. On the contrary, efficiency should not be capable of justifying certain types of age-differential treatment. In particular, it should not justify demeaning age-differential treatment. In light of these considerations, I argue that the pluralist theory of age discrimination should incorporate the idea that efficiency should not justify treatment that communicates that particular age groups have a diminished moral or social worth.

In chapter seven, I consider how courts and tribunals ought to apply the pluralist theory of age discrimination in age discrimination cases. An important argument in this chapter is that the theory of age discrimination constructed in chapter five does not contain the only considerations that a judge must take into account in assessing the proportionality of age-differential treatment – a judge must also consider the institutional limitations of courts and tribunals. A judge's institutional position means that sometimes it is appropriate to defer to the judgement of the original decision-maker if that decision-maker is in a better position to make a judgement on proportionality.

Also in chapter seven, I move on to consider how the theory of age discrimination can assist in deciding age discrimination cases. I compare and contrast the pluralist theory of age discrimination to the UK case law's approach. I assess whether the courts' moral judgements and moral principles concerning unequal treatment on the grounds of age are consistent with my own theory of age discrimination. This process demonstrates how my framework works in practice, but also, further to my method of reflective equilibrium, ensures that I assess any potential weaknesses in my approach and consider revision of the framework. This is an essential process of testing my framework. In forming a guide for age discrimination law, it is particularly important to consider the practical implications of the theory and to determine whether it can successfully guide age discrimination disputes.

In chapter eight, I test the pluralist theory of age discrimination against the method of healthcare rationing in the UK (QALY). This is a way of testing my framework to determine whether it is capable of successfully and fairly guiding the resolution of age discrimination issues. The QALY method of health rationing aims to maximise health benefits in allocating resources, but some argue that the National Institute for Health and Care Excellence's (NICE) use of the QALY method is indirectly discriminatory against older people because older people are more likely to have a low QALY score and therefore are less likely to be granted access to treatment. I argue that NICE's use of the QALY method can engage the indirect age discrimination provisions, but NICE can nonetheless justify using QALY on the grounds that they use the method as a proportionate means of achieving a legitimate aim, which is lawful under section 19(2)(d) of the Equality Act 2010. In making this argument, I consider each of the principles of the pluralist theory of age discrimination at different stages of the proportionality test and use these principles to support the position that NICE's use of the QALY method is proportionate.

Finally, in chapter nine, I summarise the main findings of this book – the value and limitations of the reflective equilibrium method – and explain the possible implications of those findings on areas outside the scope of the book, including the implications of the pluralist theory of age discrimination for understanding discrimination law more generally, the usefulness of the theory in relation to other systems than the UK and the possible value of the theory for identifying which grounds should be protected under discrimination law.

# 2

# The Legal Context

This book aims to offer a theory of age discrimination that is the best explanation for the sorts of wrongs that direct and indirect age discrimination provisions of the Equality Act 2010 should address. To create a theory of age discrimination that can guide the direct and indirect age discrimination provisions of the Equality Act 2010, we must first determine the nature and scope of the direct and indirect age discrimination duties. By understanding how the direct and indirect age discrimination provisions work, we can then begin to outline a theory that can guide how these provisions should determine people's rights.

I structure this chapter as follows: I first explain the age provisions of the Equality Act 2010; then I argue that the concept of proportionality embedded in age discrimination law requires a moral theory of age discrimination; and, finally, I consider examples of cases on the proportionality test and the unsatisfactory way this test has been undertaken to date, revealing the need for a theory of age discrimination to guide the application of age discrimination law to ensure all relevant principles are taken into account to decide cases.

In outlining the age discrimination provisions in the Equality Act 2010, I explain that age discrimination law is unique in its structure. Impugned treatment that engages the direct age discrimination provisions can be justified if it is a 'proportionate means of achieving a legitimate aim',[1] whereas impugned treatment relating to other protected characteristics, such as race and sex, can only be justified in a much narrower range of circumstances, such as when the treatment is a 'genuine occupational requirement'[2] or the treatment fits the positive action criteria under the Equality Act 2010.[3] It is important, then, to examine how the proportionality test in age discrimination law has been interpreted and applied to date. Further to this, I examine the leading cases on the proportionality test in the context of age discrimination in the UK, including *Seldon v Clarkson, Wright and Jakes*[4] (which related to the operation of the proportionality test for direct discrimination) and *Homer v Chief Constable of West Yorkshire Police*[5] (which related to

[1] Equality Act 2010, ss 13(2) and 19(2).
[2] ibid sch 9.
[3] ibid ss 158 and 159.
[4] [2012] UKSC 16, [2012] ICR 716.
[5] [2012] UKSC 15, [2012] ICR 704.

the operation of the proportionality test for indirect discrimination). These cases outline the Supreme Court's view on the sorts of aims that should be capable of justifying treatment that engages the age discrimination provisions, and they apply EU case law on age discrimination. Importantly, these cases hold that the proportionality test should operate differently for direct age discrimination even though the proportionality test in the Equality Act 2010 uses the same wording in the direct and indirect discrimination provisions. *Seldon* and *Homer*, for example, hold that impugned treatment engaging the direct discrimination provisions can only be justified by aims that concern 'public policy', such as intergenerational fairness, whereas impugned treatment engaging the indirect discrimination provision can be justified by private interests as well as public policy, such as costs reduction and improving competitiveness.

I also discuss other cases that have adopted the approaches in *Seldon* and *Homer*, including *White v Ministry of Justice*[6] (which concerned the retirement age of 70 for judges) and *Lockwood v Department of Work & Pensions & Anor*[7] (which concerned redundancy pay). I explain why these cases illustrate the problem of courts using the proportionality test without a theory of age discrimination.

I have also selected *Cross v British Airways plc*[8] and *Woodcock v Cumbria Primary Care Trust*,[9] which relate to the extent costs can justify measures that engage the age discrimination provisions. The importance of this issue and the implications for employees requires an assessment to ensure that the findings of the courts are justified by reference to sound moral principles, which the pluralist theory of age discrimination aims to offer.

I return to these cases in chapter seven to illustrate how the pluralist theory of age discrimination developed in this book can improve the legal reasoning in these cases. As explained in chapter one, I do not offer a complete survey of the UK and EU jurisprudence on age discrimination, but rather focus on a select group of cases to illustrate the key features of the age discrimination duties and select cases for an in-depth analysis and a clear communication of how the pluralist theory of age discrimination can make a difference to the legal reasoning in age discrimination cases.

## I. The Structure of Age Discrimination Law

The Equality Act 2010 prohibits direct and indirect age discrimination in relation to the following: access to employment,[10] training and education (with schooling

[6] [2014] UKET/2201298/2013.
[7] [2013] EWCA Civ 1195, [2014] 1 All ER 250.
[8] [2006] EWCA Civ 549, [2005] IRLR 423.
[9] [2012] EWCA Civ 330, [2012] ICR 1126.
[10] Equality Act 2010, pt 5.

as an exception);[11] membership of associations and clubs (with some exceptions); and provision of goods and services.[12] These provisions protect all people over 18 years of age in relation to the field of goods, facilities and services.[13] The Equality Act 2010 protects all age groups in relation to associations and work.

Direct age discrimination occurs when, because of age, an individual is treated less favourably, and this treatment is not a proportionate means of achieving a legitimate aim.[14] The Equality Act 2010 defines age as including an age group (such as people over 40 years old) and a specific age (45 years of age).[15] This means that a 25-year-old claimant can establish direct discrimination by demonstrating that they were treated less favourably than someone who is 45 years of age or by demonstrating that people below 30 years of age were treated less favourably than people above 30 years of age.

Indirect age discrimination occurs when there is an ostensibly age-neutral provision, criterion or practice that puts individuals of a particular age group at a particular disadvantage and the policy, criterion or practice is not a proportionate means of achieving a legitimate aim.[16] These provisions implement the EU Framework Directive, which requires EU Member States to pass legislation prohibiting direct and indirect age discrimination. The Framework Directive provides that Member States can permit age-differential treatment provided that the treatment is objectively justified. For example, Article 6 of the Framework Directive provides:

> Member States may provide that differences of treatment on grounds of age shall not constitute discrimination, if, within the context of national law, they are objectively and reasonably justified by a legitimate aim, including legitimate employment policy, labour market and vocational training objectives, and if the means of achieving that aim are appropriate and necessary.

Following Article 6, the Equality Act 2010 provides that both the direct and indirect discrimination provisions have proportionality tests. If a measure engages the direct or indirect discrimination provisions, it will be lawful if it is a 'proportionate means of achieving a legitimate aim'.[17] I explain the concepts of direct and indirect discrimination and proportionality in more detail below.

Exceptions to direct and indirect age discrimination include: the use of age distinctions in financial services, such as offering loans, saving accounts or mortgages;[18] charities offering proportionate assistance to particular age groups;[19]

[11] ibid pt 6.
[12] ibid pt 3.
[13] ibid s 28(1)(a).
[14] ibid s 13.
[15] ibid s 5.
[16] ibid s 19.
[17] ibid s 19(2).
[18] ibid sch 3, pt 5, para 20A(1).
[19] ibid ss 193 and 194.

proportionate action to safeguard national security;[20] using age to assess risk for the purpose of deciding what premium to charge a customer for motor or travel insurance;[21] the use of age in controlling immigration;[22] age requirements in sport;[23] companies offering holidays for particular age groups;[24] age restrictions for selling alcohol, tobacco or fireworks;[25] age-based 'concessions', including admission to associations;[26] age distinctions in offering residential mobile homes;[27] decisions relating to the content or scheduling of television or radio programmes, such as depicting particular age groups or selecting people of a particular age to take part;[28] receiving people of a particular age into a private home to offer care;[29] and exceptions to the national minimum wage permitting employers to pay lower rates for young workers.[30]

There are also exceptions for positive action measures (ie measures designed to favour disadvantaged groups).[31] For example, the Equality Act 2010 permits unequal treatment on the grounds of age when this treatment is a proportionate means to enable age groups to overcome age-related disadvantages, to meet age-related needs or to encourage people in age groups to participate in a particular activity where there are disproportionately small numbers of that age group participating in that activity.[32] This provision does not apply to recruitment and promotion.

Relating to recruitment and promotion, section 159 of the Equality Act 2010 permits employers to favour particular age groups in job recruitment and promotion opportunities if the employer reasonably believes members of the age group are disadvantaged because of their age or are a member of an age group with disproportionately low numbers participating in a particular activity, but employers can only favour particular age groups if the person benefiting from the favourable treatment is as qualified as another candidate or candidates who are competing for the job or promotion, the treatment is a proportionate means of addressing the disadvantage of the age group and the employer does not have a policy of favouring that age group in recruitment and promotion.[33]

[20] ibid s 192.
[21] ibid sch 3, pt 5, para 20A(2).
[22] ibid sch 3 pt 4, para 15A.
[23] ibid s 195(7).
[24] ibid sch 3, pt 7, para 30(B).
[25] ibid sch 3, pt 7, para 30C.
[26] ibid sch 16, para 1(2).
[27] ibid sch 3, pt 7, para 30D.
[28] ibid sch 3, para 31(1).
[29] ibid sch 3, para 15.
[30] ibid sch 9, pt 2(11).
[31] Positive action has been justified to overcome past disadvantage and to accelerate progress towards equality of particular groups. See R Dworkin, 'Affirmative Action: Is It Fair?' (2000) 28 *Journal of Blacks in Higher Education* 79.
[32] Equality Act 2010, s 158.
[33] ibid s 159. It is possible that the proportionality test in the direct and indirect age discrimination provisions renders the positive action provisions redundant. This is because case law has found that positive action measures (such as facilitating employment opportunities for disadvantaged age groups)

Further, an employer can also escape a finding of discrimination in respect of recruitment, access to promotion, transfer or training, or dismissal by demonstrating that, having regard to the nature or context of the work, being a particular age is an occupational requirement.[34] For example, old age can be an occupational requirement to act the role of King Lear, given the character's old age forms an integral part of the play's plot.

The Equality Act 2010 also protects against harassment and victimisation on the grounds of age. The Act defines harassment as occurring when a person subjects another to unwanted conduct related to age which has the purpose or effect of either violating a person's dignity or creating an intimidating, hostile, degrading, humiliating or offensive environment.[35] Victimisation occurs when a person, A, is subjected to a detriment by B because A has made or intends to make (or is suspected of making or intending to make) a claim or allegation of age discrimination, or has assisted another in their claim or allegation of age discrimination.[36]

A complainant can pursue a claim of age discrimination, harassment or victimisation in relation to the provision of services, public functions or associations through the civil courts with a deadline for bringing a claim six months from the treatment complained of or 'such other period as the county court or sheriff thinks just and equitable'.[37] In the employment context, a claim can be brought to an employment tribunal within three months of the act complained of or 'such other period as the employment tribunal thinks just and equitable'.[38]

Since this book concerns the direct and indirect age discrimination provisions of the Equality Act 2010, I outline more detail on the features of these legal concepts.

## A. Features of Direct Age Discrimination (Equality Act 2010, Section 13)

As outlined above, direct age discrimination occurs when, because of age, an individual is treated less favourably, and this treatment is not a proportionate means of achieving a legitimate aim. Less favourable treatment includes refusal of services, providing an inferior service, denial of employment, denial of promotion and disrespectful conduct. Less favourable treatment can include age-related 'banter'

are legitimate aims capable of justifying measures under the general proportionality test (see *Seldon* (n 4)). It may be possible for decision-makers to justify their positive action measures as being a proportionate means of achieving a legitimate aim without having to meet the positive action requirements in ss 158 and 159.

[34] ibid sch 9.

[35] ibid s 26.

[36] ibid s 27.

[37] ibid s 118(1).

[38] ibid s 123(1).

and jokes. For example, in *Dove v Brown & Newirth Ltd*,[39] the Employment Tribunal (ET) held that calling an employee 'gramps' amounted to less favourable treatment on the grounds of age even though these comments were not intended to be discriminatory. In *Nolan v CD Bramall Dealership Limited t/a Evans Halshaw Motorhouse Worksop*,[40] the ET found that the claimant was subject to direct discrimination after having his car number plate changed from 'OAB' to 'OAP' and being frequently referred to as 'Yoda' (a character from the film *Star Wars* described by the Tribunal as 'a small, wizened character who is several hundred years old').

An important feature of direct discrimination is that there must be a necessary link between the less favourable treatment and the protected characteristic. In other words, the less favourable treatment must be 'because of' the protected characteristic. The House of Lords held in *James v Eastleigh Borough Council*[41] that treatment will be 'because of' the protected characteristic when the complainant would have received the same treatment from the decision-maker *but for* their protected characteristic. For example, the defendant in *James* offered free access to its swimming pools for those of pensionable age. At the time of the case, Parliament had set the pensionable age at 60 for women and 65 for men. The claimant, a man, had to pay for swimming while his wife had free admission. The less favourable treatment of men did not feature in the purpose for adopting the policy. The aim of the defendant's policy was to assist those with low incomes rather than to harm men. Nonetheless, the court held that the defendant's policy was direct discrimination because the complainant would have received the same treatment as his wife but for his or her sex.[42] There can be a finding of direct discrimination in the absence of an intention, purpose or motive to treat someone less favourably because of a protected characteristic.

This means that the 'but for' direct discrimination test is satisfied when the reason for a decision and the protected characteristics are so close that they are 'indissoluble'. For example, in *James* there was a direct link between the reason for the decision (helping people of pensionable age) and the protected characteristic (the status of being a man or woman). Another example is *Hall v Bull*,[43] which concerned civil partners who booked a double room at a hotel but, on arriving at the hotel, were refused the double room because the hotel owners restricted double rooms to 'heterosexual married couples'. The majority in the Supreme Court held that this was direct discrimination because of sexual orientation. The reason for the decision (married status) was indissociable from sexual orientation because, at the time, gay people could not marry someone of the same sex but only enter a

[39] [2016] UKET/3301905/2015.
[40] [2012] UKET/2601000/2012.
[41] [1990] 2 AC 751 (HL).
[42] ibid 765.
[43] [2013] UKSC 73, [2013] 1 WLR 3741.

civil partnership. Refusing the double room to the claimant because the claimant was unmarried was tantamount, in this case, to refusing services to the claimant because they were gay.[44]

For a finding of direct discrimination, the primary decision-maker must have made the decision because of the claimant's protected characteristic. The mental processes of people other than the primary decision-maker are irrelevant. For example, in *CLFIS (UK) Ltd v Reynolds*,[45] the Court of Appeal held that when a person treats someone less favourably by relying upon information expressed by others whose motivation was discriminatory, this will not amount to discrimination if the person responsible for the decision did not also act on discriminatory reasons. In this case, the claimant argued that they were the victim of direct age discrimination when a managing director reported performance concerns to a general manager, who subsequently dismissed the claimant. The claimant argued that the managing director reported these concerns for age discriminatory reasons. The Court of Appeal held that since the general manager did not treat the claimant less favourably because of age, there was no age discrimination in the decision to dismiss the claimant.

Treating a person less favourably because of a person's *perceived* age rather than their actual age is sufficient to engage the direct discrimination provisions. For example, an employer's decision not to employ an applicant because the employer falsely believed the applicant was 65 years of age is direct age discrimination unless the employer can demonstrate that the treatment was a proportionate means of achieving a legitimate aim. The fact that the applicant was younger than their perceived age does not prevent the employer's action from constituting direct discrimination.

Furthermore, treating someone less favourably because that person associates with someone of a particular age is also an action that engages the direct discrimination provisions. For example, in *EAD Solicitors LLP v Abrams*,[46] Mr Abrams set up a company to take his place in a limited liability partnership. When Mr Abrams reached the retirement age of the partnership, the firm objected to Mr Abrams working in the firm in his role as an employee of the company he had set up. The Employment Appeal Tribunal (EAT) held that Mr Abrams's company could bring a direct discrimination claim because the company was treated less favourably for being associated with Mr Abrams, and this less favourable treatment was because Mr Abrams had reached the firm's retirement age.

Another important feature for identifying direct discrimination is that a decision-maker must put an individual in a worse position than a similarly situated person. In the context of age discrimination, courts and tribunals can identify age discrimination by making a comparison between the complainant, who is of

[44] ibid [17]–[24] (Lady Hale).
[45] [2015] EWCA Civ 439, [2015] ICR 1010.
[46] [2015] UKEAT/0054/15.

a certain age, with a similarly situated person (real or hypothetical) of a different age, and determining whether the decision-maker treated the complainant less favourably. According to section 5 of the Equality Act 2010, people who share an age are those in 'the same age group', with age group defined 'by reference to age, whether by reference to a particular age or to a range of ages'. If the claimant is 40 years of age, they can identify themselves as being in a middle-age group and compare themselves to how older people – say, those over 60 years of age – were treated. Claimants must decide which age group to compare themselves to. They need to consider whether their case is more likely to be successful by comparing themselves against a wide age gap, such as all people over 65 years of age, or to compare themselves to a narrower group, such as people 65–70 years of age.

If a decision-maker treats an individual less favourably because of age, then the treatment is unlawful unless it is a 'proportionate means of achieving a legitimate aim' or the treatment fits into one of the exceptions outlined above. The Supreme Court confirmed in *Seldon* that only 'social policy objectives' can justify treatment that engages the direct age discrimination provisions.[47] This finding applied the CJEU decision in *Age Concern*, which held that direct age-differential treatment can only be justified by social policy objectives, which are 'distinguishable from purely individual reasons particular to the employer's situation, such as cost reduction or improving competitiveness'.[48] The CJEU has held that the following are legitimate aims for the purposes of justifying direct age-differential treatment:

- promoting access to employment for younger people;[49]
- the efficient planning of the departure and recruitment of staff;[50]
- ensuring a mix of generations of staff so as to promote the exchange of experience and new ideas;[51]
- rewarding experience;[52]
- creating a financial cushion for employees who may find it hard to find new employment if dismissed;[53]
- facilitating the participation of older workers in the workforce;[54] and
- avoiding the need to dismiss employees on the ground that they are no longer capable of doing the job.[55]

[47] *Seldon* (n 4) [56]–[57] (Lady Hale).

[48] Case C-388/07 *The Incorporated Trustees of the National Council on Ageing (Age Concern England) v Secretary of State for Business, Enterprise and Regulatory Reform* [2009] ECR I-1569 [46].

[49] Case C-411/05 *Palacios de la Villa v Cortefiel Servicios SA* [2007] ECR I-8531.

[50] Joined Cases C-159/10 and C-160/10 *Fuchs and Köhler* [2011] ECR I-06919.

[51] Joined Cases C-250/09 and C-268/09 *Georgiev* [2011] 2 CMLR 7.

[52] Case C-88/08 *Hütter v Technische Universität Graz* [2006] ECR I-05325.

[53] Case C-515/13 *Ingeniørforeningen i Danmark* [2011] 1 CMLR 35.

[54] Case C-144/04 *Mangold v Helm* [2006] ECR I-09981.

[55] Case C-45/09 *Rosenbladt* [2010] ECR I-09391.

Less favourable treatment because of age cannot be justified by the proportionality test if that treatment also treats people less favourably because of another protected characteristic in the Equality Act 2010. For example, a broadcaster dismissing older women from television work cannot attempt to justify this treatment on the grounds that it is proportionate and therefore justifies age-differential treatment. The dismissal is sex discrimination in addition to age discrimination, and the Equality Act 2010 does not offer a general proportionality defence for unequal treatment on the grounds of sex or protected characteristics other than age.

## B. Features of Indirect Age Discrimination (Equality Act 2010, Section 19)

Indirect age discrimination occurs when an ostensibly age-neutral provision, criterion or practice puts individuals of a particular age at a disadvantage and that policy, criterion or practice is not a proportionate means of achieving a legitimate aim.

As such, indirect discrimination concerns the effect a measure has on people, namely the effect of creating or perpetuating disadvantage of particular social groups. The indirect discrimination provisions are 'an attempt to level the playing field by subjecting to scrutiny requirements which look neutral on their face but in reality work to the comparative disadvantage of people with a particular protected characteristic'.[56]

To engage the indirect discrimination provisions, a complainant must demonstrate that an individual is put at a particular disadvantage when compared with people of a different age. In other words, there must be a connection between the protected characteristic and the disadvantage. The Supreme Court held in *Homer* that there will be a connection between a protected characteristic and disadvantage when there is an association between the protected characteristic and any particular disadvantages.[57] For example, the defendant in *Homer* enacted a rule that a law degree was necessary to be eligible for promotion to legal advisor for the police. The claimant was 61 years of age at the time of the introduction of the rule. They argued that completing a law degree would take him beyond his retirement date and therefore he was disadvantaged because of his age. The EAT[58] and the Court of Appeal[59] held that the employer had not applied any provision, criterion or practice that disadvantaged the claimant's age group. What put the claimant at a disadvantage, the EAT and the Court of Appeal held, was his proximity to leaving the defendant's employment. The Supreme Court rejected this rigid approach and found that there was an association between the claimant's age and

[56] *Homer* (n 5) [17] (Lady Hale).
[57] ibid.
[58] [2009] ICR 223.
[59] [2010] EWCA Civ 419, [2010] ICR 987.

the disadvantage of reaching the retirement age, and this was enough to engage the indirect age discrimination provisions.

Indirect discrimination requires a comparison between groups to identify disadvantage. We can use statistics to compare different groups to reveal disadvantage, but not all disadvantages can be revealed through statistics, particularly if the sample size is very small. In *London Underground Ltd v Edwards (No 2)*,[60] the Court of Appeal held that it is enough to rely on common knowledge that people with a protected characteristic are likely to be disadvantaged. For example, the claimant in *Edwards* argued that women were disadvantaged by a change in work shifts because women were more likely to be single parents, which would make it harder to comply with the new shifts instigated by the employer. Because the claimant was the only woman affected (there were very few female train drivers), it was impossible to produce statistics to illustrate women were disadvantaged by the policy. However, the Court held that indirect discrimination was established because it was common knowledge that women are far more likely to be single parents than men, and therefore women would be far more likely to be negatively affected by the change in the work shifts.[61]

To establish indirect discrimination, there is no requirement that the claimant demonstrate the reason why a policy, criterion or practice causes disadvantage to people who have a particular protected characteristic. The Supreme Court held in *Essop and others v Home Office (UK Border Agency)*[62] that while direct discrimination requires a causal link between the protected characteristic and the less favourable treatment, indirect discrimination only requires a causal link between the policy, criterion and practice and the disadvantage suffered by people who have a particular protected characteristic. In this case, civil servants claimed indirect discrimination when statistics revealed that black people, people from other ethnic minorities and people over 30 years of age had significantly lower pass rates than white people and younger people in a test that civil servants had to pass to be eligible for promotion to the level of Higher Executive Officer. The claimants, however, were unable to show why the test disadvantaged people from certain ethnic groups and older people. The failure to prove the reason why the groups were disadvantaged did not prevent a finding of indirect discrimination.

Examples of measures likely to engage the indirect age discrimination provisions include qualification requirements that are harder for older people to obtain and redundancy schemes that have length of service as a criterion. These are age-neutral policies that disadvantage particular age groups. The facts of *Homer* illustrate an indirectly discriminatory policy. The claimant had to complete a law degree to be eligible for promotion. The Supreme Court held the rule was indirectly discriminatory because the claimant's age group (60–65 years of age) would have

[60] [1998] EWCA Civ 877, [1998] IRLR 364 [26]–[26].
[61] ibid.
[62] [2017] UKSC 27, [2017] 1 WLR 1343.

less time than younger people to obtain the degree before reaching the employer's mandatory retirement age.[63]

*Rolls-Royce plc v Unite the Union*[64] illustrates a redundancy scheme that engages the indirect discrimination provisions. The claimant operated a redundancy scheme, with the agreement of the trade union Unite, that awarded points to employees on six different criteria, one of which was length of service. Employees with the lowest points score could face redundancy. The Court of Appeal held that using length of service as part of an assessment for redundancy engages the indirect discrimination provisions because younger employees are disadvantaged in accruing length of service.

Measures that engage the indirect age discrimination provisions can be justified and lawful if the decision-maker establishes that the measure is a proportionate means of 'achieving a legitimate aim'.[65] In common with the direct age discrimination provisions, the Equality Act 2010 provides no explanation for the sorts of aims capable of justifying measures, but the case law provides guidance. The Supreme Court found in *Homer* that

> The range of aims which can justify indirect discrimination on any ground is wider than the aims which can, in the case of age discrimination, justify direct discrimination. It is not limited to the social policy … but can encompass a real need on the part of the employer's business.[66]

In other words, private interests, including business efficiency, can justify treatment that engages the indirect discrimination provisions. This applied to the CJEU case *Bilka-Kaufhaus GmbH v Weber von Hartz*,[67] which held that indirect differential treatment can be justified by objectives that serve the real need of employers in addition to social policy objectives. Also, the Supreme Court held in *Homer* that 'to be proportionate, a measure has to be both an appropriate means of achieving the legitimate aim and (reasonably) necessary in order to do so'.[68] Moreover, 'Part of the assessment of whether the criterion can be justified entails a comparison of the impact of that criterion upon the affected group as against the importance of the aim to the employer'.[69]

The proportionality test in age discrimination law is an essential concept for determining the lawfulness of measures that engage the direct and indirect age discrimination provisions. In the next section, I explain that the proportionality test requires moral reasoning. The theory of age discrimination defended in this book offers guidance on the principles that can assist in determining proportionality and can therefore assist in determining legality.

[63] *Homer* (n 5) [17] (Lady Hale).
[64] [2009] EWCA Civ 387, [2009] IRLR 576.
[65] Equality Act 2010, s 19(2)(d).
[66] *Homer* (n 5) [19] (Lady Hale).
[67] Case 170/84 [1987] ICR 110.
[68] ibid [22].
[69] ibid [24].

## II. Proportionality as Moral Reasoning

As I have established in the previous section, a measure can only be a proportionate means of achieving a legitimate aim and therefore lawful if it is (i) suitable for achieving a legitimate aim, (ii) necessary to achieve that aim and (iii) proportionate in the narrower sense: it must not impose burdens or cause harms to other legitimate interests that outweigh the objectives achieved.[70] A central contention of this book is that this proportionality test is a direction to courts and tribunals to engage in moral reasoning to determine whether the impugned measure is justified or unjustified. In other words, proportionality requires courts and tribunals to weigh and choose between competing principles and interests to determine whether the impugned measure is lawful. This book aims to assist this process by identifying the moral principles relevant to assessing the proportionality of age-differential treatment.

Proportionality requires moral reasoning from courts and tribunals (and anyone else applying the law) because the three-stage proportionality assessments are value-laden.[71] For example, identifying 'legitimate' aims to justify measures that engage the direct and indirect age discrimination provisions requires moral argument. It requires that we identify the objectives that are important enough to justify treating people unequally on the grounds of age or disadvantaging particular age groups. This requires a moral theory to identify legitimacy in the context of age discrimination. In other words, we need a theory of age discrimination to identify the principles that can work to justify age-differential treatment.

The necessity stage of the proportionality test requires assessing whether there are any alternative forms of treatment that can pursue the legitimate aims as effectively as the impugned measure, but with a lower discriminatory impact.[72] This is an empirical undertaking.[73] The final stage of the proportionality test requires balancing the value of an individual being free from less favourable treatment against the values promoted by the impugned measure. In *Homer*, the Supreme Court held that the final stage of proportionality requires comparing, contrasting and weighing the impact of the measures taken on the disadvantaged age group against the significance and importance of the decision-maker's aims, requirements and needs.[74] In other words, the final test requires weighing and choosing between competing moral considerations. Increasing harms to the interests of an individual requires proportionately greater realisations of other principles to outweigh the harm.

[70] The Supreme Court confirmed in *Seldon* (n 4) that this proportionality test applies to treatment that engages the direct age discrimination provisions. The Supreme Court confirmed in *Homer* (n 5) that this test also applies to treatment that engages the indirect age discrimination provisions.

[71] For the argument that proportionality assessments require moral reasoning, see K Möller, 'Proportionality: Challenging the Critics' (2012) 10 *International Journal of Constitutional Law* 709.

[72] ibid 713.

[73] Chapter 7 discusses the necessity stage in more detail.

[74] *Homer* (n 5) [24] (Lady Hale).

Suitability, necessity and proportionality are exactly the sorts of considerations that need to be taken into account in making moral judgements. For example, in a scenario where we consider the morality of lying to someone, the decision-making process might involve determining whether lying would pursue a legitimate goal by asking ourselves whether it is legitimate to lie to avoid hurting a person's feelings. We might then consider whether it is possible to spare someone's feelings without lying (the necessity assessment) and, finally, whether the goal of sparing feelings outweighs any competing value in telling the truth, including an assessment of whether this should trump the value of maintaining trust in the relationship (the final balancing proportionality assessment). The proportionality test therefore contains the structure of a classic form of moral reasoning. As such, the proportionality test is a process of investigating whether an impugned measure is morally justified.[75]

Moral reasoning in the proportionality test is particularly prominent when there is a clear conflict of important moral values. This occurs when there is a rights conflict. For example, the press has a right to disseminate information under Article 10 of the European Convention of Human Rights, and individuals have a right under Article 8 to be free from invasions into their private lives. Sometimes these rights conflict and judges must use the proportionality test to form a moral argument on which interest should prevail. In *Campbell v Mirror Group Newspapers Ltd*,[76] the claimant argued that the defendant infringed her right to respect for her private life when the defendant published a story with photographs of the claimant leaving a drug addiction clinic. In deciding whether the claimant's right to a private life prevailed over the defendant's rights to disseminate information, the House of Lords formed a moral argument about the value of free speech and privacy. Lord Nicholls argued that

> The need to be free to disseminate information regarding Miss Campbell's drug addiction is of a lower order than the need for freedom to disseminate information on some other subjects such as political information. The degree of latitude reasonably to be accorded to journalists is correspondingly reduced, but it is not excluded altogether.[77]

In conflicts of values like this case and many others, the courts have no choice but to form moral arguments to settle which interest should prevail.

A number of academics have supported the idea of proportionality as moral reasoning. Möller, for example, characterises the proportionality test as a procedure that guides judges through the 'reasoning process of determining whether a policy does or does not respect rights'.[78] Proportionality assessments, for Möller,

[75] M Kumm, 'The Idea of Socratic Contestation and the Right to Justification: The Point of Rights Based Proportionality Review' (2010) 4 *Law & Ethics of Human Rights* 140.

[76] [2004] UKHL 22, [2005] 1 WLR 3394.

[77] ibid 29.

[78] Möller (n 71).

'deliberately release judges from interpretative constraints and direct them to the development of a moral argument about the acceptable balance of reasons'.[79] Robert Alexy has argued that proportionality requires the weighing of values.[80] Mattias Kumm has argued that proportionality is an assessment into whether 'a public action can be demonstratively justified by reasons that are appropriate in a liberal democracy'.[81] The theory of age discrimination constructed in chapters three to six of this book aims to support this process in the context of age discrimination cases.

## III. The Possible Implications on Age Discrimination Law of the UK Exiting the European Union

The application of EU law in the UK ends on 1 January 2021 unless the terms of any agreement between the UK government and the EU Council determines otherwise.[82] The implications for UK age discrimination law include the possibility for the UK to repeal it entirely, since the UK would no longer be required by EU law to implement laws that prohibit age discrimination (although the government has not indicated any plans to repeal these laws).

The other possible implication for age discrimination law relates to the status of the CJEU case law. Section 6(5) of the European Union (Withdrawal) Act 2018 provides that CJEU decisions decided before the UK's withdrawal from the EU will have the status of Supreme Court decisions. It follows that it is possible for the UK Supreme Court to take this as an opportunity to overrule judgments of the CJEU should it consider that justice requires departure from that precedent. In chapter seven, I criticise some aspects of how the UK courts and tribunals have applied the proportionality test in age discrimination cases. The Supreme Court would have the freedom to reject the CJEU jurisprudence in their approach to the proportionality test and possibly follow the recommendations of this book on the appropriate way to apply the proportionality test in age discrimination cases.

Also, decisions of the CJEU decided after the UK has withdrawn from the EU will not bind the UK courts. This means that the UK courts can develop age discrimination jurisprudence independent of future developments of age discrimination law developed by the CJEU. UK age discrimination law may then start to differ in operation from that of the EU.

[79] ibid 717.

[80] R Alexy, 'Constitutional Rights and Proportionality' (2014) 16 *Ratio Juris* 131.

[81] Kumm (n 75).

[82] See Agreement on the withdrawal of the United Kingdom of Great Britain and Northern Ireland from the European Union and the European Atomic Energy Community, pt 4.

## IV. The Proportionality Test in UK Age Discrimination Cases

The need for a theory of age discrimination to guide the proportionality test arises because the UK courts and tribunals have failed to undertake the proportionality test in a way that ensures an open assessment of the competing interests and principles at stake in age discrimination claims. This failure is evident in the courts' and tribunals' approach to the first stage of the proportionality test – identifying the legitimate aims capable of justifying measures – and in the final stage of the proportionality test – balancing the competing interests at stake in the case.

The leading case on direct age discrimination, *Seldon*, held that, in undertaking the proportionality test, only 'social policy objectives' should be capable of justifying measures that engage the direct age discrimination provisions.[83] These objectives include a wide variety of aims related to employment policy, the labour market and vocational training. The Supreme Court divided these legitimate social policy aims into two categories. The first category includes aims that promote 'inter-generational fairness', which includes facilitating access to employment for young people, sharing work fairly between the generations and enabling older people to remain in the workforce.[84] The second category includes aims to protect 'dignity', which includes aims justifying mandatory retirement ages on the grounds of avoiding the involvement of older workers in capability assessments.[85]

The Supreme Court described the legitimacy of 'inter-generational fairness' aims as uncontroversial, but did not assess whether inter-generational fairness has a sound theoretical basis for justifying unequal treatment on the grounds of age. The Supreme Court relied on EU case law, including *Palacios de la Villa v Cortefiel Servicios SA*[86] and *Rosenbladt v Oellerking Gebaudereinigungsgesellschaft mbH*,[87] which held that measures disadvantaging older people are capable of being justified by furthering the aim of promoting youth employment. The Supreme Court also cited *Georgiev v Tehnicheski universitet – Sofia, filial Plovdiv*,[88] which held that it was legitimate to justify a retirement age by the 'encouragement of recruitment in higher education by means of the offer of posts as professors to younger people …'. It is not clear, however, from the EU cases or the reasoning in the Supreme Court in *Seldon*, why these aims should justify forcing older people out of work to provide opportunities for younger people. There is a need to explain why it is justified to prioritise the interests of younger people at the expense of older people. We might argue that inter-generational fairness aims are positive-action

[83] *Seldon* (n 4) [56]–[57] (Lady Hale).
[84] ibid [56].
[85] ibid [57].
[86] Case C-411/05 [2007] ECR I-8531.
[87] Case C-45/09 [2011] 1 CMLR 32.
[88] Case C-250/09 [2011] 2 CMLR 7.

measures designed to give assistance to the particular needs of disadvantaged age groups. But it still warrants an explanation why positive action should be capable of justifying unequal treatment on the grounds of age in the general proportionality test when positive action is only available under the more restrictive provisions of sections 158 and 159 of the Equality Act 2010 for other protected grounds, such as race and sex. A theory of age discrimination could aim to provide such an explanation.

In *Lockwood*, the Court of Appeal accepted the legitimacy of positive action in justifying age-differential treatment, but did not explain why these aims are legitimate. The Court of Appeal held that it was a legitimate aim to provide a financial cushion to older workers to cover a period until those workers find alternative employment. In this case, the claimant began working at the Department for Work and Pensions ('DWP') at 18 years of age. She continued working at the DWP for eight years until she was 26 years old. The claimant then applied for redundancy and was accepted. The redundancy scheme entitled her to £10,849.04. However, the same scheme would have entitled her to significantly more money if she were over 30 years of age and had worked the same number of years at the DWP. The claimant argued this was direct age discrimination because it treated her less favourably because she was a young employee.

In rejecting the direct discrimination claim, the Court of Appeal held the policy was justified by statistics demonstrating that it was more difficult for older people to find employment.[89] The Court of Appeal also relied on the assumption that older people need more redundancy pay because older people are more likely to have families and dependants than young people, which makes it more difficult for older workers to relocate to find employment.[90] The DWP's scheme was a positive action measure.

There was no analysis, however, explaining why it was justified to generalise about age groups in this way. Financially cushioning older workers is a form of age stereotyping because it reflects a generalisation that young people react differently to unemployment when compared to older people. The ET reasoned (which was affirmed by the Court of Appeal) that

> Individuals in the younger categories and in their twenties can generally be expected to react more easily and more rapidly to the loss of their jobs and greater flexibility can, in general, be expected of them given their lesser family and financial obligations.[91]

The ET referred to 'the average at date of marriage was 34 for women, and 36 years for men' as an explanation for why greater financial assistance was needed for people in their 30s compared to people in their 20s.[92]

[89] *Lockwood* (n 7) [50]–[51].
[90] ibid.
[91] [2010] UKET/1808694/07, 101539/08, 115515/10 [20].
[92] ibid [27].

Using race, sex and many other protected grounds under the Equality Act 2010 to grant higher redundancy pay would be unlawful. It warrants a theory of age discrimination to explain why unequal treatment on the grounds of age can be justified in this way when it is unlawful in relation to other grounds of discrimination. And a theory of age discrimination can examine whether the sorts of age generalisations in *Lockwood* are an acceptable way to identify justified age-differential treatment.

In relation to the second category of legitimate aims identified by *Seldon*, namely 'dignity' aims, the Supreme Court held in *Seldon* that retirement ages are capable of being justified by avoiding the need to involve older workers in incapacity or underperformance processes. Lady Hale expressed sympathy for the view that this aim was 'suspiciously like stereotyping' because it used age as a proxy for poor performance.[93] The Court held that they were bound by the EU case law, which held that avoiding 'unseemly debates about capacity' was a legitimate aim.[94] The Court, however, failed to offer analysis for why avoiding humiliation is enough to justify a mandatory retirement age and failed to explain why it is acceptable to assume older workers are less capable. The Court accepted stereotypes as capable of justifying unequal treatment on the grounds of age without explaining the reason why age stereotyping is legitimate.

A further example of the acceptance of age stereotyping for justifying unequal treatment is the decision in *White*, which applied the *Seldon* approach to the retirement age of 70 for judges. In finding that the retirement age for judges was justified and therefore lawful, the ET referred to a letter from the Lord Chief Justice to the Lord Chancellor that explained that this retirement age was necessary to avoid the problem of having to ask judges to retire when they have 'gone off the boil intellectually'.[95] The ET held that it was legitimate to act on a presumption that judges are likely to decline in ability after 70 years of age. This presumption, the ET held, is to ensure public confidence that they are not undergoing age-based intellectual decline. This reasoning followed the decision of the CJEU in *Commission v Hungary*, which held that a judicial retirement can be justified 'to prevent possible disputes concerning employees' fitness to work beyond a certain age'.[96] The ET offered no explanation, however, for why negative age stereotyping should be

[93] *Seldon* (n 4) [57].

[94] ibid.

[95] *White* (n 6) [24].

[96] Case C-286/12 [2013] 1 CMLR 44, para 62. Nonetheless, the courts can find a retirement age unlawful under EU law if it undermines judicial independence. For example, in Case C-619/18 *Commission v Poland* [2019] (Grand Chamber, 24 June 2019)., the CJEU held that a Polish law that lowered the judicial retirement age to 65 for men and 60 for women with the Polish President having the discretion to decide whether individual judges could continue to work as judges after the retirement age violated the Charter of Fundamental Rights and Art 2 of the EU Treaty because the law undermined judicial independence and values such as the rule of law. The CJEU rejected the argument that the policy was aimed at creating an age balance in the judiciary since the law affected about one-third of the sitting judiciary and, as a result, was likely to be an attempt to undermine judicial independence.

capable of justifying this unequal treatment. We would consider race or sex stereotyping unacceptable as a reason to remove a person from their work. A theory of age discrimination is necessary to examine age stereotyping and the reason for the acceptability or otherwise of age stereotyping.

The failure to engage openly with the principles at stake is also clear in relation to indirect discrimination claims. The Supreme Court held in *Homer* that the sorts of aims capable of justifying treatment that engages the indirect age discrimination provisions are not limited to social policy, but can encompass a real need on the part of an employer's business. No explanation, however, was offered as to why the sort of aims that can justify measures engaging the indirect age discrimination provisions are wider than the sorts of aims that can justify measures that engage the direct age discrimination provisions. A theory of age discrimination may go some way to revealing why we should treat direct and indirect age discrimination differently in identifying legitimate aims.

There is also a lack of a theoretical underpinning in the finding that costs alone cannot justify age-differential treatment. In *Cross*, the EAT held that cost savings cannot justify measures that engage the indirect age discrimination provisions unless cost savings are combined with some other aim that can be said to be legitimate.[97] The Court of Appeal in *Woodcock* held that costs alone cannot justify measures that engage the direct age discrimination provisions.[98] However, cost savings combined with a legitimate aim, the Court held, is an acceptable consideration in determining proportionality. A theory of age discrimination might explain why costs alone cannot justify age-differential treatment and explain the role costs should play in the proportionality assessment. This is currently unclear in the case law.

A further problematic aspect of the case law is the treatment of the final stage of proportionality, which requires that measures do not impose burdens or cause harms to other legitimate interests that outweigh the objectives achieved. The Supreme Court recognised in *Homer* that 'both the Age Regulations and the Equality Act recognise that difficult balances have to be struck between the competing interests of different age groups'.[99] Much of the case law, however, lacks clear transparent reasoning about the balance of competing interests.

For example, the ET reasoning in *Seldon* concerning the proportionality of a law firm's retirement age (reasoning upheld in later appeals) did little to evaluate the competing interests at stake in the case. The ET held that the partner's consent to the partnership agreement and the fact that the partner had time to financially prepare for the retirement were relevant factors to weigh in the balance of whether the retirement age was proportionate. The ET concluded that these factors lessened the harmful impact on the complainant and, therefore, on balance, the

[97] *Cross* (n 8).
[98] *Woodcock* (n 9).
[99] *Homer* (n 5) [27] (Lady Hale).

retirement age was proportionate. The ET did not, however, evaluate how and why retirement ages are harmful to the interests of individuals. Nor did it openly evaluate the weight of the claimant's interest in being free from the age stereotyping that underpinned the retirement age, including being free from the stereotype that older workers need capability assessments because older people are less capable. The ET also failed to evaluate the weight of the claimant's interest in being able to continue in socially productive work.

The lack of recognition of the burdens placed on the claimant was particularly problematic in *Seldon* because the retirement age was unlikely to do much to advance public policy objectives. The ET and the EAT acknowledged that a large number of partners choose to leave the firm before they reach the retirement age and that the firm has the option of agreeing to keep on partners who reach the retirement age. Therefore, the retirement age was likely to have only a limited effect on creating inter-generational fairness by creating promotion opportunities for younger workers.

The lack of openness about competing interests in the final stage of the proportionality test is also clear in the *Lockwood* case. The ET claimed that the respondent's aim of offering a financial cushion to older workers outweighed the discriminatory effect it had on the claimant.[100] This was upheld by the EAT and the Court of Appeal. The ET did not explain, however, why the benefits of the scheme outweighed the discriminatory effect. In particular, it did not evaluate the weight of the claimant's interest in being free from the stereotyping present in the redundancy scheme and did not explain which principles were at stake. For example, the ET did not explain why the benefit of the scheme cushioning older workers from the effects of unemployment outweighs any harm caused to the claimant by the stereotyping present in the scheme. Constructing a theory of discrimination can help to explain why the redundancy scheme in *Lockwood* would harm the interests of younger workers and this would help to weigh this interest against the objective pursued by the scheme.

## V. Conclusion

To determine the legality of measures that engage the direct and indirect age discrimination provisions of the Equality Act 2010, we must investigate whether the treatment fits into a specifically prescribed exception or whether it is a proportionate means of achieving a legitimate aim. The proportionality test requires an assessment of the competing interests of those adversely affected by the treatment against any interests promoted by the treatment. This assessment, I have argued,

[100] [2011] ET 1808694/07, 101539/08, 115515/10.

requires moral reasoning to engage with theoretical questions about the principles that determine when less favourable treatment on the grounds of age and measures that disadvantage particular age groups are justified or unjustified. I have further argued that a theory of age discrimination can assist in undertaking this proportionality test with regard to the competing principles that are at stake in an age discrimination claim.

An open assessment of the competing principles at stake in any age discrimination claim has been largely missing from many of the leading UK age discrimination cases. The courts and tribunals have failed to explain why particular aims are legitimate for the purposes of justifying unequal treatment. The courts and tribunals have also failed to provide principles for determining whether a measure is proportionate. The result is that the rationale for these decisions is often unclear. This points towards the need for guidance on the principles that should determine the legality of measures that engage the direct and indirect age discrimination provisions. This book aims to provide this guidance by outlining and defending a theory of age discrimination that should assist in determining the justifiability and therefore legality of treatment that engages the direct and indirect discrimination provisions. In chapters three to five, I examine and offer principles that can form a comprehensive theory of age discrimination. These principles determine whether a measure in an age discrimination claim pursues a legitimate aim and whether the measure has an acceptable balance between competing interests. In chapter seven, I return to the cases discussed in this chapter to demonstrate the positive difference a theory of age discrimination can make to the legal reasoning in age discrimination cases.

# 3

# Equality Principles

In the previous chapter, I argued that determining the legality of treatment that engages the direct and indirect age discrimination provisions requires determining whether the impugned treatment pursues a legitimate aim, is necessary to achieve that aim and does not impose burdens or cause harms to other legitimate interests that outweigh the objectives achieved. This proportionality test, I argued, requires courts and tribunals (and anyone else seeking to determine the lawfulness of treatment subject to the proportionality test) to engage with and choose between competing moral interests and principles that work to distinguish justified from unjustified age-differential treatment.

This chapter starts the process of identifying these principles by identifying equality norms that may assist in distinguishing justified from unjustified age-differential treatment and therefore form part of a theory of discrimination. Age discrimination is a means by which inequality is produced. It concerns treating people 'less favourably' than others and putting people at a disadvantage.[1] As argued by Kasper Lippert-Rasmussen, 'Conceptually, discrimination is tied to inequality. It is impossible to discriminate against someone unless there is some dimension in which the discriminator treats the discriminatee worse than those against whom she does not discriminate.'[2] It follows that a plausible theory of age discrimination, which this book is concerned with creating, must address what is wrong with inequality in order to have a complete account of when and why age discrimination is wrong.[3] Further to the process of creating a theory of age discrimination, this chapter identifies principles for explaining the wrongness of inequality. I argue that the principles of equality of opportunity, which requires an equal distribution of benefits and burdens except insofar as individuals

[1] As I explained in ch 2, age discrimination is a comparative concept. The definition of direct discrimination requires that an act put an individual in a worse position than a person of a different age. The definition of indirect discrimination requires a policy, criterion or practice to put an individual at a particular disadvantage in comparison to people of a different age.

[2] K Lippert-Rasmussen, 'Discrimination and Equality' in A Marmor (ed), *Routledge, Companion to Philosophy of Law* (Routledge, 2012) 569.

[3] However, many deny that equality explains the wrong of discrimination. For example, Tarunabh Khaitan argued that anti-discrimination laws are best justified by the capacity of these laws to enhance freedom of disadvantaged groups: T Khaitan, *A Theory of Discrimination Law* (Oxford University Press, 2015). And Sophie Moreau argued that the wrong of discrimination is explained by it violating liberty: S Moreau, 'What is Discrimination?' (2010) 38 *Philosophy and Public Affairs* 143.

are responsible for their condition of being worse off, and social equality, which requires conditions in which people are able to interact as equals, provides an account of the wrongness of inequality. However, it is important to note that we should not simply assume that the equality principles explain all that is wrong about discrimination. In chapter four, I verify whether the equality principles outlined in this chapter explain the wrongness of discrimination and also consider non-equality principles, such as autonomy and respect, that are important for explaining the wrongness of discrimination. Chapter five examines whether the principles can work to distinguish justified from unjustified treatment that engages the age discrimination provisions.

As I explained in chapter one, I adopt a version of the reflective equilibrium method where I consider not only my own intuitions in searching for appropriate moral principles, but also the intuitions and beliefs of a range of people who have experience with age discrimination issues. I reject the principle of equality of outcome (the idea that equality requires citizens have the same level of resources, welfare etc) on the grounds that it requires citizens to have an equal level of resources regardless of the outcomes of individual choices. Equality of opportunity, I argue, coheres better with our intuitions about personal responsibility than equality of outcome, and is supported by a plausible background theory of personal responsibility that holds that we are responsible for actions when we are capable of being responsive to reasons for acting.

A strict version of equality of opportunity, however, can be overly demanding by requiring unacceptable intrusion on people's autonomy to prevent the formation of advantages and can also be consistent with large inequalities in social status to the extent that some social groups may be in a position of dominance over others. I argue that we should revise an equality of opportunity account of equality to incorporate the social equality principle, which holds that inequality is wrong when it leads to social conditions that deny the ability of individuals to be full and equal participants in modern democratic society.[4] Finally, I argue that we should understand equality as the aim to secure access to the constitutive components of a flourishing life. Rather than selecting one value to equalise, I argue that egalitarians ought to be concerned with creating equal opportunity to experience a range of intrinsic goods, including welfare, autonomy, health and education.

## I. A Starting Point for Understanding Equality

In pre-modern times, it was typical to rank human worth according to wealth, power and social class. The modern idea of equality instead asserts that all humans

[4] David Miller and Elizabeth Anderson have defended versions of social equality or democratic principle equality: D Miller, 'What Kind of Equality Should the Left Pursue' in J Franklin (ed), *Equality* (Institute for Public Policy Research, 1997); E Anderson, 'What Is the Point of Equality?' (1999) 109 *Ethics* 287.

have an equal and objectively high moral status. This derives from the Kantian idea that the capacity for self-governance and autonomous choice is determinative of the equal status and value of human beings.[5] According to this idea, humans have an equal incomparable dignity, and to respect this dignity, we should always treat people with equal concern and respect.[6] Discrimination and other forms of unequal treatment can undermine this ideal. This version of equality is widely accepted, and discussions of equality tend to concern how this idea should inform the way we treat people.[7]

I now consider the sorts of actions and conditions that can wrongfully undermine this moral equality. I consider strict equality of outcome and conclude that it fails to support our moral beliefs about equality. I defend two equality principles – equality of opportunity and social equality – that explain when and why inequality is wrong.

## II. Strict Equality of Outcome

Strict equality of outcome requires that people hold an equal level of goods, whether that be welfare, resources or some other values. The problems with strict equality of outcome are familiar. To achieve equality of outcome would be to violate personal responsibility. We would have to distribute resources from people who are prudent – and therefore have accumulated more resources than others – to people who are wasteful. This shields the reckless and irresponsible from the consequences of their choices, and, in doing so, rewards free riders, who can unfairly exploit the prudence of others.

Another problem is that equality of outcome does not respect individual preferences. One person may be content with a moderate income if their job provides for a work–life balance, another person may want to work long hours to achieve a higher income and yet another person may be content with a low income if it means pursuing their passion for creating art. Forcing equality of outcome would have to neutralise the choice to pursue different forms of life.

To create equal outcomes, it would be necessary to constantly interfere with voluntary choices. For example, a large number of people may be happy to pay money to witness the skill of a sports star and this will inevitably result in the

[5] I Kant, *Groundwork of the Metaphysics of Morals*, M Gregor, trans, ed (Cambridge University Press, 1998).

[6] Dworkin has argued that moral equality requires treating people as equals. This principle recognises that we can treat people differently if different circumstances require this, but to treat people as equals, Dworkin argues, means that we should always show equal concern and respect in our treatment of others: R Dworkin, *Taking Rights Seriously* (Harvard University Press, 1977) 370.

[7] The belief in the equal moral worth of persons is not universal. For example, Uwe Steinhoff has argued that there is no universal duty 'of equal respect and concern' or equal worth of persons: U Steinhoff, *Do All Persons Have Equal Moral Worth?: On 'Basic Equality' and Equal Respect and Concern* (Oxford University Press, 2015) ch 8.

sports star holding a larger pool of resources than many others. But to create equality of outcomes, we would have to prevent, or at least interfere with, these voluntary choices to ensure that the sports star does not hold more resources than others.[8] This invasion of liberty in pursuit of equality is too severe.[9]

Strict equality of outcomes is also likely to lead to an inefficient economy since it offers the same outcomes for productive and unproductive behaviour, thereby removing incentives to avoid waste. We would need a huge bureaucracy to measure outcomes and to redistribute resources to ensure equal holdings for different individuals.[10] This inefficiency would lead to lower prosperity, which in turn would lead to lower welfare for society as a whole.

An account of equality that fits better with our intuitions would account for personal responsibility, welfare and liberty by ensuring that people are responsible for certain inequalities resulting from their decisions. Further to providing such an account of equality, I now consider the equality of opportunity principle.[11]

## III. Equality of Opportunity

Equality of opportunity holds that inequalities are acceptable if they result from personal choices; inequalities are unacceptable when they result from factors outside our control. For example, it is not wrong for the person who chooses to go on multiple holidays a year to end up with less resources than the person who chooses to invest their disposable income, but it is wrong for one person to be much wealthier than another simply because they were born into a wealthy family. This is the luck egalitarian version of the equality of opportunity principle, which holds that it is wrong for a person to be worse off to the extent that they are not

[8] This is Robert Nozick's famous Wilt Chamberlain argument. It demonstrates that equality of outcome would disrupt the patterns that result from free choices. Respecting liberty, Nozick argues, means we have to accept inequality of outcome. R Nozick, *Anarchy, State and Utopia* (Basic Books, 1974) 160–61.

[9] For a detailed libertarian criticism of the pursuit of equality of outcome, see F Hayek, *The Constitution of Liberty* (Routledge, 1960).

[10] Equality of outcome would require extensive government central planning. Central planning has a host of undesirable consequences, including the fact that it usually requires authoritarian government. See F Hayek, *The Road to Serfdom* (Routledge, 2014).

[11] Note, however, that some thinkers argue that we should not consider equality of opportunity in isolation from assessing equality of outcome. For example, Anne Phillips argued that we should collapse the distinction between equality of outcome and equality of opportunity when we compare different social groups: A Phillips, 'Defending Equality of Outcome' (2004) 12 *Journal of Political Philosophy* 1. She argued that 'It makes sense to start from the expectation that all groups would normally be distributed in roughly equal proportions along all measures of social activity: to expect, therefore, an equality of outcome, and to take any divergence from this as a reasonably safe indication that opportunities are not yet equal' (18). To take equality opportunity seriously, she argues, we should 'regard equality of outcome as the template against which to measure equal opportunity claims'. This argument, while sensitive to outcome, still takes equality of opportunity as its foundational equality principle.

directly responsible for their condition of being worse off.[12] It follows from this that we should try giving people initial equality of opportunity and then let people choose how and when to exercise those opportunities.

The sorts of things we are not responsible for include the circumstances we find ourselves in, including our genetics, our ethnicity and our upbringing.[13] To create equality of opportunity, we must redistribute to ensure an equal starting point in life.[14] An example might be education: some children have an unfair start in life because they have better teachers and more supportive parents than others. This early form of socialisation will place these people at a strong advantage to access higher paying employment. Equality of opportunity requires ensuring that each child has an equal chance of accessing the higher paying and rewarding work, and this requires taking measures to ensure educational benefits are roughly equal for each child. This requires higher spending for children from socially disadvantaged families to level the playing field.

Luck egalitarians, such as Ronald Dworkin, have called the negative consequences that result from unchosen circumstances brute luck, whereas inequalities that result from choice is called option luck.[15] Only the latter type of inequality, they have argued, is acceptable.[16] Dworkin's version of equality of opportunity requires initial equal division of resources, but after this initial division, the result of free choices should be borne by individuals. In contrast, we should compensate brute luck misfortune in full. For example, if a person invests in the stock market and loses wealth, then we should not compensate this loss since it is a voluntary gamble. However, the costs caused by genetic disability should not be borne by the individual since they cannot be held responsible for the disability.

The equality of opportunity principle accounts for our intuitions about personal responsibility. As Arneson has argued, 'In myriad institutional contexts we hold people responsible for the good or bad outcomes of their choices by attaching

[12] The following have defended this principle: G Cohen, 'On the Currency of Egalitarian Justice' (1989) 99 *Ethics* 906; S Segall, *Equality and Opportunity* (Oxford University Press, 2013); A Mason, *Levelling the Playing Field: The Idea of Equality of Opportunity and Its Place in Egalitarian Thought* (Oxford University Press, 2006). For critics of this principle, see Anderson (n 4); S Scheffler, 'What Is Egalitarianism?' (2003) 31 *Philosophy and Public Affairs* 5; M Fleurbaey, 'Equal Opportunity or Equal Social Outcome?' (1995) 11 *Economics and Philosophy* 25.

[13] R Arneson, 'Equality of Opportunity' in E Zalta (ed), *The Stanford Encyclopedia of Philosophy*, Summer 2015 edn https://plato.stanford.edu/archives/sum2015/entries/equal-opportunity/.

[14] This is the level playing field idea. See J Roemer, *Equality of Opportunity* (Cambridge University Press, 1998).

[15] Dworkin had distanced himself from the luck egalitarian label, although his theory of equality supports the central tenets of the doctrine.

[16] Dworkin has defined brute luck as 'a matter of how risks fall out that are not in that sense deliberate gambles': R Dworkin, 'What is Equality? Part 1: Equality of Welfare' (1981) 10 *Philosophy and Public Affairs* 185. He has defined option luck as 'a matter of how deliberate and calculated gambles turn out – whether someone gains or loses through accepting an isolated risk he or she should have anticipated and might have declined': R Dworkin, *Sovereign Virtue: The Theory and Practice of Equality* (Harvard University Press, 2002) 73.

negative and positive sanctions, punishments and rewards, to them'.[17] Adults are capable of autonomous choices if they are not under duress or suffering serious mental illness and are morally responsible for their choices. A failure to do this leads to a moral hazard where 'one person makes the decision about how much risk to take, while someone else bears the cost if things go badly'.[18]

Equality of opportunity also fits with our intuition that it is wrong for the state to interfere with the outcomes of our choices. In the discussion of equality of outcome, I argued that the problem with the doctrine is that it would require constant redistributions from the consequences of choices to artificially maintain an equal outcome, which is an unacceptable intrusion into liberty. Equality of opportunity addresses this problem by accepting that individuals should be free to choose how to exercise their opportunities. The resulting inequality, however, is acceptable.

Equality of opportunity promotes independence, self-reliance and, therefore, self-respect. A failure to ensure people are responsible for the consequences of their choices means that people will become 'dependent on others, where being dependent on others means continually looking to others to meet one's basic needs'.[19] And this means people will not shape their life, but will require others to shape it.

But why exactly is inequality of opportunity wrong? The best answer is that it coheres with our belief that inequality of opportunity is unfair.[20] Brute luck consequences should be equalised because people are not morally responsible for these circumstances, and it is unfair for people to be worse off than others due to factors outside their reasonable control. Since every person is entitled to equal concern and respect, we ought to avoid granting or permitting better conditions to particular people on an arbitrary basis, such as brute luck consequences. It follows that the value of equality requires a presumption in favour of equal access to goods unless option luck causes inequality.

However, sometimes we should not hold individuals responsible for the consequences that result from their choices. For example, a person may choose to travel to work by car knowing that there is a very small chance that a storm will arise that will lead to a car accident. The driver has made a choice to take on this risk, but it is inappropriate to hold the driver fully responsible for the damage caused by the storm since the risk resulting from a choice is so small. It is reasonable for a person to take this risk and unreasonable to hold that the individual

[17] R Arneson, 'Luck Egalitarianism: A Primer' in C Knight and Z Stemplowska (eds), *Responsibility and Distributive Justice* (Oxford University Press, 2011) 26.

[18] P Krugman, *The Return of Depression Economics and the Crisis of 2008* (WW Norton & Company, 2009) 224.

[19] A Brown, *Personal Responsibility: Why It Matters* (Bloomsbury Publishing, 2009) 19.

[20] L Temkin, 'Equality, Priority, and the Levelling Down Objection' in M Clayton and A Williams (eds), *The Ideal of Equality* (Macmillan, 2000) 126.

must cover all the costs of any negative consequences. The effects of bad luck that individuals cannot reasonably avoid should constitute brute luck and be subject to compensation.[21]

To determine when a risk cannot be reasonably avoided, we should consider the likelihood that a disadvantage will arise, the extent of the disadvantage, the likely benefits from taking a risk and the availability of other options that may reduce the risk. The person who chooses to drive despite a risk of a storm cannot reasonably avoid that risk if we assume the chance of the storm occurring is very low, the benefit to be gained from driving is very high (eg going to work) and other forms of transport are unavailable.

Importantly, there is not always a clear division between brute luck and option luck. The consequences of choices may be the result of both option luck and brute luck. For example:

> Consider a case where I can choose between two alternatives. One involves a 75% chance of having one's crop destroyed by cold weather. The other one involves a 70% chance of having one's crop destroyed by flooding. In one sense, obviously, either risk is avoidable. Yet, if one were to go for the first alternative, and if one's crops were destroyed by cold weather, it would seem odd to say that the full extent to which one becomes worse off as a result of that choice is a matter of bad option luck. After all, the chances of becoming just as badly off via a different causal route, had I chosen the other alternative, were almost as great. So it seems we should often think of a given piece of luck as a mixture of brute luck and option luck where the exact mixture depends on the extent to which one could influence the expected value of the outcome of one's choice. In the present case, I could only marginally influence the expected value of the outcome. Hence the disadvantages resulting from my choice should be seen as mostly a matter of bad brute luck.[22]

A key consideration in determining brute luck, then, is the extent we can reasonably influence the likelihood of an outcome occurring. The greater the extent we cannot influence an outcome, the greater degree we should attribute the consequences of the choice to brute luck.

## IV. Choice and Moral Responsibility

One may object to equality of opportunity on the grounds that a person's 'choices' are really indistinguishable from a person's circumstances and therefore must also

[21] Several scholars have clarified and amended Dworkin's definition of brute luck and option luck. See K Lippert-Rasmussen, 'Equality, Option Luck, and Responsibility' (2001) 111 *Ethics* 548; P Vallentyne, 'Brute Luck, Option Luck, and Equality of Initial Opportunities' (2002) 112 *Ethics* 529; P Vallentyne, 'Brute Luck and Responsibility' (2008) 7 *Politics, Philosophy & Economics* 57; M Otsuka, 'Luck, Insurance, and Equality' (2002) 113 *Ethics* 40.

[22] K Lippert-Rasmussen, 'Justice and Bad Luck' in E Zalta (ed), *The Stanford Encyclopedia of Philosophy*, Summer 2014 edn https://plato.stanford.edu/archives/sum2014/entries/justice-bad-luck/.

qualify as brute luck that should be equalised.[23] On this account, people do not choose who they are; rather, they are determined by their environment and shaped by socialisation. Traits that we associate with option luck, such as effort, ambition and prudence, are the result of socialisation by upbringing and environment. It follows from this argument that equality of opportunity is incorrect in identifying the wrong of inequality as being inequality resulting from forces apart from our choices. Our choices, so this argument goes, are also brute luck for which we are not responsible.[24] If this is true, then it is senseless to hold anyone morally responsible for any action.

The standard reply is the position of compatibilism, which acknowledges that everything we do is fixed in advance but that this determinism is consistent with free choice and responsibility.[25] If we follow this account, we need to acknowledge the undoubted truth that inequality caused by effort, ambition and prudence are, at least partly, the result of socialisation by upbringing and environment, but we must argue that the most plausible background theory of personal responsibility holds that socialisation and cultural structures can coexist with genuine choice and therefore personal responsibility. In support of this, I defend the background theory that people can be held responsible when they are reason-responsive.[26] We can define reason responsiveness as the capacity for individuals to reflect on different options and to select between those options.[27]

Our attitudes correspond to the reason responsiveness version of personal responsibility. Emotions such as gratitude, resentment, forgiveness, love and hurt feelings are all predicated on holding people responsible for their choices and tend to be displayed to people who are capable of responding to reasons.[28] For example, we usually resent a person who has killed another, but we are unlikely to have this attitude if we learn that person was suffering from a mental illness and they were acting under the influence of hallucinations. The person suffering from the mental illness is incapable of doing otherwise because their rationality has been impaired to the extent that they cannot consider and act upon a range of reasons. For a

[23] S Smilansky, 'Egalitarian Justice and the Importance of the Free Will Problem' (1997) 25 *Philosophia* 153.

[24] This is a position called hard determinism – the idea that every event is necessitated by antecedent events.

[25] David Hume, the enlightenment philosopher, supported compatibilism. The modern philosophers Peter Strawson and Harry Frankfurt also support it. See D Hume, *An Enquiry Concerning Human Understanding*, Peter Nidditch, ed (Clarendon Press, 1978); P Strawson, *Freedom and Resentment and Other Essays* (Routledge, 2008); H Frankfurt, 'Alternate Possibilities and Moral Responsibility' (1969) 66 *Journal of Philosophy* 829.

[26] There is extensive literature on the view that reason responsiveness is the foundation for personal responsibility. See D Dennett, *Elbow Room: The Varieties of Free Will Worth Wanting* (MIT Press, 1984); H Fingarette, *The Meaning of Criminal Insanity* (University of California Press, 1972); A MacIntyre, 'Determinism' (1957) 66 *Mind* 28; R Nozick, *Philosophical Explanations* (Harvard University Press, 1981).

[27] G Watson, 'Reason and Responsibility' (2001) 111 *Ethics* 374.

[28] P Strawson, 'Freedom and Resentment' (1962) 48 *Proceedings of the British Academy* 1.

similar reason, we are unlikely to condemn a person who has lied to us because they were under duress. Duress pressures and coerces people into taking a particular course of action and deprives them of the chance to act upon an appropriate range of reasons. As such, we can say they are incapable of doing otherwise and therefore we will not hold them responsible for their actions.

We accept that people who are unresponsive to appropriate rational considerations do not act under free will. But people who are responsive to a range of rational considerations are morally responsible for the decisions they make. Responsiveness to reasons requires a set of alternatives and information about those alternatives.[29]

We can test whether a person is reason responsive by considering whether they would have acted differently if the reasons to act were different. For example, the person who has lied to us because of selfishness would act differently if they were offered a considerable financial reward for telling the truth. We would therefore hold this person responsible for their actions because they were capable of acting differently by responding to reasons. In contrast, the mentally ill person and the person under duress, assuming that the illness and duress rendered these individuals incapable of valuing financial reward in those circumstances, would not change their behaviour if offered a reward and therefore could be considered to be incapable of acting differently.

This reason responsiveness theory of personal responsibility supports the position that inequality can be appropriate when it is the result of holding people appropriately responsible for their choices. However, an individual may make choices from a background of unchosen circumstances that influences their choice. For example, making choices from a position of poverty is likely to influence how we decide what to do. And since people do not choose these circumstances, they cannot be held responsible for them. The result is that the outcomes of our choices can be a mixture of both option luck and the brute luck that influences how we respond to reasons for action. To be plausible, then, equality of opportunity must accommodate adequately the impact of socialisation and reflect the impact this has on our responsibility for making decisions. Inequality resulting from choices can only be justified to the extent that it is unconnected to unequal bad brute luck circumstances.

There are a number of different ways theorists have identified the extent decisions are made from choice, for which individuals should be held responsible, and the extent decisions are made from a background of unfortunate circumstances, for which they should not be held responsible. Roemer's Pragmatic Theory of Responsibility is probably the best attempt to account for unchosen circumstances such as socialisation.[30] Roemer's theory holds that people are responsible

[29] T Scanlon, 'The Significance of Choice' (1998) 8 *The Tanner Lectures on Human Values* 149.
[30] J Roemer, 'A Pragmatic Theory of Responsibility for the Egalitarian Planner' (1993) 22 *Philosophy and Public Affairs* 146.

if they are responsive to reasons while holding that it is not justifiable for decision-makers to bear the full costs of a decision that is related to circumstances that they have not chosen. There are degrees of responsibility for the outcomes of our choices, and this depends on the control we have over those choices and their outcomes.

To evaluate the wrongness of inequality, then, we must look at all the factors that caused the individual to choose a course of action and evaluate which of these factors are in the control of the individual, and therefore option luck, and which of these factors are outside the control of the individual, and therefore brute luck. We can thus determine the proportion of option luck to brute luck. The extent to which inequality is wrong is the extent to which factors outside the individual's control caused the outcome.[31]

To demonstrate this theory, we can look at Roemer's example of a smoker who has contracted lung cancer.[32] To determine the extent of the smoker's responsibility for the illness, we need to consider the range of circumstances that influenced that person's decision to take up smoking. This can include parental influence, schooling and socio-economic status. We can then assign people into groups who have similar backgrounds and influences. We can judge people in these groups as having equivalent levels of responsibility for taking up smoking. For example, people in a higher socio-economic class who did not have parents who were smokers will have greater responsibility for taking up smoking than people in lower socio-economic classes who had parents who were smokers.

We can also think how Roemer's theory applies to talent, which is a significant cause of inequality. Genetics and supportive parents and teachers influence talent. This means that the outcomes of talent are partly the result of undeserved circumstances; therefore, inequality from talent with no redistribution is wrong.[33] However, we are at least partly responsible for the results of exercising and developing our talents because so treating our talents is a choice that falls into the option luck category. We should therefore accept reward for exercising talent, but we should also ensure that the resulting distribution reflects the fact that some people have more talent to exercise than others. In other words, we must recognise that people make decisions from circumstances where there are unequal conditions to exploit opportunities.[34]

For example, consider a person with a supportive family who exerts himself to develop his talents and, as a result, becomes wealthy. Another person, raised by negligent parents, suffers from a lack of confidence and therefore remains poor.

[31] For a criticism of Roemer's theory, see A Mason, 'XI – Equality, Personal Responsibility, and Gender Socialisation' (2000) 100 *Proceedings of the Aristotelian Society* 227.

[32] Roemer (n 30) 150–52.

[33] '[T]he extent to which natural capacities develop and reach fruition is affected by all kinds of social conditions and class attitudes.' Rawls regards natural talents as a common asset that should be shared amongst society. J Rawls, *A Theory of Justice* (Harvard University Press, 2009) 164.

[34] Phillips (n 11).

Choice has influenced the outcomes. The first person made a decision to exert himself, while the second person did not. However, unchosen circumstances influenced the choice to exert or not to exert. Due to brute luck differences (such as family background), the individuals do not face an equivalent range of options to choose from. The inequality in this example is therefore partly the result of brute luck and partly the result of option luck. The distributive consequences ought to reward the productive person, but it is wrong for the first person to have all of the positive consequences of exercising their talents while the second person suffers entirely from not exercising theirs. Equality of opportunity requires we redistribute to disadvantaged people to reflect the fact that their position is, to a considerable extent, the result of bad brute luck. Equality of opportunity requires redistributing wealth to ensure that people who have benefited from advantageous conditions contribute to assisting people who have acted against a background of disadvantage.

## V. Problems with Equality of Opportunity

The critics of equality of opportunity argue that implementation of the principle would require state agencies to make invasive moral assessments into whether individuals have made the best use of their opportunities. For example:

> In order to lay a claim to some important benefit, people are forced to obey other people's judgements of what uses they should have made of their opportunities, rather than following their own judgments. Such a system requires the state to make grossly intrusive, moralizing judgments of individual's choices. Equality of fortune thus interferes with citizens' privacy and liberty. Furthermore, as Arneson and Roemer make clear, such judgments require the state to determine how much responsibility each citizen was capable of exercising in each case. But it is disrespectful for the state to pass judgment on how much people are responsible for their expensive tastes or their imprudent choices.[35]

Further:

> Equality of fortune succeeds not in establishing a society of equals, but only in reproducing the stigmatizing regime of the Poor Laws, in which citizens lay claim to aid from the state only on condition that they accept inferior status. Poor Law thinking pervades the reasoning of luck egalitarians. This is most evident in their distinction between the deserving and the undeserving disadvantaged.[36]

Imagine I find myself unemployed despite a long search for employment. To qualify for employment benefits under the luck egalitarian version of equality of opportunity, I would have to demonstrate to the government that I am incompetent at

[35] Anderson (n 4), 310.
[36] ibid 310.

finding employment through no fault or choice of my own. This forces me to reveal something shameful about myself. Equality of opportunity prioritises fairness over other principles, including respect. Securing complete equality of opportunity would lead to widespread violations of the respect principle by imposing shameful revelations.[37]

Anderson has also argued that the attempt to eradicate brute luck inequalities can stigmatise people by expressing contemptuous pity towards them.[38] For example, we know that physically attractive people have advantages in society. It follows that equality of opportunity requires, as a matter of fairness, that attractive people compensate less attractive people for their unfortunate aesthetics. This action, however, is disrespectful and humiliating.

Another possible criticism is that equality of opportunity is very demanding when it is not balanced by other principles. We know, for example, that parents reading to their children can create educational advantages.[39] To correct the resulting inequality would require either prohibiting parents from reading to their children, somehow forcing parents to read to their children or the state taking radical remedial measures to correct the advantages that some children have. Each of these approaches could pose an unacceptable intrusion into people's autonomy. The force of the above criticisms of equality of opportunity, however, do not mean that we must abandon the fairness requirements of the principle. The criticisms are only persuasive as an argument to abandon equality of opportunity if we view the principle as a 'strong equalisandum claim, which is the sort that an uncompromising egalitarian asserts, [that] says that people should be as equal as possible in the dimension it specifies'.[40] However, we do not need to understand equality principles as absolute requirements that cannot be overridden in circumstances where the principle would lead to bad outcomes or violate important moral principles. Instead, as Temkin has argued, equality can be understood as one moral consideration among many and should give way to other principles when equality of opportunity has unacceptable consequences.[41] For example, equality of opportunity in exclusion of other principles may specify that we should make moralising judgements to distinguish the deserving from the undeserving poor. However, we can trade off the equality of opportunity demand of distinguishing the deserving from the undeserving with the respect principle, which requires that we do not make moralising judgements about people. For example, the failure to monitor the responsibility of benefit claimants in their unemployment status will provide

[37] Wolff has argued that a decent society does not impose shameful revelations on any of its members: J Wolff, 'Fairness, Respect, and the Egalitarian Ethos' (1998) 27 *Philosophy and Public Affairs* 97.

[38] Anderson (n 4), 306.

[39] J Hutton, T Horowitz-Kraus, A Mendelsohn, T DeWitt, S Holland and the C-MIND Authorship Consortium, 'Home Reading Environment and Brain Activation in Preschool Children Listening to Stories' (2015) 136 *Pediatrics* 466.

[40] Cohen (n 12) 908.

[41] '[A]ny reasonable egalitarian will be a pluralist. Equality is not the only thing that matters to an egalitarian.' L Temkin, 'Egalitarianism Defended' (2003) 113 *Ethics* 63.

conditions where people can claim a taxpayer-funded benefit without the effort of finding employment. But monitoring the claimant's behaviour can be stigmatising by passing judgement on the individual's capabilities in finding employment. We should strike a balance between these competing values. The process of distributing benefits should not be overly intrusive on an individual's private life. Equality of opportunity, on this approach, can be subject to limitations in deference to other values.

Another criticism of equality of opportunity is that the refusal to compensate bad option luck can lead to the refusal to help those who become destitute through their own choices.[42] The argument is that equality of opportunity is overly harsh. Again, this argument should not require us to abandon equality of opportunity but, as part of a pluralist framework, we should supplement equality of opportunity with a threshold of wealth below which we do not permit people to fall regardless of how culpable they are for their destitution.[43] A sufficiency principle can require a threshold of resources or welfare that people should have whatever their personal conduct. But beyond that threshold, the equality of opportunity principle should hold people responsible for losses from actions that can be properly attached to individual choice.

## VI. Social Equality

Equality of opportunity cannot reveal the full picture needed to understand the wrong of inequality. Perfect equality of opportunity will still leave us with inequality that we intuitively deem unacceptable. For example, imagine an arrangement that the top 100 hardest workers should have 90 per cent of the world's wealth. If we assume this is in conditions where people have an equal initial starting point, this is compatible with equality of opportunity. Also, imagine using a lottery to assign people into a particular caste in society. In both these examples, there is an initial equality of opportunity, but the resulting option luck leads to what we would consider wrongful inequality.[44] What is wrong in both these examples is that the inequality leads to real or potential domination of one group of people over others. Equality of opportunity is therefore consistent with the creation of hierarchies where some are subordinated and/or marginalised.

If we are to fully respect the moral equality of people, we must ensure that people are not treated as having inferior moral status and are not excluded from the valuable things that society has to offer. Equality of opportunity does not

[42] S Scheffler, 'Responsibility, Reactive Attitudes, and Liberalism in Philosophy and Politics' (1992) 21 *Philosophy and Public Affairs* 299.

[43] Paula Casal argued in favour of this approach: P Casal, 'Why Sufficiency Is Not Enough' (2007) 117 *Ethics* 296.

[44] P Vallentyne, 'Brute luck, Option Luck, and Equality of Initial Opportunities' (n 21).

guarantee people having equality of status and does not guarantee that people are participating in society.

It is clear, then, that equality of opportunity cannot be a complete theory accounting for our intuitions about all types of wrongful inequality. We need to identify a principle that can explain why, for example, oppression and subordination are wrong. To do this, we can look beyond considerations of distribution and towards inequalities that relate to how people regard one another. This is the social basis of equality that equality of opportunity overlooks.[45] Social equality, unlike equality of opportunity, does not directly concern any specific distribution. Instead, it concerns the ideal that people should be able to regard one another as equals.

As David Miller has stated:

> [Social equality] does not require that people should be equal in power, prestige or wealth, nor, absurdly, that they should score the same on natural dimensions such as strength or intelligence. What matters is how such differences are regarded, and in particular whether they serve to construct a social hierarchy in which A can unequivocally be ranked as B's superior. Where there is social equality, people feel that each member of the community enjoys an equal standing with all the rest that overrides their unequal ratings along particular dimensions.[46]

While there is widespread acceptance of certain differences of rank, power and status, including the power of employers over employees and teachers over students, there are certain types of hierarchical relationship that threaten a community founded on equal concern and respect. Slavery, aristocracy and caste systems, for example, are arrangements that make it impossible for citizens to live together as equals. Social equality requires developing a community that has proper forms of relationships between people. Any form of social hierarchies that convey a ranking of human beings is wrongful inequality on this account. This includes any forms of relationships where some can dominate, oppress or exploit others.

Oppressive relationships do not just emerge as one person oppressing another; they can also be cultural. This form of oppression relates to a societal practice where large numbers of people, over a number of generations, have together engaged in actions that subordinate less powerful groups. Beliefs, values, attitudes and assumptions in a society can reflect and maintain relations of dominance and subordination that have resulted from conditioning and socialisation.[47] This has occurred most obviously with regard to race and sex, but, as I explain in chapter five, it has also applied to age groups.

This form of oppression becomes a form of socialisation that makes the oppression very difficult to dislodge. For example, stereotypes about the inferiority of particular social groups can be passed on through generations, and the acceptance

[45] D Miller, 'Equality and Justice' (1997) 10 *Ratio* 222.
[46] D Miller, *Principles of Social Justice* (Harvard University Press, 1999) 239.
[47] K Warren, 'The Power and Promise of Ecological Feminism' (1990) *Environmental Ethics* 125.

of widespread discrimination can lead to feelings that the subordinate status of particular social groups is natural and expected. As Susan Sherwin notes, individuals can internalise these beliefs.[48] It is the aim of social equality to break down these relationships of dominance and subordination.

In addition, social equality requires we should maintain social conditions that enable each individual to be a full and equal participant in modern democratic society.[49] This means that we should aim to ensure that each individual has self-determination and does not have to regard themselves or others as inferior.

Social equality requires that each person in a diverse society has the opportunity to have their views considered on an equal basis. Excessive hierarchies in authority can create conditions in which oppression and marginalisation can thrive. According to Young, 'Oppression refers to structural phenomena that immobilize or diminish a group', where group is defined as 'a collective of persons differentiated from at least one other group by cultural forms, practices, or way of life'.[50] In essence, social equality is in opposition to disadvantages suffered due to membership of socially salient groups based on characteristics such as gender, ethnicity, religion and sexual preference. Since group affinity is a major component of individual identity, to subordinate or discriminate because of social-group membership is to cast some groups as inferior. This, in turn, can create patterns of oppression, which threaten a society of equals by reinforcing a sense of superiority among the fortunate and undermining the self-respect of the unfortunate.

According to Anderson, a society of equals requires people to participate in fair systems of cooperation.[51] Since our economy is a cooperative, joint production, then the productivity of a worker in a specific role depends not only on their own efforts, but also on other people performing their roles. It follows, Anderson argues, that every distribution in our economy should be capable of being justified to each person cooperating in a society. Social equality in this way is a requirement of reciprocity because obligations arise when people benefit from projects that result from the contributions of a group of people.[52] Those who benefit from collective projects ought to contribute to ensuring that all other people contributing to the product have an adequate outcome distribution. As a matter of fairness, reciprocity requires that the wealthy recognise the contribution of others by ensuring that low-income workers have access to goods necessary for a flourishing life, including healthcare, housing and education. These goods are essential for people participating in society's institutions as equals. To deny a section of society access

[48] S Sherwin, *No Longer Patient: Feminist Ethics and Health Care* (Temple University Press, 1992) 14.

[49] Anderson names this principle 'democratic equality' (n 4). I use the name 'social equality' because it better captures that this version of equality relates not just to participation in democracy, but also to participation in society.

[50] I Young, *Justice and the Politics of Difference* (Princeton University Press, 2011) 42.

[51] Anderson (n 4) 321.

[52] For a theory on how reciprocity gives rise to moral duties, see A Sangiovanni, 'Global Justice, Reciprocity, and the State' (2007) 35 *Philosophy and Public Affairs* 3.

to basic education would create conditions in which the educated can dominate power in democratic institutions, leading to the marginalisation of others.

Social equality requires effective societal participation, and this requires effective participation in the labour market and an adequate standard of living. We cannot, for example, participate as equals in the labour market without access to food, medical treatment and sufficient education levels. A failure to provide these goods is to permit the creation of a socially excluded underclass. Higher-status social classes will have the option to dominate and marginalise the unfortunate.

Social equality aims to guarantee sufficient baseline conditions in order that people can function and participate in society as equals. This baseline should not be lost. Equality of opportunity, in contrast, does not recognise a baseline, but adopts the position that people can lose resources because of personal irresponsibility. However, when people have enough resources to participate in society as equals, we need the principle of equality of opportunity to determine the fairness of distribution beyond the threshold. This sufficiency-constrained equality of opportunity incorporates our duties of common humanity with duties to promote personal responsibility.

## VII. Equality of What?

The 'equality of what' debate has focused on determining which particular condition of inequality should be of moral concern – for example, inequality of welfare, resources or capabilities – and explaining why we care about unequal distribution of some things but not others. The concept of equality itself cannot tell us what is important to equalise. As Joseph Raz has argued:

> We only have reason to care about inequalities in the distribution of *goods* and *ills*[,] that is of what is value or disvalue for independent reasons. There is no reason to care about inequalities in the distribution of sand, unless there is some other reason to wish to have or avoid sand.[53]

Equality theory has suggested a range of different things that are subject to equality principles.[54] The most plausible reason why equality theorists have struggled to identify one thing of value that is worthy of equalising (whether resources, welfare or capabilities) is that it is implausible that there is only one value of intrinsic worth we should attempt to equalise. There may be no value on its own that we are required to equalise, but there may be a number of values. Each argument for

[53] J Raz, *The Morality of Freedom* (Clarendon Press, 1986) 235 (emphasis added).

[54] Rawls (n 33) and R Dworkin, What is Equality? Part 2: Equality of Resources' (1981) 10 *Philosophy and Public Affairs* 283 supported an equality of resources approach. Richard Arneson has supported an equality of opportunity to welfare approach: R Arneson, 'Equality and Equal Opportunity for Welfare' (1989) 56 *Philosophical Studies* 77. Arguing for an equality of capabilities approach, A Sen, *Inequality Reexamined* (Clarendon Press, 1992).

selecting one value to equalise seems persuasive as it recognises the importance we attach to that value. However, prioritising one of these values to the total exclusion of other values has unattractive consequences. I demonstrate this by using a series of thought experiments.

Access to welfare is a commonly cited value. John Stuart Mill famously argued 'that happiness is desirable, and the only thing desirable, as an end; all other things being only desirable as means to that end'.[55] If the experience of happiness (or welfare) is the only intrinsic end, then we must try to maximise it across people. Amartya Sen uses the following example to show the unattractive consequences of this welfarist approach:

> If person A as a cripple gets half the utility that the pleasure-wizard person B does from any given level of income, then in the pure distribution problem between A and B the utilitarian would end up giving the pleasure-wizard B more income than the cripple A. The cripple would then be doubly worse off: both since he gets less utility from the same level of income, and since he will also get less income. Utilitarianism must lead to this thanks to its single-minded concern with maximizing the utility sum. The pleasure-wizard's superior efficiency in producing utility would pull income away from the less efficient cripple.[56]

The distribution of income in Sen's example is unfair because it treats person B's projects as more worthy of concern than person A's projects. The fact that person B's projects generate more utility does not, however, make them more worthy of concern. Welfare is not the only value to judge the worth of a person's life.

In a thought experiment designed to refute welfarism, Nozick asks us to imagine that we have the choice to plug ourselves into a machine that can give us whatever desirable or pleasurable experiences we want. If welfare is the only intrinsic value, then we ought to plug ourselves into the machine without hesitation. But there are reasons to live in a real life rather than an experience machine, namely 'We want to make a difference in the world' and 'it is only because we first want to do the actions that we want the experiences of doing them'.[57] Applied to Sen's example, person A may not derive much pleasure from their projects, but they can still derive value from using their income as a way of contributing something meaningful to the world. This non-welfare value is no less worthy than the welfare generated by person B.

Another commonly cited problem with equalising welfare is that it will require subsidising people to indulge their expensive tastes. This will mean giving more resources to some people simply because they need more resources in order to generate sufficient levels of welfare. For example, if person A is unable to walk

[55] JS Mill, 'Utilitarianism' in R Shafer-Landau (ed), *Ethical Theory: An Anthology* (John Wiley & Sons, 2012) 288.
[56] A Sen, 'Equality of What?' in S McMurrin (ed), *Tanner Lectures on Human Values: Vol 1* (Cambridge University Press, 1980).
[57] Nozick (n 8) 42–45.

but is happier than person B, who can only be satisfied if he consumes expensive wines, we will then have to prioritise paying for expensive wines for person B before paying for a wheelchair for person A. This certainly seems unjust, given that providing the wheelchair seems more urgent.

The problem of expensive tastes has led some egalitarians to emphasise prioritising equality of resources over equality of welfare. Dworkin, for example, has argued that we ought to give person A a wheelchair because they are inadequately resourced.[58] This approach aims to give people equal resources regardless of the fact that some may experience greater welfare than others from these resources. Sen's capability approach can explain the problem of resource deprivation as failing to provide that person with an adequate set of capabilities necessary to live a flourishing life.

But equality of resources and equality of capabilities do not seem to provide a value that must be prioritised over other values. Gerald Cohen asks us to imagine someone who can move their arms more easily than other people can but that movement leads to pain later in their life.[59] We would want to cure this pain even though that would lead to this person gaining more resources than others. Medicine that would cure the pain would not compensate for lower resources or diminished capabilities. The fact that the individual can move their arms more freely than others suggests that the individual has greater capabilities. The medicine is effective for compensating for the diminished welfare of the individual and this is a good reason to distribute more resources to the person experiencing pain.

Cohen has argued persuasively that Dworkin is wrong to have argued that expensive tastes render attempts to equalise welfare unpalatable. If expensive tastes have been deliberately cultivated, then this falls into the category of chosen circumstances – the costs of which the individual should cover. We should not subsidise expensive wines for people who have spent the bulk of their savings cultivating a taste in fine wines. But it is not unjust to fund 'tastes' that result not from option luck but brute luck. People should not be worse off in terms of welfare because of the brute luck disadvantage of requiring more resources in order to generate a sufficient level of welfare. A strict focus on equality of resources or capabilities will unfairly leave some worse off than others in terms of welfare when the individual is not at fault for that inequality.

Cohen provides the following example:

> People vary in the amount of discomfort which given low temperatures cause them, and, consequently, in the volume of resources which they need to alleviate their discomfort. Some people need costly heavy sweaters and a great deal of fuel to achieve an average level of thermal well-being. With respect to warmth, they have what Dworkin calls expensive tastes: they need unusually large doses of resources to achieve an ordinary

[58] See Dworkin (n 54).
[59] Cohen (n 12) 919.

> level of welfare. They are losers under Dworkin's equality of resources, because ... it sets itself against compensation for expensive tastes.[60]

It is unfair to refuse extra help for those who experience greater discomfort in cold weather when individuals do not choose this disability. It would be a form of involuntary disadvantage that the individual is not responsible for. Contrary to Dworkin's resources approach, we must acknowledge that 'people can be unlucky not only in their unchosen resource endowments but also in their unchosen liabilities to pain and suffering and in their unchosen expensive preferences'.[61]

In summary, each argument for selecting a value to equalise, whether that is resources, capabilities or welfare, has good reasons for support, but if we select one of these values to the exclusion of the others, this seems to have unacceptable consequences. It follows that the best approach is to strive for a pluralism of values, including access to welfare, resources and capabilities.

## VIII. Conclusion

I have outlined two theories of equality: equality of opportunity, which requires that people do not experience disadvantage when they cannot be held responsible for that disadvantage; and social equality, which requires conditions where people are able to interact as equals. We must temper the drive for equality by recognising the value of personal responsibility. To create conditions where people can live meaningful and autonomous lives, we need to ensure that people bear at least part of the costs of their choices, and we must tolerate at least some of the inequality that naturally follows from those choices.

Given that there are good reasons for valuing equality of resources, capabilities and welfare (but we are unable to directly place one value above another), we can conclude that it is prima facie wrong when there is an unequal distribution of welfare, resources or capabilities, except when the inequality arises in a way for which the person who ends up with less should properly be held responsible.

This chapter has provided a rough guide to principles of equality, which has gained some desiderata for egalitarian principles, including principles of equality of opportunity and social equality. This creates the opportunity for the next stage of constructing the theory of age discrimination, which is to identify the principles that can explain the wrongness of discrimination. Further to this, in the next chapter I assess the extent equality of opportunity and social equality can explain the wrongness of discrimination, and I examine whether any non-equality principles can also explain the wrongness of discrimination.

[60] ibid 920.
[61] ibid 932.

# 4

# The Wrongs of Discrimination

In the previous chapter, I identify the principles that explain when and why inequality is wrong, including the principle of equality of opportunity, which explains that it is wrong for someone to be worse off than others due to circumstances outside their control, and the principle of social equality, which explains that inequality is wrong when it creates conditions where people are unable to interact as equals. Since discrimination is a means by which inequality is produced, these equality principles can form a groundwork theory for determining when and why discrimination is wrong and therefore can form part of a theory of age discrimination.[1]

It is not enough, however, to identify equality principles to have a complete theory of discrimination. We must also examine whether non-equality principles can illuminate the concept. Indeed, many scholars argue that non-equality principles provide the best foundation for explaining the point of discrimination laws.[2] This chapter argues that both equality and non-equality principles contribute to explaining the wrongness of discrimination. I argue that we must identify a range of principles, including the principles of equality of opportunity, social equality, autonomy and respect, in order to acknowledge the 'messy plurality' of moral concerns that discrimination law addresses.[3]

In chapter five, I verify the extent each of the principles identified in this chapter can explain when and why age-differential treatment is wrong. This then forms a theory of age discrimination that can assist in distinguishing justified from unjustified unequal treatment on the grounds of age and therefore guide age discrimination law.

[1] K Lippert-Rasmussen, 'Discrimination and Equality' in A Marmor (ed), *Routledge, Companion to Philosophy of Law* (Routledge, 2012) 569: 'Conceptually, discrimination is tied to inequality. It is impossible to discriminate against someone unless there is some dimension in which the discriminator treats the discriminatee worse than those against whom she does not discriminate.'

[2] For example, Tarunabh Khaitan argued that the justifying norm of anti-discrimination laws is freedom not equality: T Khaitan, *A Theory of Discrimination Law* (Oxford University Press, 2016). Other freedom-based accounts of discrimination include S Moreau, 'What Is Discrimination?' (2010) 38 *Philosophy and Public Affairs* 143; J Gardner, 'On the Ground of Her Sex(uality)' (1998) 18 *OJLS* 167. For another account grounding anti-discrimination law in non-equality principles, see E Holmes, 'Anti-discrimination Rights Without Equality' (2005) 68 *MLR* 175.

[3] P Shin, 'Is There a Unitary Concept of Discrimination?' in D Hellman and S Moreau (eds), *Philosophical Foundations of Discrimination Law* (Oxford University Press, 2013).

As an important preliminary note, the review of theories of discrimination has the purpose of explaining the wrongs of treatment that constitute direct and indirect discrimination under the Equality Act 2010. This overview does not attempt to explain the concept of discrimination we use in ordinary language. As explained in chapter one, there are important differences between the ordinary language meaning of discrimination, which is treatment that is direct and motivated by prejudice, and the legal concept, which includes actions and structures that cause disadvantages without fault on the part of the decision-maker.[4]

Further to this, I apply reflective equilibrium by considering not just my own intuitions in searching for appropriate moral principles, but also the intuitions and beliefs of a range of people with experience working towards understanding the concept of discrimination. I assess particular theorists' understanding of the wrong of discrimination and then determine whether these beliefs cohere with our intuitions about wrongful discrimination and consider revising the principles when they do not cohere with our intuitions. For example, I argue that equality of opportunity and social equality fail to explain some forms of discrimination that are better explained by non-equality principles.

## I. Rejecting Unitary Theories of Discrimination

Unitary theories of discrimination identify a single core principle that should explain all forms of discrimination.[5] The attractiveness of these theories is their simplicity. If there is a single moral principle that identifies the wrong of discrimination, then, in determining whether impugned treatment is a proportionate means of achieving a legitimate aim and lawful under the Equality Act 2010, we would assess whether the impugned treatment violates the central unifying moral principle. The task for applying age discrimination law would be to determine the outcome that maximises this moral principle. For example, imagine an employer justifies mandatory retirement on the grounds that this ensures that people have an equal opportunity to access employment and promotion opportunities. Equality of opportunity would justify this policy where the retirement age would apply equally to each employee.

[4] It should be noted, however, that some theories of discrimination explored in this chapter were intended to explain the ordinary language concept of discrimination. For example, Benjamin Eidelson's theory of discrimination is concerned with direct rather than indirect forms of discrimination: B Eidelson, *Discrimination and Disrespect* (Oxford University Press, 2015). Eidelson argues that 'indirect discrimination' should be understood as distinct from the wider concept of discrimination because incorporating indirect discrimination into the concept of discrimination can obscure a clear understanding of the distinct wrong of direct discrimination.

[5] eg S Segall, 'What's So Bad about Discrimination?' (2012) 24 *Utilitas* 82.

However, for unitary theories of discrimination to be successful, they must rely on a core moral principle that has plausible explanations of a range of different types of discrimination, including direct and indirect discrimination, race and sex discrimination.[6] While unitary theories of discrimination have persuasive features that explain discrimination (as I demonstrate in this chapter), they also have unattractive implications when applied against particular instances of discrimination. Unitary theories of age discrimination, I argue, are invariably under-inclusive. I demonstrate this by working through a number of principles that can explain the wrong of discrimination, and I conclude that a pluralist approach to discrimination is a better approach for capturing all the wrongs of discrimination.

Pluralist accounts of discrimination that recognise that discrimination wrongs people for a number of different overlapping reasons are the best way we can capture the multiple wrongs of discrimination and therefore the best way to guide the application of discrimination law.[7] Value pluralism in the context of discrimination law should be unsurprising. We cannot expect that one idea can encapsulate every wrong of discrimination when the legal definition of discrimination has such a wide scope, ranging from direct and indirect discrimination and spanning across very different protected characteristics.[8]

The difficulty of trying to grapple with different conflicting principles might explain why so many thinkers have attempted to create unitary theories of discrimination. However, this difficulty is an inescapable feature of moral decision-making, whether at a personal level or at a societal level. In our personal lives, we often have to choose between the principle of honesty and the need to tell 'white lies' to avoid hurting people's feelings. At a societal level, we need to decide on an appropriate balance between equality, autonomy, prosperity, security, welfare and many other values that do not always align perfectly. There is inevitable complexity in moral decision-making. Any attempt to simplify decision-making by deciding on one principle will lead to important principles being overlooked. It is better to have a complex but true moral theory than an oversimplified untrue moral theory.

[6] For an outline of these criteria for a successful theory of discrimination, see R Segev, 'Making Sense of Discrimination' (2014) 27 *Ratio Juris* 47.

[7] The following are pluralist accounts of discrimination: Shin (n 3); Segev (n 6); S Fredman, *Discrimination Law* (Oxford University Press, 2011).

[8] Value pluralism is defined as the position that there are multiple values that cannot be reducible to one super value. John Stuart Mill defended a version of value pluralism in his argument that there are distinct and incommensurable types of pleasure. See JS Mill, 'Utilitarianism' in R Shafer-Landau (ed), *Ethical Theory: An Anthology* (John Wiley & Sons, 2012). The other major moral philosopher in Western philosophy, Immanuel Kant, offered a unitary account of morality. His moral philosophy holds that there is a core fundamental principle of morality, based on human autonomy, on which all moral duties are founded. I Kant, *Groundwork of the Metaphysics of Morals*, M Gregor, trans, ed (Cambridge University Press, 1998). A famous modern pluralist account is Isaiah Berlin's argument that there are multiple and incommensurable types of liberty. See I Berlin, *Four Essays on Liberty* (Oxford University Press, 1969).

# II. Explaining the Wrong of Discrimination

## A. Equality of Opportunity

In chapter three, I provided a general defence of this principle as an explanation for when and why inequality is wrong. I now verify the extent to which this principle can explain the wrongness of discrimination. Shlomi Segal has argued that 'discrimination is bad as such … because and only because it undermines equality of opportunity'.[9] All forms of wrongful discrimination, he has argued, are wrong because they cause inequality of opportunity.[10]

Equality of opportunity seems to account for many of our intuitions about discrimination. A major reason why we find discrimination wrong is that we recognise it is unfair to impose a comparative disadvantage on the grounds of a characteristic that the individual cannot change by choice. Many of the protected characteristics in the Equality Act 2010, such as race, sex and nationality, are traits that people cannot change by mere choice.

The equality of opportunity principle also explains the indirect discrimination provisions of the Equality Act 2010. An action engages the indirect discrimination provisions when it has the effect of causing disadvantage to people who share a particular protected characteristic. This is exactly the sort of action the equality of opportunity principle rules out. Further, equality of opportunity, like the definition of indirect discrimination, locates the wrong of discrimination not in any fault or intentions of a discriminator, but in the effect that a policy, criterion or practice has on people.

However, the equality of opportunity principle fails to explain a number of examples of discrimination that seem intuitively wrong. Consider an example introduced by Deborah Hellman of a lecturer who separates their students so that black students move to one side of the lecture hall and white students move to the other side.[11] The action, despite not causing disadvantage, seems to be wrong because it demeans the black students. It does this, Hellman argues, because of the cultural history of segregation being used to mark people with racial inferiority.

Another example that challenges the equality of opportunity account of discrimination is the example of the prison policy in South Africa during apartheid that required black prisoners to wear shorts and white prisoners to wear long trousers. Hellman has argued that this policy actually does not disadvantage

[9] Segall (n 5) 82.

[10] For criticisms of this view, see Moreau (n 2); D Hellman, *When Is Discrimination Wrong?* (Harvard University Press, 2008); M Cavanagh, *Against Equality of Opportunity* (Clarendon Press, 2002); Holmes (n 2); L Alexander, 'What Makes Wrongful Discrimination Wrong? Biases, Preferences, Stereotypes, and Proxies' (1992) 141 *University of Pennsylvania Law Review* 149; R Arneson, 'What Is Wrongful Discrimination' (2006) 43 *San Diego Law Review* 775.

[11] This example is discussed by Hellman (n 10) 27–29.

black prisoners (in fact, it advantaged them because shorts provided greater comfort in the hot South African climate), yet we would consider the policy treated black prisoners less favourably because it represented an attempt to demean them.[12]

Furthermore, consider the US case *Palmer v Thompson*.[13] Following legislation requiring desegregation, the city of Jackson decided that rather than desegregate the city's swimming pools, it would close all the pools. The mayor of Jackson did not want white people and black people swimming together. This is undoubtedly wrongful treatment, but the policy does not create inequality of opportunity because the pools were closed to everyone. Instead, the insulting message it sends to the black community explains the wrongness of the policy.

Sophia Moreau provides another example of discrimination that equality of opportunity fails to explain. She presented a hypothetical of a community with restaurants each of which refuses entry to people of different religious groups.[14] Moreau added that there are an equal number of restaurants catering to each religious group in the community, thus ensuring that people of different religions have an equal opportunity to access restaurants. Despite not creating disadvantage, this treatment seems wrong, and we need to identify a principle other than equality of opportunity to explain why it is wrong.

In defending the equality of opportunity theory of discrimination, Segall acknowledged that the above examples are morally wrong, but denied that they undermine the equality of opportunity theory. In his view, they are not forms of discrimination and therefore do not need to be explained by equality of opportunity.[15] However, the examples almost certainly engage the legal definition of direct discrimination in the Equality Act 2010 and therefore form part of the legal concept of discrimination that must be accounted for. The restaurants turning people away on the grounds of religion is less favourable treatment on the grounds of religion and engages the direct discrimination provisions. Closing all the city's swimming pools is a more contentious example because, on its face, it seems to treat people equally. However, the action does constitute less favourable treatment towards black people because the policy was a direct insult to them. Likewise, the example of a lecturer dividing students by race and the clothes policy in South African prisons are also actions that treat black people less favourably by humiliating them. A complete theory of discrimination should be capable of explaining these examples.

[12] ibid 5.

[13] 403 US 217 (1971).

[14] Moreau (n 2) 172–74.

[15] Segall (n 5) cites the Supreme Court reasoning in *Palmer* (n 13) allowing the mayor's racist decision to stand. In this case, Justice Black wrote: 'Nothing in the history or language of the Fourteenth Amendment nor in any of our prior cases persuades us that the closing of the Jackson swimming pools to all its citizens constitutes a denial of the "equal protection of the laws".'

## B. Social Equality

In chapter three, I provided a general defence of this principle, which requires conditions that ensure people can interact as equals. I now verify the extent to which this principle can explain the wrongness of discrimination. Discrimination can clearly offend social equality because it can entrench power inequalities that can cause people to have insufficient social or political influence. This undermines the aims of social equality to eliminate hierarchies of social status.[16] For example, race discrimination has had the effect of restricting access to power, wealth and political influence by erroneously ascribing the biological status of distinctness and otherness to groups of people.[17]

Some jurisdictions have used the social equality principle as a means of identifying wrongful discrimination. An example is *United States v Carolene Products Company*.[18] The US Supreme Court, in a famous footnote, held that the courts should offer a heightened scrutiny of laws that disadvantage 'discrete and insular minorities'. The Court justified this approach on the grounds that these socially excluded groups are vulnerable to subordination from the political process and therefore ensuring equal protection of the law between citizens requires protecting vulnerable groups through heightened scrutiny of the legal process.

The social equality principle explains many paradigm cases of discrimination. For example, social equality holds that denying someone a job because of race is wrong because it undermines the applicant's status as an equal to their employer.[19] The employer here is at fault because 'He would rather retain some personal benefit (be it the satisfaction of a taste for discrimination or the realization of dollars-and-cents profits) than avoid contributing to a subordinating system'.[20]

Social equality finds that indirect discrimination can be wrong because structures may perpetuate the social domination of certain groups even if no individual deliberately tried to harm those subject to disadvantages.[21] In this way, social equality is not concerned with finding fault, but instead is concerned with the effects measures have on excluded social groups that continue patterns of social subordination. Social equality identifies the wrongs of indirect discrimination in the structural barriers which can contribute to creating oppressive relations. And the legal definition of discrimination does not require finding any fault on the part of the discriminator.

[16] For a similar account of discrimination, see C Sunstein, 'The Anticaste Principle' (1994) 92 *Michigan Law Review* 2410. For Sunstein, discrimination is wrong when 'highly visible differences' become markers of low status due to systematic social disadvantage caused by discrimination.

[17] A Smedley and B Smedley, 'Race as Biology Is Fiction, Racism as a Social Problem Is Real: Anthropological and Historical Perspectives on the Social Construction of Race' (2005) 60 *American Psychologist* 16.

[18] 304 US 144 (1938).

[19] S Bagenstos, 'Employment Law and Social Equality' (2013) 112 *Michigan Law Review* 225.

[20] S Bagenstos, 'Rational Discrimination Accommodation, and the Politics of (Disability) Civil Rights' (2003) 89 *Virginia Law Review* 825, 858.

[21] S Moreau, 'The Wrongs of Unequal Treatment' (2004) 54 *University of Toronto Law Journal* 291.

Social equality as an explanation of discrimination, however, is limited by its presupposing that the wrongfulness of discrimination is necessarily located in its effects on social groups. Certainly, discrimination can have bad effects, but the wrongness of direct forms of discrimination lies, at least partly, in what brings about the effects.[22] For example, it is usually explained that laws that limit marriage to opposite-sex couples is wrong because, in refusing gay people the right to recognise their relationships as 'marriages', it sends the message that same-sex couples are inferior to heterosexual couples.[23] Therefore, in locating the wrong of discrimination, we need to look not just at its effects, but also at the message conveyed by the discriminator.

Another limitation of social equality is that there are examples of wrongful discrimination which do not perpetuate oppressive social relations. We would consider it wrong if a member of a disadvantaged group discriminated against a privileged group for an important opportunity, for example, a black employer rejecting a job applicant for being white as a result of the employer's animus towards white people. Despite this being unlikely to reinforce the dominance of privileged groups, we still consider this treatment wrong, and a complete account of discrimination should be able to explain this wrong. A better explanation for this type of discrimination is the respect account, ie that we consider this form of discrimination wrong because it takes on the meaning of an insult.

It is clear from this chapter so far that the equality principles defended in chapter three cannot provide a complete explanation of the wrongness of discrimination. I now go on to consider the extent to which non-equality principles can explain the wrongness of discrimination.

## C. Irrelevance

A commonly identified non-equality principle for explaining the wrong of discrimination is that treating someone disadvantageously because of their race, sex or religion is to wrongfully act on an arbitrary trait.[24] Selecting one person over another for a job because they are white and the other applicant is black is wrong because skin colour is irrelevant to the hiring decision. Harry Frankfurt is a defender of this view and a critic of equality accounts of discrimination.

[22] Gardner (n 2) argued that much of what we consider wrong about paradigm cases of discrimination is in the actions of the discriminator.

[23] See the South African case *Minister of Home Affairs v Fourie* [2005] ZACC 19. The South African Supreme Court held that no provision made for same-sex marriages amounted to unfair discrimination. In the majority, Judge Sachs adopted the respect account of discrimination to justify his ruling: 'To penalise people for being who and what they are is profoundly disrespectful of the human personality and violatory of equality. Equality means equal concern and respect across difference' [60].

[24] Anthony Flew argued that racism is wrong because it treats people on the basis of traits that 'are strictly superficial and properly irrelevant to all, or almost all, questions of social status and employability': A Flew, 'Three Concepts of Racism' (1990) 75 *Encounter* 63.

He has argued that 'failing to respect somebody is a matter of ignoring the relevance of some aspect of his nature or rationality … Pertinent features of how things are with him are treated as though they had no reality'.[25] Thus, he concludes, the alternative to discrimination 'is not equality. It is relevance.'

However, we should reject the relevance principle as an account of discrimination. There are many cases of wrongful discrimination that we cannot explain by relevance. For example, an employer aiming to maximise profits may choose to cut costs by dismissing a woman on maternity leave. Despite pregnancy being a relevant trait, this is still wrongful discrimination because it forces women to incur a disproportionate burden of reproduction, and this will lead to reduced opportunities for women in the workforce. Gardner also offers the example of race being a relevant (albeit immoral) reason to refuse black people entry to a pub if customers will desert the pub when the black people come in.[26]

## D. Autonomy

John Gardner has argued that maximising autonomy is the justification for discrimination laws.[27] His argument concerns the rationale for discrimination laws rather than attempting to cover all the reasons why discrimination is wrong. Nonetheless, Gardner's argument can give insight into why discrimination is harmful, which can be useful for constructing a theory of discrimination. In his theory of discrimination, Gardner has argued that discrimination can harm people when the discriminator diminishes the discriminatee's opportunities for autonomous agency. He defines autonomy as 'the ideal of a life substantially lived through the successive valuable choices of the person who lives it, where valuable choices are choices from among an adequate range of valuable options'.[28]

Gardner has argued that discrimination violates autonomy when the discrimination is related to immutable characteristics and fundamental choices.[29] Discrimination because of immutable traits, such as race and sex, violates autonomy because it results in restricting the choices of the victim of discrimination:

> Because these choices are based on our immutable status, our own choices can make no difference to them. And where the discrimination is endemic enough, we are left with too few valuable options to choose among and we are deprived of valuable choice over large swathes of our own lives.[30]

[25] H Frankfurt, *Necessity, Volition, and Love* (Cambridge University Press, 1999) 152.
[26] J Gardner, 'Liberals and Unlawful Discrimination' (1989) 9 *OJLS* 168.
[27] Gardner (n 2).
[28] ibid 170.
[29] This autonomy account of discrimination has been present in the UK case law. For example, Lady Hale in *Ghaidan v Godin-Mendoza* [2004] UKHL 30, [2004] 2 AC 557 [130] adopted Gardner's position by explaining that race and sex discrimination were wrong 'because [they were] based on an irrelevant characteristic which the woman or the black did not choose and could do nothing about'.
[30] Gardner (n 2) 170.

Gardner has explained that discrimination on the ground of fundamental choices (such as religion) violates autonomy by attaching costs to an individual choosing between available valuable options. In this way, discrimination has the effect of foreclosing some meaningful choices. For Gardner, discrimination law offers people the opportunity to make their own valuable choices, rather than have their lives dictated by others.[31]

Gardner has also argued that indirect discrimination violates autonomy because it exacerbates the low autonomy levels of groups who have been subject to widespread discrimination in the past.[32] The indirect discrimination provisions enhance autonomy by removing disadvantages that attach to people's immutable traits and fundamental choices.

Discrimination can also reduce autonomy when victims of discrimination internalise the damaging stereotypes that motivate discrimination. For example, the stereotype that women are less intellectually capable than men persisted for centuries and resulted in women becoming socialised into a subordinate position. Because of the stereotype, women were typically less educated than men and were less likely to pursue intellectual activities that would develop their autonomy. And the acceptance of this as a natural gender difference reduced the opportunities of women to make contributions in intellectual fields.

In a similar account to Gardner, Sophia Moreau has argued that discrimination is wrong when it attaches costs to people's choices.[33] For Moreau, 'people should not be constrained by the social costs of being one race rather than another when they deliberate about such questions as what job to take or where to live'.[34] On this account, discrimination law protects people's freedom to go about their lives with their choices being insulated from traits that are morally irrelevant, such as race and sex. An important limitation of the autonomy account of the wrongness of discrimination, however, is that – in common with the other accounts of discrimination that locate the wrong of discrimination in its effects on people – it fails to account for our intuition that a major feature of why we object to discrimination lies in the insulting or demeaning treatment of a person. For example, our objection to racist treatment is at least partly rooted not just in the autonomy harms it has on the victims, but also in the fact that the racist treatment is a communication that a person has a degraded moral status.

## E. Discrimination and Disrespect

As I have argued above, to account for our intuitions about the wrong of discrimination, we must also identify the wrong of many forms of discrimination not

[31] Gardner (n 2) 171.
[32] Gardner (n 2) 187.
[33] Moreau (n 2).
[34] ibid 148.

in the effects that the action has, but in the disrespect manifested by the action. The respect account of discrimination relates to the Kantian principle that certain acts are intrinsically wrong because they pursue 'impermissible ends'.[35] The impermissible ends can include judgements of prejudice and hostility that send the message that a person has lower social worth and usefulness, including acts of racism, sexism and ageism.

The respect account encompasses a number of subtly different accounts of discrimination. One version locates the wrong of discrimination in the thought process of the discriminator; another version locates the wrong in the loss of self-respect of the victim of discrimination; and another locates the wrong in the 'social meaning' of the act of discrimination. I assess each of these accounts and their strengths and weaknesses as explanations of discrimination.[36]

The first account of the respect principle is that discrimination is wrong when a discriminator is motivated by prejudice.[37] Prejudice occurs when a person acts on the belief that another person deserves less respect than others because of their membership of a particular social group: for example, the belief that black people can be treated less well because black people are inferior. Prejudice covers a range of different attitudes, including animus, dislike and indifference.[38]

This respect principle is a subjective account because it locates the wrong of discrimination in the thought process of the discriminator. For example, Richard Arneson identifies the wrong of discrimination as occurring when 'an agent treats a person identified as being of a certain type differently than she otherwise would have done from unwarranted prejudice or animus against persons of that type'.[39]

This account captures our abhorrence to racist and sexist treatment. However, not all wrongful discrimination is motivated by prejudice towards particular groups. It is possible for someone to wrongly discriminate even though they have no beliefs about the moral worth of the people they are discriminating against. Consider 'rational' discrimination. Imagine if the community as a whole had preferences for white lawyers. A law firm declines to employ black people because a

[35] Kant (n 8).

[36] The Supreme Court of Canada in *Law v Canada (Minister of Employment and Immigration)* [1999] 1 SCR 49 adopted a combination of these respect accounts for distinguishing justified from unjustified differential treatment. The Court held that wrongful discrimination is 'where the differential treatment reflects the stereotypical application of presumed group or personal characteristics, or otherwise has the effect of perpetuating or promoting the view that the individual is less capable, or less worthy of recognition or value as a human being or as a member of Canadian society'. This approach has been subsequently overruled in *R v Kapp* [2008] 2 SCR 483, 2008 SCC 41.

[37] John Ely defended this account by holding that discriminatory acts are those that are motivated by prejudice: J Ely, *Democracy and Distrust* (Harvard University Press, 1980). Similarly, Cavanagh (n 10) 166 identified wrongful discrimination as treating people 'with unwarranted contempt'.

[38] 'Ethnic prejudice is an antipathy based upon a faulty and inflexible generalization. It may be felt or expressed. It may be directed toward a group as a whole, or toward an individual because he is a member of that group': G Allport, *The Nature of Prejudice* (Addison Wesley, 1954) 9.

[39] Arneson (n 10) 787.

black person will find it harder to gain clients due to the racist attitudes in the community. The employer does not share the widespread racism in the community, but considers this community racism in rejecting black job applicants because the employer is seeking to maximise profits. Despite the 'rationality' of the employer's decision, the action still violates the principle of respect because the employer acquiesces in the racist preferences of the community. As Owen Fiss has argued, 'rational discrimination' can be as disrespectful and demeaning as animus-based discrimination because 'to the victim of the employment decision the appearance of the conduct is identical, whether the use of race is efficiency-related or not'.[40] In using the racism of their customers as a reason to discriminate, the employer is affirming that racism by acting on the community's demeaning attitudes.[41] To give credence to these attitudes is to disrespect and insult the black job applicant. This example demonstrates that we need to incorporate into the respect account actions that acquiesce in the prejudice of third parties.

Another limitation of the prejudice account is that it fails to explain examples of disrespectful and wrongful discrimination that are not motivated by prejudice, for example, the lecturer who instructs black students to move to one side of the lecture hall and white students to move to the other side because the lecturer likes the aesthetic it produces rather than being motivated by any form of prejudice. Despite benign motives, we would still view this as offensive conduct. Hellman has argued that the reason why the lecturer's actions are wrong is that it demeans the students regardless of the motives of the lecturer.[42] Classifying people into race groups is demeaning because of the cultural history of expressing inferiority by race classification.

Another version of the respect account of discrimination is the theory that discrimination is wrong because it undermines the victim's self-respect. As Rawls has argued, disrespectful treatment is likely to undermine the self-respect of people subject to the action since how other people treat us affects our self-esteem. And, for Rawls, self-respect is 'perhaps the most important primary good'.[43] Discrimination can lead to injuring people's dignity by humiliating the victims. Further, once racism, sexism and other forms of prejudice become endemic in society, then the false ideas about the diminished moral and social worth of victims of discrimination can be internalised and shape how people think about themselves, leading to diminished self-respect.[44] Being a victim of discrimination

[40] O Fiss, 'A Theory of Fair Employment Laws' (1971) 38 *University of Chicago Law Review* 235, 260.

[41] Employers often tried to justify discrimination on the grounds that they were simply responding to market principles, such as profit maximisation, rather than acting on prejudice. For example, paying women lower wages was justified on the grounds that this decision was concerned with profit.

[42] Hellman (n 10) 27–29.

[43] J Rawls, *A Theory of Justice* (Harvard University Press, 2009) 440.

[44] Susan Sherwin argued that cultural beliefs about social groups become 'so well established that they have been internalized by both those who suffer under them, and those who benefit from them; they remain invisible to many of the people': S Sherwin, *No Longer Patient: Feminist Ethics and Health Care Philadelphia* (Temple University Press, 1992) 14.

can lead to a sense of shame about one's social identity leading to a personal sense of feeling inferior.[45] However, as Segall notes, this account of discrimination fails to account for wrongful discrimination of which the victim is unaware. Think of an employer secretly paying higher salaries to male employees. Women employees 'are unlikely to experience a reduction of self-respect and yet we probably think that they are nevertheless discriminated against'.[46]

Hellman has defended a different respect account of discrimination that locates the wrong of discrimination in the 'social meaning' of the discriminator's actions rather than in the thought process of the discriminator or the impact discrimination has on individuals or groups. Hellman has argued that to demean is wrongful 'whether or not the person affected feels demeaned, stigmatized, or harmed'.[47] Discrimination demeans, on this account, when the action conveys the message that the victims of discrimination have a diminished moral and social worth. The message can demean because actions, like words, can take on a particular meaning regardless of the motivation of the actor. Social meaning can be determined by 'the context and culture' which invests certain classifications and distinctions with the meaning that certain people lack moral worth or are socially useless. Wrongful discrimination occurs, on this account, when classifying people by a trait that has been invested with the meaning of an offensive insult.

A similar account is Iyiola Solanke's argument that discrimination is wrong when it stigmatises people.[48] Stigma is a social construct to shame or humiliate people. Discrimination stigmatises by communicating the message that particular social groups have a diminished moral or social worth. For example, people are stigmatised by discrimination when a discriminatee possesses a trait (eg skin colour, nationality, sex) that has taken on the societal meaning of an undesirable difference. On this account, discrimination wrongs people by reinforcing the negative social meaning of possessing particular traits. Stigma can also emerge from negative stereotypes and prejudice that reinforce the social subordinate position of particular social groups.

This theory and Hellman and Solanke's respect account explain why discrimination law has selected protected grounds such as race, sex, gender, religion and political belief. These forms of unequal treatment have, in many contexts, taken on the meaning of a demeaning insult and it has become stigmatising to classify people based on these traits. The law must prohibit employers and providers of goods and services from acting on certain classifications because the very act of using them risks demeaning people.[49]

[45] Lawrence Blum discussed how racism can lead to feelings of inferiority: L Blum, *'I'm Not a Racist, but …': The Moral Quandary of Race* (Cornell University Press, 2002).

[46] Segall (n 5) 87.

[47] Hellman (n 10) 8.

[48] I Solanke, *Discrimination as Stigma: A Theory of Anti-discrimination Law* (Bloomsbury Publishing, 2017).

[49] Mark Kelman argued that discrimination is wrong when it imposes stigma on subordinated group members: M Kelman, 'Market Discrimination and Groups' (2001) 53 *Stanford Law Review* 833. He contrasts this with other wrongful conduct, such as an employer refusing to hire someone because

Hellman's account is also able to explain why discrimination is wrong when it is directed at dominant social groups, such as white men. This is because subordinate groups can disrespect and demean members of a dominant group by discriminating against them. For example, we would consider it wrong for a discriminator to reject a white male job applicant on the grounds that they consider that white men to have less empathy than other groups. This discrimination is wrong primarily because it sends insulting messages. The respect account holds that the fact that white men tend to have greater social and political influence does not prevent this discrimination from being wrong.

Hellman's respect account of discrimination also succeeds in explaining why discrimination laws permit forms of positive action.[50] Positive action typically represents an attempt to redistribute resources or opportunities to disadvantaged groups. On the respect account, positive action may be justified because, even though it treats people unequally on the grounds of a protected characteristic, it does not always communicate demeaning messages about particular people.[51]

Hellman's account also explains why we recognise many forms of wrongful discrimination that are not motivated by animus. Demeaning discrimination can occur when people act on unconscious biases from stereotypes. People stereotype (consciously or unconsciously) by identifying particular social groups and attaching particular characteristics to these groups in the form of expected behaviours.[52] These assumed characteristics can include ideas that confirm the diminished moral and social worth of members of these social groups. For example, stereotyping can demean by being founded on assumptions that certain racial groups are, say, less intelligent and capable.[53]

the applicant reminds the employer of their hated stepfather. This action, unlike wrongful discrimination, 'does not confirm traditional status-based hierarchies … or demean the victim'. The employer is being stupid rather than discriminatory.

[50] Equality Act 2010, ss 158 and 159 permit some forms of positive action.

[51] For this argument, see R Dworkin, 'Affirming Affirmative Action' (1998) 45 *New York Review of Books* 1. However, note that some argue that affirmative action is unjustified because it can demean. In the US Supreme Court case *Grutter v Bollinger* 539 US 306 (2003), Clarence Thomas, in arguing against affirmative action, held that 'The [US] Constitution abhors classifications based on race, not only because those classifications can harm favoured races or are based on illegitimate motives, but also because every time the government places citizens on racial registers and makes race relevant to the provision of burdens or benefits, it demeans us all'.

[52] An explanation for why we stereotype is that it is a mechanism in our brains to cope with information overload. Rather than have to consider the individual characteristics of every person we encounter before making a judgment, our brains instead make generalisations on some obvious characteristics, like age, sex or race. We perceive people based on their social category rather than as individuals. See N Macrae, C Stangor and M Hewstone (eds), *Stereotypes and Stereotyping* (Guilford Press, 1996).

[53] The UK case law has recognised this account of discrimination. For example, Lord Walker held in *R (Carson and Reynolds) v Secretary of State for Work and Pensions* [2005] UKHL 37, [2006] 1 AC 173 [40] that 'Discrimination on the ground of sex or race demeans the victim by using a sexual or racial stereotype as a sufficient ground for unfavourable treatment, rather than treating her as an individual to be judged on her own merits'.

Demeaning treatment can include relatively accurate generalisations about a group of people when that generalisation reinforces ideas that particular social groups have a lower moral and social worth. For example, if we assume taking maternity leave is likely to reduce that person's productivity compared to men over the long term, and an employer uses this as a reason to discriminate on the grounds of pregnancy by claiming that pregnancy is relevant when maximising profits, this is disrespectful discrimination because it reinforces the sexist idea that it is women's responsibility to incur a disproportionate burden of reproduction.

Stereotypes are often used to legitimise existing social arrangements, which, in turn, justifies keeping certain groups 'in their place', with corresponding demeaning attitudes towards these disfavoured groups. For example, people may correctly perceive certain ethnic groups as occupying lower social strata. They may conclude from this that the explanation for these groups occupying the lower social strata is that these groups are unintelligent, lazy etc. And from these stereotypes, they may conclude that it is justified to discriminate against these groups. In doing so, the discriminator is denying a benefit based on an assumption of lesser social worth of certain individuals and is thus treating those individuals with disrespect.

Importantly, however, some accurate generalisations are not necessarily disrespectful. For example, the assumption that women may need separate sports competitions because of physiological differences between men and women is unlikely to be considered demeaning because it can be justified as promoting the opportunity for women to compete successfully in sporting events. In this way, the generalisation enhances equality of opportunity and can be justified on this basis. Also, as I argue in chapter eight in the context of healthcare rationing, it is not necessarily disrespectful to make generalisations about groups when the purpose of the generalisation is to maximise an important social good. For example, distributing free flu vaccinations to over 65s on the grounds that this age group is more likely to be vulnerable to the illness does not imply that this age group are more valuable; rather, it represents an attempt to distribute resources to those who may need them the most.

In a subtlety different respect account, Eidelson has argued that unjust discrimination can be explained by the failure to respect the individuality of a person or the autonomy of a person.[54] This can occur when a discriminator acts on a generalisation or stereotype that imposes costs on an individual by assuming that individual has a trait even in circumstances where the individual may not in fact have that trait. This is disrespectful treatment because relying on generalisations can fail to take the person's individual choices seriously by not paying attention to the way the person has constructed their life.[55] However, for Eidelson, it can be justifiable

[54] Eidelson (n 4).
[55] ibid 138.

to discriminate on the basis of traits for which people are personally responsible. He also argues that it is not disrespectful to rely on statistical generalisations when information about individuals is not reasonably available.[56] This can mean that it can be justified, for Eidelson, to use generalisations where the use of the generalisation is much more efficient than assessing each person individually.[57]

The respect account of discrimination, however, has a harder time explaining why the legal concept of discrimination does not protect some forms of demeaning discrimination, such as discrimination on the grounds of weight, appearance or height.[58] Denying a person a job on the grounds of weight is likely to be demeaning, offensive and hurtful in a similar way to denying a person a job based on sex, yet it is not a protected characteristic in discrimination law in the UK or most other jurisdictions.[59] It is unlikely that we can explain this omission on the grounds that weight discrimination is less widespread than sex discrimination: there is a great deal of evidence that weight discrimination is prevalent and harmful.[60]

Also, the respect account does not seem to be a complete account of the wrong of discrimination because denial of moral or social worth is not a necessary condition for explaining the wrongfulness of discrimination. Some forms of discrimination are wrong even though the discrimination does not convey any disrespect. For example:

> Consider employers who refuse to employ a certain racial group, explicitly on the ground that they consider them to be too good for the unskilled jobs they have to offer. Even though there are jobs going, they would sooner leave them vacant. Given the rationale offered, it seems clear that this is not disrespectful, but the effects could be catastrophic for the group concerned. Suppose, for instance, that these views reflect the employers' upbringings at a time when this group was predominantly employed as artisans, in trades that have now disappeared. This group will now be destitute as a result of the employers' actions, which they will not alter, being very set in their views of the dignity of the group, even when made aware of the consequences. The absence of disrespect does not seem sufficient to prevent this from being a case of unjust discrimination.[61]

[56] ibid 157.

[57] This is a major justification of the QALY method of healthcare rationing, which I evaluate in ch 8. I explain that the efficiency of the QALY method can justify the disadvantages it places on older people because the method's reliance on generalisations is not disrespectful and does not communicate that older people's lives are worth less than younger people's lives.

[58] This criticism is made in Segall (n 5).

[59] Note, however, that discrimination on the ground of weight can be unlawful if a person's weight amounts to a disability. For example, a Northern Ireland tribunal in *Bickerstaff v Butcher* [2015] 92/14 FET held that obesity can amount to a disability. The claimant successfully claimed he was unlawfully harassed because of his weight.

[60] US studies have found discriminatory attitudes and behaviours against overweight people, including in the areas of employment, education and healthcare. See R Puhl and K Brownell, 'Bias, Discrimination, and Obesity' (2001) 9 *Obesity* 788. One study found that weight/height discrimination 'is relatively close to reported rates of racial discrimination, particularly among women': R Puhl, T Andreyeva and K Brownell, 'Perceptions of Weight Discrimination: Prevalence and Comparison to Race and Gender Discrimination in America' (2008) 32 *International Journal of Obesity* 992.

[61] C Knight, 'The Injustice of Discrimination' (2013) 32 *South African Journal of Philosophy* 55.

A further limitation of the respect account of discrimination is that it fails to adequately account for the indirect discrimination provisions.[62] The respect principle cannot explain the wrongness of some forms of indirect discrimination. Consider an employer that requires job applicants to pass a test to be considered for a particular role. The employer hires one of the candidates who passed the test and rejects all the candidates who failed it. After a statistical analysis, it is revealed that younger employers passed the test in significantly higher numbers than older applicants. In using the test in application procedures, the employer did not have a preference for younger applicants and did not foresee that it would disadvantage older age groups. Assuming that the employer cannot demonstrate the test is a proportionate means of achieving a legitimate aim, the test is indirectly discriminatory against older employees. However, the policy was not motivated by prejudice or stereotypes, and does not send the message that older employees have a diminished moral or social worth. A respect account of discrimination does not, therefore, explain this discrimination. As Segall notes, 'Such cases show that some action may constitute wrongful discrimination even if there was no discriminatory intent and even if there was no loss of respect, either manifested or incurred'.[63] The wrong of indirect discrimination is better explained by the equality of opportunity and social equality principle, namely that the policy, criterion or practice has the effect of imposing disadvantages on particular groups, resulting in fewer members of that group accessing a valuable resource or opportunity and potentially leading to social exclusion of that group.

Further, the respect conception of the wrongness of discrimination cannot adequately explain the full extent of inequality and disadvantage in society that discrimination law can help address. Much inequality is not caused directly by demeaning treatment of people, but by deep, systematic patterns of exclusion that work to ensure that people remain disadvantaged. We need the social equality account in order to ensure that discrimination law is concerned not just with demeaning treatment, but also with eliminating indirectly discriminatory treatment that works to sustain disadvantage and subordination of particular social groups. Discrimination law does not merely protect people from humiliating and insulting treatment; it can also aim at a transformation of society to ensure that disadvantaged groups can overcome barriers.

## III. Conclusion

This chapter, by identifying the principles that explain the wrong of discrimination, has provided the opportunity to construct a theory of age discrimination that can guide age discrimination law. I have argued that each explanation for the

[62] Eidelson's (n 4) theory relates to direct rather than indirect discrimination. The theory is not attempting to explain indirect discrimination.

[63] Segall (n 5) 95.

wrongness of discrimination is incomplete because there are examples of wrongful discrimination that each principle fails to account for. This does not mean that we cannot theorise about the wrongness of discrimination. Each account is important to our explanation because they each offer plausible reasons for the wrongness of some common forms of discrimination. The fact that we cannot find a single complete explanation means that it is more appropriate to acknowledge that there are many different reasons for considering discrimination wrong. This pluralism coheres better with our intuitions than accounts of discrimination that are limited to one principle. In building a moral framework for applying age discrimination law, we must consider the range of principles outlined in this chapter to determine whether an instance of age discrimination wrongs people.

It follows that we should adopt a pluralist account of discrimination consisting of equality of opportunity, social equality, autonomy and respect. These principles resist expression in terms of a unifying value, but the principles are each necessary to capture a full understanding of the wrongs of discrimination, and it is important to take this plural account in understanding and applying discrimination law to capture the complexity and richness of discrimination as a concept. A failure to do so will ensure that we overlook certain moral principles, with the potential result of failing to achieve justice when applying discrimination law.

Requiring that age discrimination law should take into account all four principles to determine when impugned treatment is wrong will clearly lead to debate about the priorities between these underlying concerns when they clash. For example, social equality can be in tension with the respect account of discrimination. Social equality may permit positive action in favour of a disadvantaged group, such as lower-grade entry requirements to university for black students, to promote the integration of disadvantaged racial groups. However, many argue that it is inherently demeaning to people to classify them on the grounds of race. How should courts approach this value pluralism and decide among these different conceptions of the wrong of inequality and discrimination? To reiterate from chapter one, the conclusion reached in any case-specific scenario will have to be a matter of judgement. The principles operate prima facie, which means that each principle is relevant to determining whether the impugned treatment is unjustified discrimination even though some principles may not be prioritised in making this judgement. In other words, the conclusion should not be inferred from any particular belief, but from looking at the sum total of the principles that would be infringed by the impugned measure, related to the sum total of the principles that would be advanced. A judge must choose and, in so choosing, certain principles of my moral framework are promoted or vindicated while others are subordinated or sacrificed.[64] Courts and tribunals must consider the most just outcome of a case,

[64] Chapter 7 illustrates how courts and tribunals can use the theory of age discrimination outlined in this book to decide cases.

provide the reasons in support of it and consider whether these reasons are more convincing than the reasons that support an alternative decision.

Further to forming a theory of age discrimination, the next chapter verifies whether the principles in this chapter that explain the paradigm examples of discrimination can also explain age discrimination. I also consider whether we need to introduce any new principles to explain age discrimination. This is an essential part of the method of reflective equilibrium of building coherence between our beliefs on a range of scenarios, including building coherence between our beliefs on paradigm forms of discrimination and beliefs on age discrimination that also cohere with a background theory of ageing.

# 5

# Forming a Pluralist Theory of Age Discrimination

In chapter four, I argued in favour of adopting a framework of principles to determine the wrong of discrimination, including the principle of equality of opportunity (the idea that inequality is wrong when it makes people worse off on grounds that someone cannot be held responsible for), social equality (the position that it is wrong when conditions produce hierarchies of status), respect (prohibiting expressions of insults or messages that certain people are less worthy of concern and respect) and autonomy (prohibiting actions that unfairly diminish a person's opportunities for autonomous agency). These principles form a groundwork theory of discrimination. In this chapter, I examine whether and how these principles can identify unjustified unequal treatment on the grounds of age and treatment that is disadvantageous to particular age groups. This, then, forms a pluralist theory of age discrimination that should guide the direct and indirect age discrimination provisions of the Equality Act 2010.

The uniqueness of age as a phenomenon reveals the importance of verifying which of the anti-discrimination principles identified in the previous chapter are capable of explaining age discrimination. We must first explain in detail the meaning of age and then evaluate how the unique features of age can inform when and why age-differential treatment is wrong. Further to this, I argue that a background theory of age and ageing reveals a number of potential benefits that age distinctions may have that can work to justify this treatment. I then apply the principles outlined in chapters three and four to issues of age and ageing to determine when and why unequal treatment on the grounds of age and treatment that is disadvantageous to particular age groups is wrong and how these principles can also work to justify the treatment.

I later test the plausibility of this pluralist theory of age discrimination in chapters six and seven by comparing and contrasting the theory against the views and beliefs identified in important sources, including the views of UK governments responsible for introducing age discrimination laws and the views expressed in court judgments. In chapter eight, I test the pluralist theory of age discrimination against the UK method of healthcare rationing. Throughout this process, I remain open to revising the theory if it reveals weaknesses in my approach.

I apply the reflective equilibrium method in this chapter to form a theory of age discrimination. Reflective equilibrium requires identifying moral principles that support our moral beliefs about age discrimination and ensuring that these beliefs cohere with a background theory of age and ageing. In advancing a background theory of the meaning of age and ageing, I explain that age is both a biological and social concept connected to the passing of time. Physical, emotional and intellectual changes occur as one ages and, therefore, age can be a proxy for these traits. By using age as a reliable proxy, we can maximise efficiency in generating many social goods.[1] For example, compulsory education for children up to 16 years of age can maximise learning because that covers the age when people are most capable of learning certain skills. Also, health resources directed to age groups who are vulnerable to particular health problems is a more efficient use of resources than an age-neutral policy. The nature of age distinctions as promoting efficiency goes some way to supporting the belief that some forms of age distinctions are justifiable.

I explain that the background theory of age and ageing reveals that age distinctions can force people to sequence and order their lives chronologically: for example, structuring people's lives to be involved with education in youth, productive work in adulthood and retirement in older age. This encourages, and sometimes forces, people to undertake tasks at a time of life when there is the greatest benefit to the individual and society. Further to the requirement of reflective equilibrium that moral beliefs should cohere with background theories, I revise my theory of discrimination to incorporate the efficiency principle, which can explain why and when age distinctions are justified.

The background theory of age and ageing also reveals that age distinctions promote equality of opportunity when they form stable policies over time that are likely to be experienced by people at some point in their lives. This can justify age distinctions and should be part of a theory of age discrimination. However, our intuitions reveal that age distinctions can be wrong even if they secure equality over people's complete lives. We must return to the principles outlined in chapters three and four to explain that age distinctions can be wrong even if efficient or compatible with equality of opportunity. Age-differential treatment can be wrong when based on negative stereotypes and prejudice about an oppressed age group, by allowing dominant groups to profit by the oppression of disadvantaged groups and by reducing the autonomy of age groups.

To determine when age-differential treatment is justifiable, we must determine if the promotion of moral principles, including efficiency, equality of opportunity, social equality, autonomy and respect, outweigh the costs to any potential violations of these principles.

## I. A Background Theory of Age and Ageing

We can understand age as a biological phenomenon and as a social phenomenon. I explain these different meanings of age and later examine how they reveal both the benefits of age-differential treatment and its harms.

[1] Richard Posner argued that this feature can justify age discrimination in the workplace: R Posner, *Aging and Old Age* (University of Chicago Press, 1995) 204.

## A. Age as a Biological Process

People occupying different points in the life cycle have different physical features and functioning which is caused by the ageing process. Age-related changes that are beneficial to securing autonomy are 'developments', while age-related changes that are detrimental and relate to deterioration constitute 'ageing'.[2] Through the process of development, people gain the physical and mental attributes that are necessary to maintain independence. Development includes growth in height and weight, development of coordination, balance etc, and development of the capacity for logic, communication, memory and certain emotional developments, such as the capacity for empathy and compassion.[3] Illness and disease may disrupt or eliminate some of these developments, but all people experience a development of at least some of these traits and capabilities.

Developments tend to occur at particular ages. At about the age of four years, for example, children generally develop the capacity to recognise emotions in others and the capacity to understand how others are feeling.[4] Major physical and mental changes occur during the adolescent years, including changes in body shape, achieving fertility, greater aerobic power reserves and blood pressure changes.[5] Ageing is a different process to development. It relates to decline and, eventually, loss of autonomy.[6] Ageing has the effect that people become more susceptible to the things that will lead to death.[7] It is a universal process experienced by everyone except those who die young. Features of ageing include declines in physical strength, hearing and fertility, skin wrinkling and the loss of hair pigment, height, working memory and vision. While ageing brings about declines, it also provides the benefits of experience. In far advanced age, however, the declines associated with ageing are more likely to outweigh the benefits of experience.[8]

The effect of ageing also varies according to different capabilities. Athletes, for example, tend to 'retire' before reaching middle age (indicating that physical strength and stamina deteriorate rapidly in adulthood), while judges are usually competent into old age (indicating intellect can persist into old age).

[2] J Bond, P Coleman and S Peace (eds), *Ageing in Society: An Introduction to Social Gerontology* (SAGE Publications, 1993) 21.

[3] ibid.

[4] L Kutner, 'How Children Develop Empathy' (PsychCentral, 2018) https://psychcentral.com/lib/how-children-develop-empathy/.

[5] W Marshall and J Tanner, 'Variations in Pattern of Pubertal Changes in Girls' (1969) 44 *Archives of Disease in Childhood* 291; W Marshall and J Tanner, 'Variations in the Pattern of Pubertal Changes in Boys' (1970) 45 *Archives of Disease in Childhood* 13.

[6] Bond et al (n 2) 21.

[7] J Maynard Smith, 'Review Lectures on Senescence. I. The Causes of Ageing' (1962) 157 *Proceedings of the Royal Society of London B: Biological Sciences* 115.

[8] Posner (n 1) 204.

## B. Age in the Social Structure

Age is more than a biological process; it is also a major component of the social structure linked to the assignment of status, social roles and responsibilities.[9] Age-related roles have emerged, ensuring that the meaning of age has become a social construct.[10] According to gerontology, 'ageing and old age are socially constructed within educational, family, legal, welfare and healthcare institutions'.[11]

Age roles have arisen from the structures of society and have changed according to societal developments. Pre-modern societies did not have a sharp distinction between age groups divided by chronological age. For example, in pre-industrial Britain, society did not identify old age so much with chronological age, but with the fact of a person being dependent on others.[12] People 40 years of age, for example, were considered old if they were no longer able to undertake manual labour. Society also did not view childhood as being a distinct stage of life. Instead, children were just small adults who had to do manual work.[13] This attitude reflected the economic necessity of children supporting the economy.

The emergence of industrialisation and formal education in Britain brought about a greater connection between chronological age and social roles. Age stratification provided 'an effective division of labour … establishing a social mechanism for maintaining the economy, the educational system, the family system, and the military, political and religious systems'.[14] Age-related structures also divided people's lives into different social roles, with 'age groups' being treated as distinct stages of the life cycle. Society assigned young people to education, adults to productive labour and elderly people to retirement.

With the affluence resulting from industrialisation, it became possible to stop child labour, and this resulted in the emergence of the modern concept of childhood, with children being understood as occupying a separate stage of life.[15] This followed with symbols of childhood, such as the emergence of children's

[9] See S Eisenstadt, *From Generation to Generation: Age Groups and Social Structure* (Transaction Publishers, 1956); B Bernardi, *Age Class Systems, Social Institutions and Politics Based on Age* (Cambridge University Press, 1985); T Parsons, 'Age and Sex in the Social Structure of the United States' (1942) 7 *American Sociological Review* 604.

[10] Social constructions are 'contingent aspects of our social selves' which our society creates according to its values, needs and interests. See P Boghossian, 'What is Social Construction?' (*Times Literary Supplement*, 23 February 2001) https://as.nyu.edu/content/dam/nyu-as/philosophy/documents/faculty-documents/boghossian/Boghossian-Paul-socialconstruction1.pdf.

[11] S Katz and B Marshall, 'New Sex for Old: Lifestyle, Consumerism, and the Ethics of Ageing Well' (2003) 17 *Journal of Ageing Studies* 3.

[12] Bond et al (n 2) 320.

[13] R Lowe, 'Childhood through the Ages' in T Maynard and N Thomas (eds), *An Introduction to Early Childhood Studies* (SAGE Publications, 2004) 65.

[14] D Neugarten (ed), *The Meanings of Age: Selected Papers of Bernice L Neugarten* (University of Chicago Press, 1996) 60.

[15] Lowe (n 13).

clothing, children's games and a valuation of childhood innocence.[16] The introduction of age-regimented education has reinforced the modern idea of childhood as a period of learning.

Today in Britain, the idea of distinct age groups is firmly in place and age stratification has become pervasive, with the classification by age becoming a hugely significant part of people's identity. For example, age classification determines when we are 'supposed to enter school, leave school, marry, drink, vote, smoke, get called up for military duty in a real column, draw a retirement pension, and a great deal else in between the registered birth and the registered death'.[17] This structuring of society means age is now used as a proxy for a wide range of characteristics, including

> intellectual and emotional maturity (eg minimum ages for entering school), readiness to assume adult responsibilities (eg minimum ages for voting, drinking, driving and marriage), physical strength or speed of response (eg maximum ages for policemen, bus drivers, or air-line pilots), economic productivity (eg age of retirement), and various types of debility (eg ages for eligibility for medical services and social services).[18]

The emergence of the welfare state has further contributed to the cultural division of age groups. Governments have deliberately created policies combined to create, enhance or maintain economic dependency in old age.[19] These policies have associated late chronological age with retirement from productive work. Given the high status our culture attaches to productive work, this has led to the association between old age and low social status.

Age norms define the appropriate time in people's lives for major events and achieving, such as leaving home, marrying and having children, and retirement.[20] Age norms exert pressure on people by casting non-conforming behaviour as deviant. This occurs when behaviour does not match our culturally defined age roles. For example, our society stigmatises teenage mothers and women who reach the age of 50 but have not married, as well as certain types of relationships – for example, the stigma attached to marriage between a young husband and older wife or work relationships where the boss is younger than the workers.[21]

Certain forms of emotional expression are considered appropriate to particular age groups. For example, while a baby can cry, to do so later in life may lead to criticism for immaturity. And young people are not supposed to be despondent as they have 'their whole life ahead of them'.[22]

[16] ibid.

[17] M Young, *The Metronomic Society: Natural Rhythms and Human Timetables* (Thames and Hudson 1988) 109.

[18] Neugarten (n 14) 822.

[19] Bond et al (n 2) 280.

[20] G Elder, 'Age Differentiation and the Life Course' (1975) 1 *Annual Review of Sociology* 165.

[21] See S Reinharz, 'The Embeddedness of Age: Toward a Social Control Perspective' (1987) 1 *Journal of Aging Studies* 77, 88.

[22] ibid 88.

This pervasiveness of age norms influences people's self-evaluation. As Reinharz has argued, 'Because age is embedded in a society's system of social control, it is internalized and applied by socialized individuals to themselves'.[23] For example, an older person, socialised in the idea that older people are to withdraw from society, may feel bound to retire, and this, in turn, can negatively influence the person's self-esteem.

Part of the explanation for the pervasiveness of age norms is that a person's age is usually apparent from physical features and can be determined after face-to-face interactions.[24] We can easily judge a person against an age norm because we can determine an approximate age simply by looking at someone.

Given the pervasiveness of age-based structures in our society, we can ask what this background theory of the meaning of age has for understanding the acceptability or otherwise of age-differential treatment.

## II. The Efficiency Value of Age-Based Social Organisation

What the above discussion reveals is that age can be a proxy for certain attributes and abilities, whether biologically or socially constructed.[25] Intellectual skills and physical changes develop over time, and this development can approximate to certain points in a person's life cycle, which means we can use age as a proxy for these traits.[26] For example, the National Institute for Care and Health Excellence recommend that there should be restricted access to in vitro fertilisation for women over 43 for the reason that it is unlikely to be successful for these women. Age here is used as a (relatively) reliable proxy for the possibility of the procedure resulting in pregnancy.[27] Flu vaccines are distributed free on the National Health Service to people over 65 years of age because this age group tend to be more vulnerable to the illness than other age groups. England and Wales has a criminal age of responsibility set at 10 years old because younger children below this age

[23] ibid 87.

[24] E Goffman, 'The Interaction Order' (1983) 48 *American Sociological Review* 1.

[25] The usefulness of age distinctions has prompted judges to hold that age discrimination is more easily justifiable than unequal treatment on other protected grounds. For example, Advocate General Mazák in his opinion in Case C-388/07 *The Incorporated Trustees of the National Council on Ageing (Age Concern England) v Secretary of State for Business, Enterprise and Regulatory Reform* [2009] ECR I-1569 said that 'Age is not by its nature a "suspect ground", at least not so much as for example race or sex. Simple in principle to administrate, clear and transparent, age-based differentiations, age-limits and age-related measures are, quite to the contrary, widespread in law and in social and employment legislation in particular.'

[26] For a discussion of age as a reliable proxy, see A Gosseries, 'What Makes Age Discrimination Special? A Philosophical Look at the ECJ Case Law' (2014) 43 *Netherlands Journal of Legal Philosophy* 59.

[27] National Institute for Health and Care Excellence, 'Fertility Problems: Assessment and Treatment' (2013).

are unlikely to have the capacity to understand what they have done wrong and why.[28] While some children under 10 years of age have the mental capabilities to be responsible for crimes, a large proportion do not.

The value of using age as a proxy in these examples is that age can be a more objective and measurable target than the thing age is a proxy for, and this reduces costs and therefore increases the efficiency of pursuing the objectives of the policies.[29] This can ensure that there are more resources that can be dedicated to attain appropriate outcomes. For example, without an age proxy for criminal responsibility, we would have to assess the mental capacities of each child under 10 suspected of a crime. It is less costly to assume that all children under 10 have no criminal responsibility since we know that most children at this age lack this trait. Further, it is less costly to assume women over 43 years of age are unlikely to benefit from in vitro fertilisation than it is to assess each woman's likelihood of benefiting from the treatment. To spend resources on assessing each woman would mean fewer resources to spend on healthcare generally. It should be noted, however, that the reliability of age proxies depends on which ages we consider. As Gosseries notes,

> the reliability of age as a proxy is certainly strong at very early and very advanced ages (eg, the working ability of those below 14, the emotional maturity of those below 16, the driving ability of those below 25, the physical strength of those above 50, the health condition of those above 85). In contrast, when comparing people within the middle range (eg, a 35 and a 45 years old), many other factors often play a more significant role and intra-age-group variability then often becomes stronger than interage-groups variability.[30]

Age distinctions can also be efficient in other ways. As I explained in section I of this chapter, society has become age-regimented, with different roles assigned to different age groups. We expect children to be in education, adults in work and older people retired. This age-based structure ensures that we organise the chronological order of people's life activities to ensure they gain skills before having them put into practice. For example, we force children to start learning early in their lives because it is efficient that they learn skills necessary for work life before engaging in employment.[31]

[28] The Children and Young Persons Act 1933, ss 23 and 24. There is now widespread agreement that the criminal age of responsibility is too low. See T Bateman, 'Criminalising Children for No Good Purpose: The Age of Criminal Responsibility in England and Wales' (National Association for Youth Justice Campaign, 2012); C McDiarmid, 'An Age of Complexity: Children and Criminal Responsibility in Law' (2013) 13 *Youth Justice* 145; B Goldson, 'Counterblast: "Difficult to Understand or Defend: A Reasoned Case for Raising the Age of Criminal Responsibility"' (2009) 48 *Howard Journal of Criminal Justice* 514.

[29] Advocate General Mazák's opinion in the CJEU Case C-411/05 *Palacios de la Villa v Cortefiel Servicios SA* [2007] ECR I-8531 [62] argued that age-differential treatment is different to other forms of discrimination because it is 'common in social and employment policies'.

[30] Gosseries (n 26) 64.

[31] ibid.

Efficient age proxies and sequencing people's lives by age may explain why we consider many age-based social policies justified, including free flu vaccinations for over 65s, a criminal age of responsibility, restrictions on IVF treatments and compulsory education for children. However, efficiency is not always enough to justify differential treatment. For example, an employer may refuse to hire women because women are more likely to need to spend time out of the labour market. Even if this policy is efficient, it is unjustified because it violates a number of principles, including undermining equality of opportunity and social equality between men and women. Further, the fact that something can be a reliable or efficient proxy does not necessarily justify its use as a proxy. In a sexist society where women are often confined to the domestic sphere, sex might be a reliable proxy for under-developed workplace skills, but it would be unjustified for employers to refuse to hire women when that reinforces the subordinate position of women. What this illustrates is that efficiency can be valuable when it reduces the costs of pursuing an outcome that improves welfare or some other important or useful goal, but it is unjustifiable if the efficiency contributes to an unjust or generally undesirable outcome.

When we evaluate whether an age distinction is justified or unjustified, we should evaluate whether an age distinction is efficient, but also consider whether the age distinction causes some unjustifiable discriminatory impact. In the next section, I outline the principles that explain why and when age-differential treatment can be unjustified, which includes age distinctions that violate the principles of respect, equality of opportunity, social equality and autonomy.

## III. Age Discrimination and Equality of Opportunity

Equality of opportunity requires an equal distribution of benefits and burdens except when inequality arises in a way for which the person who ends up with less should be held responsible. In chapter four, I argued that this principle offers part of the reason why discrimination is wrong since many paradigm cases of discrimination cause disadvantages to people based on traits that they cannot or should not be held responsible for. Race discrimination, for example, denies people opportunities on the grounds of a trait people are powerless to change. We might, therefore, posit equality of opportunity as providing an explanation for why age discrimination is wrong.

However, equality of opportunity can actually justify age distinctions due to the nature of age. Age, like race, is a trait people cannot control because at any one time a person is a particular age. However, age is different to traits such as race (and many of the other protected characteristics in the Equality Act 2010) because age is changeable and we each experience the different age groups in turn. The nature of age means that people may experience the different advantages and disadvantages associated with different age groups. This means that age-differential treatment can be compatible with equality of opportunity measured over a complete life.[32] For example, while a young person is likely to have less wealth than a middle-aged person, they will likely gain the benefits of middle age as they move into that age group. Or imagine 'a health care policy that rations life-preserving care made available to the very old in order to reduce the extent to which expensive medical technology extends the lifespans of very old people with reduced quality of life' and prioritises 'health care policies toward saving the lives of very young people threatened with premature death'.[33] These policies are consistent with equality of opportunity when we measure access to resources over people's complete lives (assuming that all individuals live to the same old age).[34] This means that if we measure distributive equality over a complete life – from birth to death – then we can justify age-differential treatment if it is likely to secure equal resources or welfare distributed over a complete life, particularly if the policy is efficient in allocating resources.[35] This can also partly explain intuitions about age distinctions that we usually consider to be justified. Returning to the examples discussed earlier in the chapter, free flu vaccination to people 65 years of age or older can be justified because, assuming it is a stable policy, it would benefit every person as they reach the age subject to the policy, in addition to the policy being efficient in distributing health resources to people with particular health vulnerabilities. Compulsory education under the age of 16 ensures that people will experience education at an age when it is likely to have the most beneficial effect to the individual and to society. The policy can also be justified because it offers an equal number of years for people to benefit from the policy.

But is this complete-life version of equality of opportunity the most plausible account of equality of opportunity? We could, instead, interpret the principle of

[32] The compatibility of age discrimination with equality norms is discussed in detail by N Daniels, *Am I My Parents' Keeper?* (Oxford University Press, 1998); D McKerlie, 'Equality and Time' (1989) 99 *Ethics* 475; D McKerlie, 'Justice between the Young and the Old' (1999) 30 *Philosophy and Public Affairs* 152.

[33] R Arneson, 'Equality of Opportunity' in E Zalta (ed), *The Stanford Encyclopedia of Philosophy*, Summer 2015 edn.

[34] For example, Norman Daniels argued that the lives of people as a whole would be better if we rationed resources by age: N Daniels, 'Is There a Right to Health Care and, If So, What Does It Encompass?' in H Kuhse and P Singer (eds), *A Companion to Bioethics*, 2nd edn (Wiley-Blackwell, 1998) 81.

[35] This argument has been used in *R (Carson and Reynolds) v Secretary of State for Work and Pensions* [2005] UKHL 37, [2010] ECHR 338 to justify adopting a lower level of scrutiny for age distinctions than sex or race distinctions. Lord Walker justified this position on the grounds that age is different: 'Every human being starts life as a tiny infant, and none of us can do anything to stop the passage of the years' [80]. Younger people will eventually benefit from a provision which favours older employees and older employees will already have benefited from a provision which favours younger people. The major equality theorists adopt this complete-life version of equality of opportunity. Thomas Nagel, for example, argued that 'the subject of an egalitarian principle is not the distribution of particular rewards to individuals at some time, but the prospective quality of their lives as a whole, from birth to death: T Nagel, *Equality and Priority* (Oxford University Press, 1991) 69. Ronald Dworkin argued for assessing 'resources over an entire life', rather than 'at particular points in time', and that 'Our final aim is that an equal share of resources should be devoted to the lives of each person': R Dworkin, 'What is Equality? Part 2: Equality of Welfare' (1981) 10 *Philosophy and Public Affairs* 283, 289.

equality of opportunity as requiring equal opportunities at any moment in time. This version of equality of opportunity, however, has unattractive features and is much less plausible as a moral principle than the complete-life version. It would have the unattractive implication that it would be wrong to distribute a benefit at one time while failing to simultaneously give the same benefit to other people at the same time. Contrary to this version of equality of opportunity, we consider inequalities at particular moments to be acceptable. For example, parents giving birthday gifts on each child's birthday is acceptable even though it means one child will have a gift when the other children will have to wait until their own birthdays to get a gift. There also does not seem anything wrong with giving people the opportunity to drive at 17 years of age when this will mean people who are 16 years of age do not yet have the opportunity to drive.

The justification for the complete-life version of equality of opportunity is that each individual receives benefits and bears burdens at different life stages. We can compensate detriments at one time of life with gains at another time of life. Therefore, when determining if there is wrongful inequality of opportunity, we should add up the benefits and burdens in each life and make a comparison.

However, age-differential treatment does not always secure complete equality of opportunity over people's complete lives. Age distinctions can affect people differently. For example, people who die young will have fewer opportunities to benefit from age distinctions than people who live until old age. Someone dying at 15 years of age, for example, will never have the opportunity to vote in a general election. And age distinctions will cause some inequality of opportunity if they are changed or removed.[36] For example, a company may remove a mandatory retirement age with the result that employees who had not yet reached the retirement age no longer have to face the detriment of being forcibly retired, unlike the already retired employees. Even very stable policies, such as voting age, can be subject to change.

Nonetheless, age distinctions can contribute to equality by making opportunities more equal than they would otherwise be.[37] For example, market conditions may result in a particular age cohort having a higher unemployment rate than an older cohort experienced at an equivalent age. A mandatory retirement age might aim to redistribute opportunities from older people who have already experienced favourable employment opportunities to younger people who, due to market conditions, have had fewer of these opportunities. This policy may aim to reduce inequalities in access to jobs across cohorts.[38]

[36] See A Gosseries and M Hungerbühler, 'Rule Change and Intergenerational Justice' in J Tremmel (ed), *Handbook of Intergenerational Justice* (Edward Elgar Publishing, 2006) 106.

[37] In line with this reasoning, the Supreme Court in *Seldon v Clarkson, Wright and Jakes* [2012] UKSC 16, [2012] ICR 716 accepted the legitimacy of inter-generational fairness aims that are designed to create a fair balance between opportunities available to different age groups. The Court found that inter-generational fairness aims included measures designed to help young people enter the workforce or to create promotion opportunities for younger workers.

[38] Gosseries (n 26).

It is clear from this discussion that there are equality reasons as well as efficiency reasons for finding age-differential treatment justified. We must therefore incorporate equality of opportunity and efficiency into the theory of age discrimination as principles that can potentially justify age-differential treatment.

However, it is clear that age-differential treatment can still be wrong even if it promotes equality of opportunity. For example, policies that create severe disparity in resources and welfare between the young and the old can be compatible with equality of opportunity measured over people's complete lives, but can still be wrong. These policies may, for example, redistribute wealth to the young, leaving older people in poverty. What this example shows is that age distinctions can be wrong in treating people badly at a particular moment in time regardless of whether the policies secure equality of opportunity over complete lives. For example, the fact that people may experience the same levels of poverty over their complete lives does not make the poverty justified.[39] We must therefore invoke other principles to explain why this type of age discrimination wrongs people. To explain why and when age discrimination is wrong, we must identify the principles that explain why and when it is morally wrong to treat people less favourably on the grounds of age even if this means all people have equal opportunities over a complete life. In the next section, I argue that the social equality principle can provide an important grounding for explaining why and when age discrimination is wrong.

## IV. Age Discrimination and Social Equality

As I outlined in chapter four, social equality holds that discrimination is wrong when it creates conditions where people are unable to interact as equals. Age discrimination can clearly undermine social equality. As Neugarten notes, age is 'one of the bases for the ascription of status'.[40] Unequal treatment on the grounds of age can undermine the social status of particular age groups by reinforcing age-based hierarchies of social status.

There are a number of examples of age-differential treatment that can undermine social equality. Mandatory retirement, for example, can lock older people out of work, and this may lead to the social exclusion and marginalisation of older people. Our society links work to social status and therefore removing people from work because of age can have the effect of assigning older people to a lower

[39] As a similar example demonstrating the limitation of the equality of opportunity principle, Dennis McKerlie described a marriage in which 'circumstances dictate that first the husband and then the wife take turns in being dominant and subordinate': D McKerlie, 'Equality between Age-Groups' (1992) 21 *Philosophy and Public Affairs* 275. Even though the husband and wife each have an equal amount of dominance, this is still an unjustified form of inequality.'

[40] B Neugarten, J Moore and J Lowe, 'Age Norms, Age Constraints, and Adult Socialization' (1965) 70 *American Journal of Sociology* 710.

social status. As Sandra Fredman points out, 'Departure from the labour force frequently gives the impression that individuals are no longer active contributors to society'.[41] The fact that a mandatory retirement age might promote equality of opportunity over people's complete lives does not prevent the policy from wronging people by undermining their social status. Age discrimination can also harm the status of young people, as some examples of age stereotyping show. For example, young people are perceived as less reliable, less committed and less motivated in their work. Young people can be discriminated against on these grounds, which can make it harder for them to be taken as seriously as older age groups. This can also have the effect of making it harder for young people to find employment and achieve promotion. Due to the unique nature of age, social marginalisation caused by age-group status is likely to be restricted to parts of the life cycle. People move into new age groups over time and therefore gain (or lose) age-based opportunities over the life course.

Social equality can justify some forms of age-differential treatment. For example, positive action in favour of disadvantaged age groups can be a means to achieve social equality, rather than a breach of the principle. Positive action, such as offering work training to young people or initiatives to help older people back into employment, can facilitate the participation of marginalised age groups.[42]

Returning again to examples of efficient age proxies, we can explain that these policies can be justified partly by their respecting the social equality principle. For example, the policy of free flu vaccinations to people 65 years of age or older is justified partly because it supports social equality by distributing resources to vulnerable groups to ensure that these groups can continue to participate in society. Compulsory education under the age of 18 can ensure that people are equipped with skills to participate in the workforce and society as equals with others. In this way, these policies are justified partly because they aim to support social equality.

It is clear that social equality should play an important role in a theory of age discrimination as it explains why age-differential treatment may be wrong even though it can be efficient and can promote equality of opportunity.

## V. Autonomy and Age Discrimination

In chapter four, I argued that a major reason for the wrongness of discrimination is that it diminishes people's opportunities for autonomous agency. This autonomy

[41] S Fredman, 'What Do We Mean by Age Equality' (2001) Paper presented to the IPPR Seminar on Age as an Equality Issue, 30.

[42] As I outlined in ch 2, positive action is lawful if it meets the requirements under ss 158 and 159 of the Equality Act 2010. However, in *Seldon* (n 37), the Supreme Court held that positive action measures which aim to share opportunity between generations are legitimate for the purposes of justifying age-differential treatment. This finding means that decision-makers may not have to meet the stricter requirements of ss 158 and 159 to justify positive action.

principle can also explain the wrongness of many forms of age discrimination. For example, a mandatory retirement age wrongs older workers by forcing them out of work. The policy therefore undermines older workers' capacity to have control over their working lives.

Age discrimination can also undermine autonomy in the health sphere. For example, a doctor deciding that older patients do not have priority for certain drugs can lead to those people missing out on treatment that could help them retain their independence at a time of life when they face health challenges to their autonomy.

Another example is the age barrier to training for certain professions, such as medicine, which prevents older workers from having control over their lives. Laws restricting voting rights, driving and drinking alcohol significantly curtail young people's autonomy.

The age stereotyping that underpins and sustains age discrimination can also harm autonomy. In chapter four, I explained that stereotyping can lead to losses of autonomy when the messages of stereotyping become internalised and accepted as 'natural'. Our ability to exercise autonomy depends on how we are understood by others. For example, Caroline Dunn notes autonomy harms from the widespread set of negative perceptions of old age.[43] In Western society, the stereotyping of older people generally contains messages that they are in decline, lack productivity, and are irrelevant and a burden to society. If these messages become internalised, then it is easy to imagine how older people are less likely to take action to, say, remain in the workforce or to further develop their capabilities to increase their agency.

To be autonomous, people must view themselves as being the authors of their lives. If people internalise the message that older people are incompetent, then older people are likely to lose self-esteem, potentially resulting in a lack of confidence to act with conviction at a time of life when they are facing health challenges to their autonomy and could be missing out on treatment that could help them to retain their independence.

## VI. Age Discrimination and Disrespect

I argued in chapter four that a core reason for when and why discrimination is wrong is that it can send disrespectful messages. There are various ways such messages can be communicated, including as a result of the discriminator acting on prejudice, dislike or hostility towards members of a particular social group,[44] when the discrimination undermines the self-respect of the discriminatee,[45]

[43] C Dunn, 'The Effects of Ageing on Autonomy' in H Lesser (ed), *Ageing, Autonomy and Resources* (Ashgate, 1999) 7.

[44] M Cavanagh, *Against Equality of Opportunity* (Clarendon Press, 2002).

[45] J Rawls, *A Theory of Justice* (Harvard University Press, 2009) 440.

when the social context means that the discrimination can be interpreted as a communication that the discriminatee deserves less concern and respect than others,[46] and also when the discriminator fails to acknowledge the individuality or the autonomy of a person as a result of relying on a generalisation or stereotype that imposes costs on an individual.[47]

Some have argued that this respect principle does not explain the wrongs of age discrimination because age discrimination has not been a practice marked by prejudice, dislike and hostility. For example, Samuel Issacharoff and Erica Worth Harris have argued that age discrimination laws in the USA, which protect older people from discrimination, do not protect any group that is socially reviled, penurious, cut off from the mainstream of society and/or marked by the badge of social opprobrium.[48] However, while the degree of animus towards age groups has perhaps been less than that directed towards other groups, age discrimination often reveals attitudes that ascribe negative worth to particular groups. Both young and old, for example, have been subject to demeaning ideas about their worth as human beings. Age discrimination can demean older people by conveying that they are burdensome to society by taking up too many resources.[49] The young, in contrast, are stereotyped as immature, unruly and violent. Such stereotyping can be motivated by prejudice and can be interpreted as a communication that particular age groups have a lower moral and social worth. As Grimley Evans has highlighted, 'Ageist prejudice is deeply and widely pervasive in British society', and 'It is treated as in some way "natural," even by many older people'.[50] Empirical evidence demonstrates that age stereotypes – directed against the old and young – are widespread and harmful in a variety of contexts, including the workplace and healthcare settings.[51]

Further, age stereotypes can mean that people are disadvantaged by a generalisation even in circumstances where the individual does not conform to the generalisation. For example, the stereotype that older workers are less productive can result in productive older workers being dismissed from employment, which fails to respect the individuality of the worker.

[46] D Hellman, *When Is Discrimination Wrong?* (Harvard University Press, 2008).

[47] B Eidelson, *Discrimination and Disrespect* (Oxford University Press, 2015).

[48] S Issacharoff and EW Harris, 'Is Age Discrimination Really Age Discrimination: The ADEA's Unnatural Solution' (1997) 72 *New York University Law Review* 780.

[49] For an example of this stereotyping, see D Willetts, *The Pinch: How the Baby Boomers Took Their Children's Future – and Why They Should Give It Back* (Atlantic Books, 2011).

[50] G Evans, 'Age Discrimination: Implications of the Ageing Process' in S Fredman and S Spencer (eds), *Age as an Equality Issue* (Hart Publishing, 2003) 20.

[51] For evidence of age stereotyping in the workplace, see W Chiu et al, 'Age Stereotypes and Discriminatory Attitudes Towards Older Workers: An East–West Comparison' (2001) 54 *Human Relations* 629. For evidence of harmful stereotyping in the context of healthcare in the UK, see D Robertson et al, 'Negative Perceptions of Aging and Decline in Walking Speed: A Self-Fulfilling Prophecy' (2015) 10 *PloS One*; B Levy et al, 'A Culture–Brain Link: Negative Age Stereotypes Predict Alzheimer's Disease Biomarkers' (2016) 31 *Psychology and Aging* 82.

Age stereotypes, however, are not always negative. For example, the idea that older people have 'wisdom' is a positive stereotype. Nevertheless, acting on positive stereotypes can still wrong people because a positive stereotype can imply negative attitudes to others. For example, hiring an older person because they have greater wisdom implies that younger people are less likely to have this positive characteristic. In this way, acting on positive stereotypes still communicates disrespect.

As I have argued in chapter four, discrimination can undermine the self-respect of victims of discrimination when the negative messages conveyed by the discrimination become internalised by the victim. There is considerable evidence that older people, for example, can internalise the negative messages of age discrimination, leading to them having negative ideas about their own age, which, in turn, can undermine their self-respect.[52]

Even 'efficient' age discrimination when an employer is motivated to maximise profits, rather than by prejudice or negative stereotypes, can demean people. For example, consider an employer who refuses to employ older lawyers because the wider community prefers younger lawyers. By acting on the prejudice of the community, the employer acquiesces in the demeaning attitudes of the community and shows indifference to the moral worth of older lawyers. The employer indirectly reinforces those negative judgements.

Although it is clear that age discrimination can disrespect people, there are examples of age classifications we accept as useful or efficient rather than demeaning. As I argued earlier in this chapter, our society creates and sustains age-based structures with the goal of pursuing the efficient attainment of social goods.[53] Age-differential treatment can be respectful and justified when the treatment is not intended to maliciously lock people out of opportunities. For example, a voting age of 18 years is far less offensive than disenfranchising black people or women. It permits people to wait to have the opportunity to participate in democratic elections. In contrast, denying black people and women the right to vote conveys that these groups should not have the right to participate in an essential feature of the society in which they live.

Returning to the examples of efficient age proxies discussed earlier in the chapter, free flu vaccinations to people over 65 years of age distributes resources to people who are particularly vulnerable to health problems rather than reflecting or reinforcing harmful stereotypes or prejudice, and age restrictions in accessing

[52] See B John, 'Patterns of Ageism in Different Age Groups' (2013) 4 *Journal of European Psychology Students* 16.

[53] The legal treatment of age discrimination in the USA reflects this position. For example, the US Supreme Court held in *Massachusetts Board of Retirement v Murgia* 427 US 307, 312 (1976) that age distinctions are constitutional provided they have a rational basis. The Court explained that, in evaluating the constitutionality of age-differential treatment, the courts should adopt a low level of scrutiny because older age groups have not experienced a 'history of purposeful unequal treatment' or been 'subjected to unique disabilities on the basis of stereotyped characteristics not truly indicative of their abilities' [313].

IVF treatments on the National Health Service distributes scarce resources to people who are most likely to benefit from the treatment rather than expressing disrespect to age groups who cannot access the treatment.

To summarise, determining whether age-differential treatment is disrespectful and therefore wrong requires that we determine whether it is motivated by prejudice or stereotyping or can be interpreted to convey a message that certain age groups have a diminished moral or social worth.

# VII. Conclusion

The Equality Act 2010 requires distinguishing justified from unjustified treatment that engages the age discrimination provisions and holds that only the former are lawful (unless the treatment fits into a specifically prescribed exception). This chapter has established a pluralist theory of age discrimination to undertake this analysis. I have argued that age-differential treatment can have numerous benefits, including promoting efficiency, equality of opportunity and social equality, which can work to justify the treatment. However, it is still possible that these practices are unjustified if they contribute to oppressive social relations, are based on inaccurate or negative stereotyping and prejudice, and significantly interfere with the autonomy of individuals.

This pluralist theory of age discrimination creates the opportunity to determine the legality of treatment that engages the age discrimination provisions of the Equality Act 2010. In chapter seven, I demonstrate how this theory can settle age discrimination claims by comparing and contrasting the theory of age discrimination outlined in this chapter with the approaches adopted by the UK courts in age discrimination claims.

In applying the law, we should consider the extent to which impugned treatment promotes or violates each of the five principles of the pluralist theory of age discrimination. The principles may pull in different directions, but determining the proportionality, and therefore legality, of treatment requires that we determine which of the various arguments are most compelling to find the treatment justified or unjustified.

To simplify the process of applying the pluralist theory of age discrimination, we can divide age-differential treatment into three categories. In considering the legality of treatment that engages the age discrimination provisions, we should consider which of the following categories it falls into.

## A. Demeaning Age Discrimination

Demeaning age discrimination conveys to people of a particular age group that they have a degraded moral worth or lower social worth because of their age.

Measures that communicate that a person has a lower moral worth include age distinctions that are motivated by prejudice, animosity, hostility and dislike. Measures that communicate that a person has lower social worth include treatment founded on harmful age stereotypes, such as stereotypes that certain age groups are useless, inflexible, less productive, senile etc. While it may be true that some age group members are less productive or are inflexible, subjecting people to stereotypical judgements that may not be accurate for the individual is wrong.

## B. Efficient Age-Differential Treatment

As I argued in section II, age-differential treatment can reduce the costs of attaining some social goods, particularly when age can be used as a proxy for certain characteristics and age is more measurable and objective than the thing that age is a proxy for. For example, offering free flu vaccinations to people 65 years of age or older is an efficient way to direct health resources to people who are vulnerable to the illness because it is much harder and more expensive to measure each person's vulnerability to the illness before offering the vulnerable free vaccinations. Using age in the distribution of healthcare and education to maximise health and educational benefits is a good way to maximise welfare for society as a whole, and can justify age-differential treatment. Such policies can be unjustified, however, if they have unacceptable discriminatory impacts, such as violating equality of opportunity, social equality, respect and autonomy to an unacceptable degree.

## C. Age-Differential Treatment Aimed at Advancing Equality and/or Autonomy

Age discrimination can aim to satisfy equality and autonomy principles and therefore reflect a desire to ensure fairness. Examples include age distinctions that aim to ensure that people have equal shares of benefits and burdens over their complete lives. This satisfies the principle of the complete-life version of equality of opportunity, which holds that inequality is only wrong if there are unequal benefits over people's complete lives and this inequality is not connected to personal responsibility for that inequality.

Nonetheless, age discrimination that advances equality and/or autonomy principles may be unjustified should it violate other moral principles. For example, even if we secure equal welfare and resources over people's complete lives, this can still harm the principle of social equality when it results in people being unable to participate in society as equals. For example, restricting the benefits offered to older people denies them access to things that provide for equal participation in society. If the complete-life account of equality of opportunity conflicts with social equality, autonomy or respect, judges should weigh up the benefit and burdens of a policy by considering the extent to which it promotes one principle or violates another, and then make a decision on which principles should prevail.

Age-differential treatment can also aim to advance the social equality principle. For example, positive action aims to promote social equality by integrating people from age groups that typically suffer from social exclusion or low levels of autonomy. It can also promote the respect principle by granting people the opportunity to overcome negative stereotypes. Positive age discrimination is particularly contentious because it can undermine the interests of other groups. For example, the young usually suffer much higher levels of unemployment than other age groups and positive age action in favour of the young can invite young people to overcome their disadvantages and reduce youth unemployment. The difficulty in favouring the young in this way, however, is that it may disadvantage older people, who also suffer from social exclusion. Positive age discrimination, therefore, promotes one age group over others. A judge must weigh up the extent to which positive action advances the interests of one age group and the potential costs it has on any other age groups, and then make a decision on whether it should be considered justified and therefore lawful.

# 6

# Legislative History of Age Discrimination Law and Its Relevance to Interpreting and Applying the Equality Act 2010

I have now formed a pluralist theory of age discrimination that should guide the direct and indirect age discrimination provisions of the Equality Act 2010. This theory should operate as a guide to distinguish justified from unjustified age-differential treatment and therefore assist in determining the proportionality and lawfulness of impugned treatment.

The method of this book, reflective equilibrium, requires that I review the approaches to age discrimination from a range of sources to identify those principles that should underpin age discrimination law. Further to this, I now review the legislative history of age discrimination law, including the rationales of age discrimination law found in the consultation papers and ministerial statements, and consider whether judges should use the ideas within these materials in applying age discrimination law. The value of this exercise is that these materials contain research and ideas from people with experience in approaching the problem of age discrimination and may therefore have value as sources of knowledge on age discrimination that could feed into the theory of age discrimination developed in this book. The legislative history I consider includes the following: documents by the European Commission outlining the need for EU Member States to enact age discrimination laws;[1] documents by the UK government departments on the rationales for introducing age discrimination laws in the UK;[2] consultation documents on implementing the EU Directive prohibiting age discrimination;[3]

[1] Commission, 'Towards a Europe for All Ages – Promoting Prosperity and Intergenerational Solidarity' COM (1999) 221 final.

[2] Discrimination Law Review, *A Framework for Fairness: Proposals for a Single Equality Bill for Great Britain* (2007); Government Equalities Office, *Equality Bill: Making it Work. Policy Proposals for Specific Duties* (2010); Government Equalities Office, *The Equality Act 2010: Banning Age Discrimination in Services* (2011).

[3] Department of Trade and Industry, *Equality and Diversity: Age Matters* (2003); Department of Trade and Industry, *Equality and Diversity: Coming of Age* (2005).

the consultation document on the removal of fixed retirement ages;[4] and Hansard statements relating to age discrimination law. These documents contain research and ideas from people with experience in approaching the problem of age discrimination and may therefore have value as sources of knowledge on age discrimination.[5]

I argue that judges should not defer to the approaches to age discrimination in the legislative history. To defer to the legislative history as binding authority would be to treat the ideas in the documents as binding, and this is inappropriate because these ideas are not law and have not secured democratic backing in the parliamentary enactment process. Further, deferring to the consultation documents risks creating a misleading account of the point and value of age discrimination law because the consultation documents may not reliably represent the genuine rationales for this law.

I then consider whether the pluralist theory of age discrimination should incorporate the approaches to age discrimination law identified in the legislative history. I argue that it should not do so because the consultation documents place an inappropriate emphasis on efficiency as a rationale for age discrimination law. The efficiency account of the wrongness of age discrimination adopted in the documents is problematic because it can lead to the position that efficiency can always justify age-differential treatment. I argue that efficiency should not be capable of justifying certain types of age-differential treatment. In particular, it should not justify demeaning age-differential treatment that reflects stereotypes or prejudice or that communicates that particular age groups have a diminished moral and social worth. In light of this, I revise the pluralist theory of age discrimination to incorporate the principle that efficiency should not justify treatment that communicates that particular age groups have a diminished moral or social worth.

I also argue that we should not revise the pluralist theory of age discrimination to adopt the approach to age discrimination in the Hansard statements on the prohibition on age discrimination. The Hansard statements indicate that age

[4] Department for Work and Pensions, *Workforce Management Without a Fixed Retirement Age* (2011).

[5] Other sources that may be useful for identifying principles to underpin age discrimination law include position papers by non-governmental organisations and professional organisations. For example, see the reports by the Centre for Policy on Ageing: 'The Likely Costs and Benefits of Legislation to Prohibit Age Discrimination in Health, Social Care and Mental Health Services and Definitions of Age Discrimination that might be Operationalised for Measurement' (2007); 'Ageism and Age Discrimination in Primary and Community Health Care in the United Kingdom' (2009); 'Ageism and Age Discrimination in Secondary Health Care in the United Kingdom' (2009); 'Ageism and Age Discrimination in Mental Health Care in the United Kingdom' (2009); 'Ageism and Age Discrimination in Social Care in the United Kingdom' (2009). For useful position papers by professional organisations, see Royal College of Psychiatrists, 'A Collective Responsibility to Act Now on Ageing and Mental Health: a Consensus Statement' (Mental Health and Older People Forum 2008); Royal College of Psychiatrists, 'The Need to Tackle Age Discrimination in Mental Health – A Compendium of Evidence' (2009).

discrimination law should allow service providers to deny services to particular age groups if the service provider has had previous negative experiences with that age group.[6] I argue that this approach would permit wrongful negative age stereotyping and prejudice in denying services.

## I. The Legality of Using Legislative History in Adjudication

Legislative history includes any materials created in forming legislation. This includes consultation documents on the introduction of age discrimination law and parliamentary debates published in Hansard. Before reviewing the legislative history, we must determine whether it is permitted for judges to use this legislative history in applying age discrimination law.[7]

For centuries, the courts refused to consider using parliamentary statements as aids to statutory interpretation and application.[8] However, there are now some exceptions to this exclusionary rule. In *Pepper v Hart*, the House of Lords held that 'reference to Parliamentary material should be permitted as an aid to the construction of legislation which is ambiguous or obscure or the literal meaning of which leads to an absurdity'.[9] In *Wilson v Secretary of State for Trade and Industry*, the House of Lords clarified that only statements made by a minister or other promoter of legislation can be assessed by the court in determining the mischief legislation is aimed at correcting.[10] In *McDonnell v Congregation of Christian Brothers Trustee*, the House of Lords held that 'it is permissible to use Hansard to identify the mischief at which the statute is aimed'.[11]

It follows that courts and tribunals can refer to ministerial parliamentary statements to determine the mischief that the age provisions of the Equality Act 2010 are aimed at correcting. The direct and indirect age discrimination provisions of the Equality Act 2010 require judges to determine whether an impugned measure is a 'proportionate means of achieving a legitimate aim'. These provisions leave unclear the principles and interests that are relevant to determining proportionality and therefore legality. The proportionality test also does not tell us anything about how to weigh different interests and principles. Assessing

[6] HL Deb 17 July 2012, vol 739, cols 83–86.

[7] For a detailed discussion of the UK approach compared to the US approach, see J Brudney, 'Below the Surface: Comparing Legislative History Usage by the House of Lords and the Supreme Court' (2007) 85 *Washington University Law Review* 1.

[8] See, eg *Millar v Taylor* (1769) 4 Burr 2303, 98 ER 201. The Court excluded any consideration of legislative history as irrelevant to the meaning of the statute. Judges Willes said: 'The sense and meaning of an act of parliament must be collected from what it says when passed into law, and not from the history of changes it underwent in the house when it took its rise.'

[9] [1993] AC 593 (HL) 634.

[10] [2003] UKHL 63, [2004] 1 AC 110.

[11] [2003] UKHL 40, [2004] 1 AC 816 [29] (Lord Steyn).

ministerial statements in Hansard may clarify the rationales of the age provisions of the Equality Act 2010. In this chapter, I determine whether the courts or tribunals should defer to the understanding of age discrimination in these statements.

The other major source of legislative history is the consultation documents on the introduction of age discrimination law. The courts have allowed the use of pre-legislative materials – such as consultation documents – to determine the purpose of legislation. For example, in *Eastman Photographic Materials Co Ltd v Comptroller-General of Patents, Designs and Trademarks*, the House of Lords held that it is appropriate for courts to study pre-legislative extra-parliamentary materials as a method of determining 'the evil or defect' which the legislation is intended to remedy.[12] Further, in *Pepper v Hart*, Lord Browne-Wilkinson observed that the courts are now accustomed to relying on White Papers and official government documents as aids in determining how to interpret and apply the law.[13] Judges are therefore not excluded from using government consultation documents to identify the principles that explain the rationales for age discrimination law as a guide to applying the law.

In the next section, I explore what the consultation documents and parliamentary statements reveal about the government's rationales for age discrimination law.

## II. Legislative History of Age Discrimination Law

The EU provided the initiative for introducing age discrimination law. In 1999, the European Commission produced a document outlining the need for legislation prohibiting age discrimination.[14] The document explained that EU Member States must adapt to the ageing population in Europe and its impact on economic growth. The ageing population, the document explained, will have a number of potential consequences that EU Member States must prepare for, including the relative decline of the working age populations,[15] pressures on pension systems from a growing number of retired people[16] and a growing need for healthcare.[17]

The document highlighted both economic and equality reasons for age discrimination laws. It explained that legislation banning age discrimination can be part of a strategy to address the consequences of an ageing population by enabling and motivating older people to remain in work and to be involved in

[12] [1898] AC 571 (HL).
[13] *Pepper v Hart* (n 9) 630.
[14] Commission (n 1).
[15] ibid 8–11.
[16] ibid 12–18.
[17] ibid 18–21.

social life. Banning age discrimination, the documents said, would also promote the social inclusion of older people, which would tap into the talent and experience of that age group.

The EU passed the Employment Equality Framework Directive (Directive 2000/78/EC) on 27 November 2000. This legislation required EU Member States to implement domestic legislation to make age discrimination unlawful (subject to exceptions).[18] In response, the UK government started a consultation process on introducing age discrimination legislation. In December 2001, the government published a consultation document entitled 'Towards Equality and Diversity'.[19] The document had one chapter on implementing a ban on age discrimination. In justifying the creation of this ban, the document explained that legislation is needed to 'have a real impact in removing unfair discrimination',[20] and laws designed to tackle unfair discrimination would go some way to preventing discrimination that cannot be achieved by merely relying on voluntary (non-legal) methods. The consultation further explained:

> [Age discrimination] leads to assumptions about younger and older workers that create and perpetuate inappropriate recruitment, selection, training, promotion and retirement practices. In tandem with developing legislation, we plan to increase promotional activities to change attitudes on age in the workplace and to challenge the unthinking prejudice that blights lives and is so costly to our economy.[21]

The two primary rationales for age discrimination law outlined in the document were, first, that legislation can promote economic efficiency and, secondly, that legislation can reduce age discrimination that harms people through age stereotyping. The latter principle mirrors the respect principle of the pluralist theory of age discrimination, which holds that age discrimination is wrong when it demeans people through stereotyping and prejudice.

The document places greater emphasis on the harmful effect of age discrimination on the economy than its harmful effect on individuals. Age discrimination, the document says, has a 'negative impact on productivity and profits' and 'denies employers access to valuable knowledge, experience and skills'.[22] The emphasis on the economy in the document is likely to reflect government attempts to convince a sceptical business community to accept age discrimination laws as being in businesses' self-interest. It is unclear whether the government actually believed that economic reasons are the best rationale for introducing age discrimination laws.

In the consultation 'Age Matters' of July 2003, the government again took an economic approach to age discrimination.[23] The document stated that 'Legislation

[18] While the UK remains in the EU, it will be obligated to maintain age discrimination laws in line with EU Directives. As I explained in ch 2, after withdrawal from the EU, the UK can repeal age discrimination laws.

[19] Department of Trade and Industry, *Towards Equality and Diversity* (2001).

[20] ibid para 3.1a.

[21] ibid para 15.3.

[22] ibid para 1.4.

[23] Department of Trade and Industry, *Equality and Diversity: Age Matters* (2003).

on age discrimination is likely to result in increased participation rates for older and younger workers',[24] and that 'This will lead to a wider pool of workers whose abilities and talents better match the requirements of employers when recruiting and developing their staff'.[25] The document highlighted that 'about £16 billion a year in lost GDP' and '£3–5 billion in extra benefits and lost taxes' results from people over 50 years old leaving the workforce.[26] The document also stated that age discrimination can 'perpetuate inaccurate stereotypes'.[27]

In 2005, the government drafted the Employment Equality (Age) Regulations 2006 to implement the Framework Directive. It produced a consultation draft on this legislation called 'Equality and Diversity: Coming of Age'.[28] This document argued that legislation banning age discrimination can help to generate business efficiency by ensuring that people fulfil their work potential and therefore employers can ensure that they are 'delivering the best service to their customers'.[29] The report went on:

> Over time, there will be overall net economic (not to mention social) benefits from the legislation, with potentially large effects on tax and national insurance receipts, and the long run potential of the economy. We believe that these benefits will arise principally due to increased employment rates and better matching of jobs to people.[30]

The government had plans to create new equality legislation that would bring together the array of anti-discrimination legislation in one place. Further to this, the government introduced the Equality Bill. The consultation on the Equality Bill, 'Framework for Fairness', published in June 2007, recognised that many forms of age distinction are justified and should not be unlawful.[31] Legislation banning age discrimination, the document states, should not prohibit age distinctions that enable 'services to be delivered more efficiently and effectively'.[32] This reflects the efficiency principle of the pluralist theory of age discrimination, which recognises that age-differential treatment can promote good consequences.

The document also stated that age discrimination is wrong when it denies some older people 'access to services the rest of the population take for granted'.[33] This reflects the social equality principle of the pluralist theory of age discrimination, which requires conditions where different age groups have equal capacity for participation in social, economic and political life.

[24] ibid para 1.11.
[25] ibid.
[26] ibid para 1.12.
[27] ibid para 7.2.
[28] Department of Trade and Industry, *Equality and Diversity: Coming of Age* (2005).
[29] ibid para 1.13.
[30] ibid para 1.14.
[31] Discrimination Law Review, *A Framework for Fairness: Proposals for a Single Equality Bill for Great Britain* (2007).
[32] ibid para 9.5.
[33] ibid para 9.11.

The document also argued that age discrimination laws will help change discriminatory attitudes and behaviours, which are responsible for 'hampering wider government plans to improve health and social care and local council services such as transport for older people'.[34] The document noted that age discrimination laws can challenge behaviour that treats older people with a lack of dignity in environments such as hospitals. This reflects the respect principle of the pluralist theory of age discrimination. The government also referred to the respect principle as a reason to ban age discrimination in the consultation document 'The Equality Act 2010: Banning Age Discrimination in Services' of March 2011.[35] The document called for legislation to put an 'end to old-fashioned stereotyping of people because of their age and recognising the valuable contribution people of all ages'.[36] The document also identified the autonomy principle as a reason to ban age discrimination by stating that age discrimination prevents 'greater freedom, mobility and choice'.[37]

The consultation on the removal of fixed retirement ages, called 'Workforce Management Without a Fixed Retirement Age' and published in January 2011,[38] also revealed rationales for age discrimination laws. The document explained the rationale for removing fixed retirement ages as promoting business efficiency because 'Older employees can bring valuable experience and knowledge to a business' and older people 'can use their know-how to train and mentor less experienced colleagues, and may welcome the opportunity to work more flexibly to cover extended or unsocial business hours'.[39]

We can find further insight into the rationales for age discrimination laws in the discussions of the exceptions to the ban on age discrimination. For example, in the consultation 'Equality and Diversity: Age Matters',[40] the Department of Trade and Industry provided the following examples of legitimate aims capable of justifying the use of age distinctions:

- health, welfare and safety – for example, the protection of younger workers;
- facilitation of employment planning – for example, where a business has a number of people approaching retirement age at the same time;
- the particular training requirements of the post in question – for example, air traffic controllers, who have to undergo 18 months of theoretical and practical training at the College of Air Traffic Control, followed by further on-the-job training;

[34] ibid para 9.12.

[35] Government Equalities Office, *The Equality Act 2010: Banning Age Discrimination in Services* (2011).

[36] ibid ministerial foreword.

[37] ibid para 8.5.

[38] Department for Work and Pensions, *Workforce Management without a Fixed Retirement Age* (2011).

[39] ibid introduction.

[40] Department of Trade and Industry, *Equality and Diversity: Age Matters* (2003).

- encouraging and rewarding loyalty; and
- the need for a reasonable period of employment before retirement – for example, an employer who has exceptionally justified a retirement age of 65 might decline to employ someone only a few months short of 65 if the need for, and the cost and length of, training meant that the applicant would not be sufficiently productive in that time.

From this outline of legitimate aims, there is a recognition that age distinctions can produce positive social outcomes. Some of the listed legitimate aims are examples of promoting business efficiency ('rewarding loyalty'), but others relate to efficiently promoting social goods, including health, welfare and safety. This reveals that the government of the time believed that age discrimination laws should not interfere with efficient measures.

Further, the consultation document 'Making it Work', of January 2010, argued that as individuals' circumstances are different, it can be justifiable to treat individuals of different ages differently.[41] The document stated that 'treating people differently based on their age is sometimes beneficial or otherwise justified, as people's needs, expectations and circumstances change with their age'.[42] Should a particular age group have a particular need, it is rational and justifiable to treat this age group differently to satisfy that need. Linking back to earlier arguments on identifying the wrongness of age discrimination, we can understand that when age distinctions satisfy genuine age-based needs, these distinctions promote social goods while treating individuals fairly by taking into account their real circumstances in a way that is neither demeaning nor exclusionary.

In summary, the consultation documents, in identifying the rationales for age discrimination laws, refer to the principles of the pluralist theory of discrimination as identifying wrongful age-differential treatment, including equality of opportunity, social equality, autonomy, respect and efficiency. The documents, however, are vague about the meaning of these principles, and there is a lack of consistency in identifying them – some documents strongly emphasise business efficiency while others have more emphasis on fairness.

Hansard also reveals principles underpinning age discrimination law. On 12 June 2012, Lynne Featherstone, the Minister for Equalities, made a ministerial statement in Parliament explaining the government's intentions to ban age discrimination in the provision of services.[43] In common with the rationales identified in the consultation documents, the Minister emphasised both economic and fairness rationales for the ban. She stated that 'Equality of opportunity is a core coalition objective' and 'It is fundamental to building a strong economy and a strong society'.

[41] Government Equalities Office, *Equality Bill: Making it Work. Policy Proposals for Specific Duties* (2010).

[42] ibid executive summary.

[43] HC Deb 12 June 2012, vol 546.

In the House of Lords debate on the introduction of the ban on age discrimination in the provision of services, Baroness Verma, the Lords Spokesperson for Equalities and Women's Issues, discussed some examples that, in her opinion, were likely to count as a proportionate means of achieving a legitimate aim, including the example of 'a holiday cottage owner not wishing to rent to very young adults because their cottage had been damaged by such people in the past' and 'a car rental company that has had several of its cars written off by drivers aged under 25 or over 75' deciding 'not to rent cars to people in those age groups or perhaps to charge them a little more'.[44] The service provider could justify this age-differential treatment, Baroness Verma said, by 'the need to reduce road accidents generally' and the need to run the 'business efficiently'. These statements recognise that efficiency should justify actions that would otherwise constitute age discrimination and that it is justifiable to use age generalisations to justify this treatment.

## III. Using the Legislative History as Aids in Adjudication

As I argued in chapter two, the direct and indirect age discrimination provisions of the Equality Act 2010 require courts and tribunals to distinguish justified from unjustified age-differential treatment as part of an assessment into whether an impugned measure is proportionate and therefore lawful. In making this judgement, a court or tribunal must identify moral principles that determine when and why age-differential treatment wrongs people and principles that can justify age-differential treatment. Judges may use their own judgement to identify such principles or they can identify these principles in the legislative history to find rationales for the legislation.

The strongest argument for using the legislative history is that this can reveal the rationales for age discrimination law and therefore inform judges of the sorts of considerations for identifying unlawful discrimination. The legislative history can help the courts and tribunals further the purpose of age discrimination law.

The legislative history can also offer guidance in undertaking the proportionality test by highlighting the principles that determine when aims are legitimate and offering guidance on balancing the principles in the final proportionality assessment. The Equality Act 2010 offers no guidance on the principles relevant to undertaking the proportionality test. Many argue that this is a threat to the rule of law because the proportionality test fails to offer an adequate level of certainty and predictability in adjudication. For example, Stavros Tsakyrakis has argued that proportionality is 'a characteristically *impressionistic* assessment of the relative

[44] HL Deb 17 July 2012, vol 739, cols 83–86.

weights of competing considerations, which does not lend itself to a rational reconstruction of the argumentative path that has led to a particular decision'.[45] Judges deferring to the principles highlighted in the legislative history will help avoid judgments based purely on their own subjective moral ideas and can make decisions more predictable by making clear the principles the courts are relying on to decide cases.

The legislative history can simplify the job of adjudicating. As should now be evident from this book, age discrimination is morally complex. Understanding all of the relevant issues in an age discrimination claim is a difficult task. A judge has limited time and resources to consider the advantages and disadvantages of different rulings. The legislative history can simplify the judge's task by identifying the relevant moral principles in a claim.

Despite these possible benefits, however, judges should not defer to the approach to age discrimination found in the legislative history at the expense of judges' own considered views. Deferring to the approaches in the legislative history would be to treat the documents as having a binding force. However, the legislative history is not law and should not bind judges. As Aileen Kavanagh has argued:

> Law is not made in virtue of lawmakers discussing the matters to be legislated or hoping or aspiring to achieve certain aims. Nor is it determined by what the lawmaker would have directed, given a chance to do so. In order to be made into law, it must be endorsed by the law-making institutions on whose authority it is supposed to rest.[46]

To treat the legislative history as binding authority would be to 'enforce intentions and ideas that do not have legal binding force' and, in doing so, 'subvert the rationale of the enactment process'.[47] The enactment process has a democratic rationale. For a Bill to become law, it must win the support of the majority of MPs. This gives the law its authority. Legislative history does not have this democratic backing and therefore lacks authority to bind judges.

A major purpose of the parliamentary process of law-making is to aim to find consensus on a particular issue that is being legislated. If judges defer to the ideas and intentions expressed in the legislative history of age discrimination law, then the courts and tribunals will be deferring to ideas that have not necessarily secured a consensus by the majority in Parliament.

Furthermore, relying on the consultation documents risks creating a misleading account of the point and value of age discrimination law. The consultation documents may not represent the genuine rationales for introducing age discrimination law. The documents are directed at businesses, including retailers, insurance companies, financial services firms and banks. The explanations of the rationales

[45] S Tsakyrakis, 'Proportionality: An Assault on Human Rights?' (2009) 7 *International Journal of Constitutional Law* 468, 482 (emphasis added).

[46] A Kavanagh, 'Original Intention, Enacted Text, and Constitutional Interpretation' (2002) 47 *American Journal of Jurisprudence* 255.

[47] ibid 275.

of age discrimination law may represent attempts to persuade stakeholders of the beneficial nature of the legislation to businesses and charities. This may explain why the documents have greater emphasis on business reasons for introducing age discrimination laws than rationales about preventing harm to individuals. If judges defer to the consultation documents, there is a danger they will overemphasise the interests of collective bodies at the expense of individuals.

Another reason to avoid deferring to the legislative history is that the government may not have intended the consultation documents and the Hansard statements to represent a complete account of age discrimination. There is nothing in the documents to suggest that the principles discussed in the documents were the only relevant rationales for age discrimination law. While the governments responsible for introducing age discrimination law may envisage certain particular applications of the law, there may be approaches to age discrimination law that were overlooked in the documents. Further, the use of the general phrase 'proportionate means of achieving a legitimate aim' in the Equality Act 2010 reveals a discretion for judges to adopt a wider range of approaches to age discrimination law than envisaged by the authors of the law or by the authors of the consultation documents.

In summary, the legislative history of age discrimination law may be helpful in providing some principles and ideas that are relevant in applying age discrimination law, but it is important for courts and tribunals not to constrain their decision-making to defer to approaches outlined in the documents.

In the next section, I evaluate the approach to age discrimination offered in the legislative history and consider whether the pluralist theory of age discrimination ought to incorporate this approach.

## IV. Evaluating the Approach to Age Discrimination Revealed in the Legislative History

As I explained in the introduction to this chapter, the legislative history contains research and ideas from people experienced in approaching the problem of age discrimination. It is worth considering whether we should revise the pluralist theory of age discrimination to accommodate the approach to age discrimination revealed in the legislative history. Further to this, I evaluate the following approaches revealed in the legislative history: the efficiency approach to age discrimination; the instrumentalist understanding of age discrimination rights; and the idea that age generalisations should be capable of justifying age-differential treatment.

### A. Efficiency as the Rationale for Age Discrimination Laws

The Tony Blair New Labour government (1997–2007) was responsible for introducing age discrimination law in the UK, and the consultation documents reflect the 'third way' ideology of that government.[48] The third way set itself apart from other ideologies by holding that rights are complementary to business efficiency, leading to wider economic gains.[49] It attempts to balance justice concerns with the aim of supporting entrepreneurship and economic growth.[50] The attempt was a synthesis between justice and economic goals. Further to this, the documents claim that a ban on age discrimination will increase business efficiency and prosperity, but also prevent conduct that harms the dignity of people. They argue that age discrimination laws are functional to the market by correcting the irrational under-utilisation of older people in the workforce and their talent. The documents claim that requiring employers not to take into account age will, in many cases, lead to more effective services that, in turn, will benefit the wider economy.

The consultation documents consider age discrimination wrong because it wastes valuable resources, among other reasons. We can frame this argument in utilitarian terms: the greater wealth created by a more efficient economy will, in turn, produce a greater sum of utility among members of the population.[51]

The pluralist theory of age discrimination also has an efficiency principle, but it works in a different way to the efficiency principle in the consultation documents. It explains that age-differential treatment can be particularly effective in promoting valuable social goods and this can justify age-differential treatment. The pluralist theory of age discrimination, unlike the consultation documents, does not explain the wrongness of age-differential treatment as being rooted in inefficiency. In contrast, it explains the wrong of age discrimination as rooted in its harms to individuals, including autonomy harms, harms to equality of opportunity and harms connected to disrespectful treatment.

The danger with the efficiency rationale in the consultation documents is that if efficiency is the primary explanation for having age discrimination laws (as implied by the documents), then this would mean that even very demeaning age-differential treatment should be lawful so long as it is efficient. The efficiency rationale for age discrimination laws assumes we can use people as a means to promote some collective goals. As such, it treats people as being of instrumental value.

[48] The third way was the Labour Party's attempt at finding an ideology that would distinguish it from the party's previous adherence to socialism. It emphasised a move away from an ideology of class conflict and towards a business friendly but socially liberal approach to government. See A Giddens, *The Third Way: The Renewal of Social Democracy* (John Wiley & Sons, 2013).

[49] S Fredman, 'Transformation or Dilution: Fundamental Rights in the EU Social Space' (2006) 12 *European Law Journal* 41.

[50] P Smith and G Morton, 'New Labour's Reform of Britain's Employment Law: The Devil Is Not Only in the Detail but in the Values and Policy Too' (2001) 39 *British Journal of Industrial Relations* 119.

[51] We can interpret the demand from efficiency as being a consequentialist demand to maximise welfare. For example, efficient business practices promote profits, wealth and employment, which, in turn, may lead to a maximisation of welfare. If welfare is a priority, then judges must try to maximise the good consequences (welfare).

However, as Rawls argues in his rejection of utilitarianism, people are separate and no individual can experience the general welfare of the group.[52] It is important, therefore, that we understand that human life is a thing that has value in itself and is not simply of instrumental value in promoting a good state of affairs.

The problem with the efficiency rationale in the consultation documents is that it would lead to treating people's interests as being vulnerable to contingencies of promoting economic gains, and therefore can justify sacrificing individual interests for the sake of such gains. The consequence for this approach is that it could be used to defend a range of unjust treatments. For example, it can justify dismissing older workers on efficiency grounds because older workers usually earn more than younger workers.

In contrast to the approach in the consultation documents, there ought to be justice and fairness limits to the pursuit of community goals like efficiency and wealth maximisation. We ought to treat people in accordance with their intrinsic value. This restricts the interests we can take into account in what we ought to do. As I argued in chapters four and five, the respect principle should govern our deliberations (and judges deciding cases) on the ends and interests that individuals and societies may legitimately pursue. It is wrong to subject people to humiliating treatment founded on oppressive ageist beliefs. This includes unequal treatment on the grounds of age that is motivated by negative judgements concerning the moral or social worth of older people. In these circumstances, gains in welfare (such as that which results from gains in efficiency) should not be capable of legally justifying age-differential treatment.

The respect principle requires we challenge prejudice and stereotypes in order to maintain a just society. This means we should apply age discrimination laws to remove actions based on derogatory beliefs about the worth of individuals. It is essential to achieving this that judges hold that business efficiency does not justify acting on those beliefs. This is particularly important because many stereotypical beliefs and prejudices can seem natural to people. It is only when we challenge these practices and beliefs that we can transform society to tackle ageist treatment.

The pursuit of collective goals such as business efficiency and wealth maximisation should not treat individuals as if they have a degraded moral worth because of their age. Age discrimination law should first aim to eliminate these forms of unjust treatment before considerations of efficiency. Only after it has been established that unequal treatment is not demeaning and does not convey a diminished moral status to individuals can we move on to consider efficiency as being capable of justifying unequal treatment on the grounds of age. The pluralist theory of age discrimination should be revised to account for the intuition that efficiency should not justify age-differential treatment that is demeaning by communicating that particular age groups have a diminished moral or social worth.

[52] J Rawls, *A Theory of Justice* (Harvard University Press, 1999) 164.

If it is established that age-differential treatment does not convey that an individual has a diminished or degraded moral status, then we can move on to consider efficiency as a factor capable of justifying unequal treatment on the grounds of age.[53]

We can further criticise the consultation documents for identifying economic costs as a major explanation for why age discrimination is wrong. Most people would not consider discrimination wrong because it is bad for business. Instead, we can only account for our intuitions about the wrongness of certain forms of age discrimination if we account for the injustice it does to individuals through prejudice, stereotyping, autonomy and equality harms.

The other major weakness of the approach of the consultation documents is that they state that a major value of age discrimination laws is increasing profits and economic growth. This reflects a wealth maximisation principle.[54] But wealth is only a value if it promotes other important moral values and therefore should not be thought of as a major rationale for age discrimination law.[55] Wealth is a means to an end. It only has an instrumental value in granting conditions to experience valuable things.[56] Dworkin argues effectively in dismissing the idea that wealth maximisation is intrinsically valuable:

> Suppose … that an individual faces a choice between a life that will make him happier (or more fulfilled, or more successful in his own lights, or whatever) and a life that will make him wealthier in money or the equivalent of money. It would be irrational of him to choose the latter. Nor – and this is the crux – does he lose or sacrifice anything of value in choosing the former. It is not that he should, on balance, prefer the former, recognizing that in the choice he sacrifices something of value in the latter. Money or its equivalent is useful so far as it enables someone to lead a more valuable, successful, happier, or more moral life. Anyone who counts it for more than that is a fetishist of little green paper.[57]

Since wealth maximisation is an instrument of creating value, it is not enough to point to increases in wealth itself as something that can justify a ban on age discrimination. It is important to provide evidence that wealth creation causes an increase in important values, such as welfare or fairness. Any claim that wealth

[53] Efficiency should be capable of justifying measures that are not demeaning or do not have some unacceptable violation of equality principles. We do not wish to abolish the preference to save resources, although we recognise that sometimes the employer should be required to incur some reasonable costs to remove requirements that might disadvantage people of a particular chronological age.

[54] For a defence of a wealth maximisation theory, see R Posner, 'Utilitarianism, Economics, and Legal Theory' (1979) 8 *Journal of Legal Studies* 103. Posner argued that wealth maximisation is more attractive than other goals, such as utilitarianism and Kantianism. For criticisms of this view, see A Kronman, 'Wealth Maximization as a Normative Principle' (1980) 9 *Journal of Legal Studies* 227; R Dworkin, 'Is Wealth a Value?' (1980) 9 *Journal of Legal Studies* 191.

[55] Wealth can promote the value of autonomy by giving people freedom to choose how to live their lives. It can also promote welfare by improving people's quality of life.

[56] J Coleman, 'Efficiency, Utility, and Wealth Maximization' (1979) 8 *Hofstra Law Review* 509.

[57] R Dworkin, *A Matter of Principle* (Harvard University Press, 1985) 245–46.

should trump the interests of individuals should demonstrate that this wealth advances an independent goal or value.

Posner, in defending a wealth maximisation principle, has argued that judges should aim to maximise wealth because this will 'produce an ethically attractive combination of happiness, of rights (of liberty), and of sharing with the less fortunate members of society'.[58] However, because we value liberty, equality and happiness as intrinsic goods, and value wealth only as an instrumental good, it is better for judges to aim to promote the intrinsic goods of, say, liberty, equality and welfare than to directly advance wealth as Posner suggests.

## B. Instrumentalist Understanding of Age Discrimination Rights

Instrumental conceptions of rights describe rights as instruments for achieving particular community goals, such as wealth maximisation and the efficient distribution of goods and services. The consultation documents adopt this understanding by explaining the rationale for age discrimination rights as the promotion of economic efficiency by ensuring that people are selected for jobs based on merit rather than age. This approach resembles a form of rule utilitarianism where respecting rights is justified because it (usually) leads to gains for the community.[59]

The weakness of this understanding of rights is that if the primary rationale for age discrimination rights is efficiency, we can override those rights whenever efficiency demands, then individuals do not have any meaningful 'right' against discrimination at all. If we justify age discrimination rights because of efficiency, then it is implicit in this approach that we should set aside the interests of individuals when efficiency demands this.

The pluralist theory of age discrimination should reject the economic approach to age discrimination rights adopted in the consultation documents because that approach fails to account for what we understand as essential features of what it means to have a right, which is that the right against discrimination forecloses certain ways of treating individuals that might otherwise be justified in the pursuit of the common good.[60] This means that some interests of individuals should have greater weight than the pursuit of efficiency or wealth maximisation.

[58] R Posner, 'The Ethical and Political Basis of the Efficiency Norm in Common Law Adjudication' (1979) 8 *Hofstra Law Review* 487, 487.

[59] For a defence of rule utilitarianism, see B Hooker, *Ideal Code, Real World: A Rule-Consequentialist Theory of Morality* (Oxford University Press, 2000).

[60] Ronald Dworkin has argued that rights are 'trumps'. When someone has a right, this means that the community must respect that right even if a refusal to do so diminishes collective goals such as wealth maximisation. Dworkin's theory means that certain interests of individuals should trump collective goals. See R Dworkin, 'Rights as Trumps' in J Waldron (ed), *Theories of Rights* (Oxford University Press, 1984) 153.

## C. Age Generalisations Justifying Age-Differential Treatment

The Hansard statements by Baroness Verma reveal the approach that age generalisations ought to be able to justify denying services to particular age groups. Verma stated that it is justifiable for a service provider to deny services to a particular age group if it has had bad experiences with that age group in the past.[61] An example of this, she stated, was a holiday cottage owner denying young people the chance to stay in the property because the property had been damaged by young people in the past.[62]

This approach to age discrimination violates the respect principle by holding that it is objectively justified for service providers to make negative generalisations about particular age groups and to deny services on these generalisations. The holiday cottage owner denying young people a service is an example of negative stereotyping because it assumes that young people cannot be trusted to avoid damaging the property. In chapter five, I argued that negative stereotyping and prejudice should not justify age-differential treatment. It is wrong to deny black people services because the service provider had bad experiences with black people in the past; similarly, it is wrong to deny services to particular age groups because of the assumption that these groups are troublesome. If courts and tribunals were to adopt the position adopted by Verma's parliamentary statement, then the effectiveness of the Equality Act 2010 in tackling ageism will be reduced. It would mean service providers would be capable of justifying demeaning treatment.

# V. Conclusion

The consultation documents reveal a dual approach to justifying age discrimination laws, with arguments that the legislation will both promote business efficiency and tackle unfair treatment of individuals. I have argued that it would be inappropriate for courts and tribunals to rely on the rationales set out in these documents for deciding age discrimination cases. I have also argued that the government is mistaken in identifying efficiency as a plausible rationale for age discrimination laws. Age discrimination is a moral concern because, in certain cases, it can create inequality of opportunity and social exclusion, and it can foster stigma and demean people.

In light of evaluating the government's explanations of the rationales for age discrimination laws, I have argued that the pluralist theory of age discrimination should account for the intuition that the pursuit of efficiency should not justify age-differential treatment that communicates demeaning messages.

[61] HL Deb 17 July 2012, vol 739, cols 83–86.
[62] ibid.

# 7

# The Pluralist Theory of Age Discrimination and Age Discrimination Claims

The pluralist theory of age discrimination outlined so far should assist in identifying unlawful age discrimination. It consists of a framework of principles that can distinguish justified from unjustified age-differential treatment. These principles include efficiency, equality of opportunity, social equality, autonomy and respect. In the previous chapter, I argued that efficiency should not justify discrimination that communicates that particular age groups have a diminished moral or social worth.

This chapter demonstrates how the pluralist theory of age discrimination can successfully guide age discrimination disputes. Further to this, I explain how each of the principles of the theory can assist in undertaking the proportionality assessment of age discrimination law. I then compare and contrast this approach to the approach adopted in the UK case law. I return to the case law discussed in chapter two, including *Seldon*,[1] *Lockwood*,[2] *White*,[3] *Homer*[4] and *Woodcock*.[5] These cases are illustrative of a general problem of a lack of open and transparent reasoning on the competing principles and interests at stake in age discrimination claims. *Seldon* is the leading UK authority on direct age discrimination and *Homer* is the leading UK authority on indirect age discrimination. *White* and *Lockwood* are examples of cases that have adopted the approach of these leading authorities. *Woodcock* concerns whether costs alone should be capable of justifying age-differential treatment.

By comparing and contrasting the pluralist theory of age discrimination to the reasoning in these cases, this chapter demonstrates that the theory can improve the openness and transparency of legal reasoning by articulating the principles and competing interests that are relevant to determining the legality of impugned treatment. In particular, I show that the theory provides much greater scrutiny of employer aims than the current UK case law's approach.

[1] [2012] UKSC 16, [2012] ICR 716.
[2] [2013] EWCA Civ 1195, [2014] 1 All ER 250.
[3] [2014] UKET/2201298/2013.
[4] [2012] UKSC 15, [2012] ICR 704.
[5] [2012] EWCA Civ 330, [2012] ICR 1126.

In applying age discrimination law, I argue that courts and tribunals should also consider the institutional limitations of the judicial process, including the need for deference to the original decision-maker. The proportionality test of the Equality Act 2010 requires judges to consider whether the impugned measure is suitable for achieving a legitimate aim and necessary to achieving that aim, and whether there is an appropriate balance between the aim and any discriminatory effects of the measure. Sometimes the original decision-maker is better placed to determine one or more of these considerations, and it is therefore appropriate for courts and tribunals to accord weight to the original decision-maker's assessment of these issues.[6] Factors for determining whether the original decision-maker is in a better position include where the court or tribunal has less competence or expertise to address the issue than the original decision-maker and where the original decision-maker has democratic backing for their decision.[7]

My method – reflective equilibrium – requires that I revise the pluralist theory of age discrimination if any ideas and approaches from the case law in this chapter reveal new considerations or ideas that a theory of age discrimination should incorporate. Reflective equilibrium recognises that new considerations can destabilise the theory, which requires adjusting the theory to recover stable equilibrium.[8] However, the UK case law reveals a lack of moral reasoning in deciding the age discrimination claims, including a failure to explain why particular aims are legitimate and a failure to offer principles for establishing the proportionality of impugned treatment. Therefore, the UK case law does not destabilise the pluralist theory of age discrimination. This chapter works as a demonstration of the value of the pluralist theory of age discrimination constructed from the reflective equilibrium method.

# I. A Preliminary Account of How the Pluralist Theory of Age Discrimination can Assist Age Discrimination Claims

In chapter two, I outlined the structure of age discrimination law in detail. I briefly return to this structure to provide a foundation for explaining how the pluralist theory of age discrimination can assist in applying age discrimination law.

[6] I draw on the work of Alan Brady, who has argued for integrating a theory of deference into the proportionality test. See A Brady, *Proportionality and Deference under the UK Human Rights Act: An Institutionally Sensitive Approach* (Cambridge University Press, 2012).

[7] Aileen Kavanagh argued that judges should always be sensitive to both substantive reasons for a decision and institutional concerns about the appropriateness of judges adjudicating a particular issue: A Kavanagh, 'Judicial Restraint in the Pursuit of Justice' (2010) 60 *University of Toronto Law Journal* 23. Substantive reasons are reasons that relate to the content of rights. These reasons should not always be decisive. Judges should weigh the limitations of the judicial process against the relevant substantive reasons.

[8] F Schroeter, 'Reflective Equilibrium and Anti-theory' (2004) 38 *Noûs* 110.

We can divide the process of identifying unlawful age discrimination into four stages.[9] The first stage is to determine whether the impugned treatment engages the direct or indirect age discrimination provisions. If the treatment does engage these provisions, then we must assess whether the treatment is a proportionate means of achieving a legitimate aim or fits into a specifically prescribed exception. In the second stage, we must determine whether the treatment is suitable for achieving a legitimate aim.[10] If it is not suitable, the treatment is unlawful. If the treatment promotes a legitimate aim, then we move to the third stage to assess whether the treatment is necessary to achieve that aim. A measure will only be necessary if there are no alternative forms of treatment that can achieve the legitimate aim without the equivalent discriminatory impact. If the treatment is unnecessary, it is unlawful age discrimination. If it is necessary, however, then we move to the fourth stage, which requires an assessment into whether the impugned treatment is proportionate in the narrower sense: the treatment must not impose burdens or cause harms to other legitimate interests that outweigh the objectives achieved. If the treatment passes each of these stages and is proportionate, then it is lawful. The five principles of the pluralist theory of age discrimination should assist in each of these stages. In the next section, I detail how the principles assist in the four stages to provide an open and structured assessment of the interests at stake in age discrimination claims.

## Stage 1: Does the Impugned Treatment Engage the Direct or Indirect Age Discrimination Provisions?

When a decision-maker treats an individual less favourably because of age, this treatment will engage the direct discrimination provisions.[11] The pluralist theory of age discrimination can help identify when an individual is treated less favourably and therefore it can determine when measures engage the direct discrimination provisions. For example, denying an individual a job because of their age violates autonomy by reducing the job applicant's valuable options on the grounds of a trait that they are powerless to change. It also violates equality of opportunity by denying an opportunity that other age groups can access. And social equality is undermined if the treatment is directed at historically disadvantaged age groups (for example, older people) by reinforcing the dominant position of privileged age

[9] For a detailed argument of this structured approach to proportionality, see M Elliot, 'Proportionality and Deference: The Importance of a Structured Approach' (2013) University of Cambridge Faculty of Law Research Paper No 32.

[10] In *Seldon* (n 1), the Supreme Court confirmed that the proportionality test described in this chapter should apply to treatment that engages the direct age discrimination provisions. The Supreme Court confirmed in *Homer* (n 4) that this proportionality test should also apply to treatment that engages the indirect age discrimination provisions.

[11] Equality Act 2010, s 13.

groups. In addition, the principle of respect identifies less favourable treatment as treatment that is offensive, insulting, based on prejudice or age stereotyping, or any conduct that communicates that the discriminatee has a diminished moral or social worth.[12]

Measures will engage the indirect discrimination provisions when a policy, criterion or practice is age-neutral but has the effect of disadvantaging particular age groups.[13] The pluralist theory of age discrimination can determine if treatment disadvantages particular age groups and therefore can determine when impugned treatment engages the indirect discrimination provisions. For example, the equality of opportunity principle can identify treatment that engages the indirect discrimination provisions as age-neutral structures that deny particular age groups access to valuable resources. Autonomy identifies indirect discrimination as structures that work to foreclose the valuable choices of disadvantaged age groups. And social equality identifies indirect discrimination as structures that work to marginalise vulnerable age groups.

## Stage 2: Is the Impugned Treatment Suitable for Achieving a Legitimate Aim?

The pluralist theory of age discrimination recognises that there are multiple different legitimate aims, including the pursuit of efficiency and the aim of promoting equality of opportunity, social equality and autonomy. Aims are legitimate when they promote one or more of the principles of the pluralist theory of age discrimination unless they communicate demeaning messages. The original decision-maker should be able to select the aims the impugned treatment was pursuing, but they must demonstrate that there is a rational connection between the age-differential treatment and the aims.[14]

As an illustration of how the pluralist theory of age discrimination can assist at this stage, we can return to the three categories of age-differential treatment identified in chapter five. The first category – demeaning age-differential treatment – includes age-differential treatment that pursues aims that reflect stereotypes,

[12] The case law has adopted this approach by finding that disrespectful conduct amounts to less favourable treatment. For example, the ET held in *Dove v Brown & Newirth Ltd* [2016] UKET/3301905/2015 that nicknaming someone 'gramps' amounted to less favourable treatment because these comments were disrespectful and hurtful. In *Nolan v CD Bramall Dealership Ltd t/a Evans Halshaw Motorhouse Worksop* [2012] UKET/2601000/12, the ET held that age-related 'banter', including introducing an employee as the '104 year old Service Team Leader' and changing that employee's number plate from 'OAB' and to 'OAP', was less favourable treatment on the grounds of age. In *James v Gina Shoes Ltd* [2011] UKEAT/0384/11/DM, the EAT held that it was less favourable treatment to make remarks reflecting age stereotypes, including the remark directed at the complainant 'you can't teach an old dog new tricks'.

[13] Equality Act 2010, s 19.

[14] Alexy calls this structural deference. R Alexy, *A Theory of Constitutional Rights* (Oxford University Press, 2009) 393.

prejudice or aims that communicate that particular age groups have diminished moral and social worth.[15] The respect principle operates as a deontological constraint. No one should suffer from communications that they have an inferior status because of their age. Even if age-differential treatment aims to promote ostensibly legitimate aims such as efficiency and equality, these aims should not be capable of justification if they communicate demeaning messages to particular age groups.[16]

The second category of age-differential treatment – efficient age-differential treatment – aims to maximise the attainment of social goods. For example, using age in the distribution of healthcare and education to maximise health and educational benefits is a good way to maximise welfare for society as a whole. Aims that promote efficiency in attaining social goods are legitimate unless they violate the respect principle by demeaning people. An example of possible efficient age-differential treatment that is also demeaning would include an employer dismissing all staff over 60 years of age in order to reduce wage costs during a recession. This treatment may be efficient as a method of ensuring financial stability by removing employees who tend to command higher salaries; however, it is illegitimate because it sends the demeaning message that older workers are dispensable.

The third category of age-differential treatment – age-differential treatment aimed at advancing equality and/or autonomy principles – includes treatment that aims to ensure that people have equal shares of benefits and burdens over their complete lives and/or measures designed to benefit disadvantaged or marginalised age groups. Examples include aims to facilitate access to employment for young people or aims to share work fairly between the generations. These aims attempt to promote the principles of the pluralist theory of age discrimination and therefore should be legitimate unless, again, they contain demeaning messages about particular age groups.

The suitability stage of the proportionality test requires an assessment into whether the impugned treatment is actually capable of promoting the legitimate aims. Sometimes it is appropriate to defer to the original decision-maker on this assessment. For example, deference is appropriate where there is considerable uncertainty about whether the impugned treatment actually promotes the legitimate aim. This form of deference is what Robert Alexy calls empirical epistemic deference.[17] Courts and tribunals should offer empirical epistemic

[15] Unfortunately, the UK courts have not treated all forms of age stereotyping as illegitimate. As I discuss below, the Supreme Court accepted in *Seldon* (n 1) that it is legitimate for employers to dismiss older workers to avoid the need to involve older workers in incapacity or underperformance processes. The Supreme Court acknowledged that this aim was 'suspiciously like stereotyping', but decided they should follow the CJEU jurisprudence in holding this aim legitimate. With the exit of the UK from the EU, and therefore the UK courts no longer having to follow the findings of the CJEU, it is possible for the Supreme Court to overturn the precedent.

[16] I make this argument in ch 6.

[17] Alexy (n 14).

deference when there are difficulties finding evidence relating to parts of the proportionality assessments.

If it is established that a legitimate aim promotes one or more of the principles of the pluralist theory of age discrimination, then we move to the next stage of proportionality – the necessity test. If the measure conveys demeaning messages and/or does not promote the principles of the pluralist theory of age discrimination, then the treatment is not rationally connected to a legitimate aim and therefore should be held to be unlawful age discrimination under section 13 of the Equality Act 2010 (for treatment engaging the direct discrimination claims) or section 19 of the Equality Act 2010 (for treatment engaging the indirect discrimination claims).

## Stage 3: Is the Treatment Necessary to Achieve the Legitimate Aim?

This stage of the proportionality assessment is an empirical enquiry. It requires assessing whether there are any alternative forms of treatment that can pursue the legitimate aims as effectively as the impugned measure but with a lower discriminatory impact.[18] If there is such treatment available, then the impugned measure is disproportionate and therefore unlawful. Importantly, the necessity stage does not mean the defendant must always select the means that have the least discriminatory impact. The courts and tribunals can find impugned treatment necessary to achieve a legitimate aim when alternative measures are available that have lower discriminatory impact but have some significant disadvantage or difficulty in implementation that would make it ineffective or impractical as a way to achieve the legitimate aim.[19] Also, an impugned measure can be deemed 'reasonably necessary' and therefore pass the necessity stage if it is within a range of options available to the defendant that can offer more or less a similar balance between securing the legitimate aim and its discriminatory impact.

For example, in *Seldon*, the Employment Appeal Tribunal (EAT) held that the Employment Tribunal (ET) could quite properly conclude that the defendant law firm's mandatory retirement age of 65 years of age was 'reasonably necessary' to achieve the aims of intergenerational fairness and ensuring that older workers do not have to undergo capability assessments even though the law firm could have adopted a higher retirement age which would have had a (slightly) lower discriminatory impact on the claimant.[20] The EAT held that a retirement age of

[18] K Möller, 'Proportionality: Challenging the Critics' (2012) 10 *International Journal of Constitutional Law* 709, 713.
[19] ibid 714.
[20] *Seldon v Clarkson Wright and Jakes* [2014] UKEAT/0434/13/RN.

65 years of age was 'reasonably necessary' because it would balance the effectiveness of achieving the legitimate aims with minimising the discriminatory impact to more or less the same degree as other suitable ages for the retirement age, including 64 and 66 years of age.[21] The defendant had the latitude to choose within this range.

The pluralist theory of age discrimination plays a role in the necessity stage of the proportionality test because it identifies the interests that the courts and tribunals should identify in assessing whether the impugned measure is necessary to achieve a legitimate aim. For example, if a court or tribunal finds that there are alternative methods that can promote the principles of efficiency, equality of opportunity, social equality and/or autonomy more effectively than the impugned treatment but with a lower violation of these principles, then the impugned treatment is unnecessary and therefore unlawful. If, however, the court or tribunal calculates that the measure is necessary to achieve the legitimate aim, then we must move to stage 4, which requires determining whether the seriousness of the interference with the claimant's interests is proportionate to the benefits gained in pursuit of the legitimate aim.

It is appropriate for the courts and tribunals to acknowledge their institutional limitations by deciding not to substitute their views for that of the original decision-maker on the question of necessity when that decision-maker has superior expertise and information on which to determine the effectiveness of the impugned treatment in promoting the legitimate aim.[22] As Jeffrey Jowell notes, 'There will be occasions where other bodies, whether Parliament, the executive or a non-departmental public body containing specialist expertise, will be better equipped to decide certain questions [than courts]'.[23]

For example, efficiency is a goal of healthcare rationing in the UK, but this can disadvantage older age groups.[24] A court would have difficulty assessing whether the current UK method of healthcare rationing – the Quality-Adjusted Life Year method – is necessary for maximising the legitimate aim of efficient healthcare allocation because courts lack the medical expertise to determine whether any alternative healthcare allocation method can be more effective in health promotion. In contrast, the National Institute of Health and Care Excellence, which is responsible for offering guidance on rationing healthcare, is in a better position than the courts to decide how to distribute health resources because it is staffed by medical professionals. The courts should therefore defer to the expert group in their judgement of whether the method is necessary.

In addition to public institutions, there can be good reasons for a court or tribunal to offer deference to businesses. For example, an employer may have

[21] ibid [26]–[27].
[22] Alexy (n 14) 388–425.
[23] J Jowell, 'Judicial Deference: Servility, Civility or Institutional Capacity?' [2003] (Winter) *PL* 592.
[24] I discuss this example in detail in ch 8.

inside knowledge about their own business that may put them in a better position than a court or tribunal to assess whether an age distinction is necessary to achieve a legitimate aim.

Further, judges may consider it appropriate to defer to the judgement of the original decision-maker where there is uncertainty about the realisation of particular circumstances. As Jeff King notes, judges 'may be unsure of the reliability of evidence, expert witness credibility or the likely effect of the judgment on patterns of behaviour'.[25] For example, the question of whether a retirement age is necessary to create promotion opportunities within a firm depends upon the financial health of that firm at a future date and whether the retirement age is likely to prompt people in the firm to make the decision to create new promotion opportunities. Judges may not be able to make a reliable prediction on these issues. It is appropriate for judges to recognise their fallibility in making predictions and avoid imposing their predictions over that of the original decision-maker.

This should not mean that the courts and tribunals offer no scrutiny in relation to the question of necessity. There are circumstances where the original decision-maker may have expertise but they also have incentive to act selfishly to deny someone's rights. For example, private employers typically aim to maximise profit, but this does not necessarily coincide with fair treatment of their employees.[26] An employer may use age distinctions to marginalise particular age groups. For example, an employer may dismiss older workers and replace them with younger and cheaper ones. Courts and tribunals must therefore be particularly wary in deferring to private employers and must evaluate whether the employer is using their expertise to genuinely promote legitimate aims or is using it as an excuse to act in a way which is not justifiable on grounds of necessity.

The deference factors I have discussed in this chapter do not mean that the courts should merely adopt a reasonableness test rather than the proportionality test. Wednesbury unreasonableness – the method courts use to determine the legality of administrative decision-making in judicial review claims – rules out decisions that are so unreasonable that no reasonable person acting reasonably could have made them.[27] In contrast, the necessity stage of the proportionality test is a form of merits review requiring the court or tribunal to strike down measures when the court or tribunal determines that there are other identified methods that could more effectively pursue legitimate aims. The reasonableness test permits measures in pursuit of a legitimate aim if the measure is not 'So outrageous in its defiance of logic or accepted moral standards that no sensible person who had applied his mind to the question

[25] J King, 'Institutional Approaches to Judicial Restraint' (2008) 28 *OJLS* 425.

[26] This point is made by A Davies, 'Judicial Self-Restraint in Labour Law' (2009) 38 *Industrial Law Journal* 278.

[27] *Associated Provincial Picture Houses Ltd v Wednesbury Corporation* [1948] 1 KB 223.

to be decided could have arrived at it'.[28] Proportionality is different from this reasonableness review because courts and tribunals should only defer in the necessity stage of the proportionality test when the courts and tribunals do not have the knowledge (or do not have as much knowledge as the decision-maker) to calculate whether the impugned measure is the most effective way to pursue a legitimate aim.

The courts and tribunals should not consider the deference factors entirely separately from the substantive principles. The level of deference should depend on the severity of a violation of the principles of the pluralist theory of age discrimination. For example, if the court can calculate that a measure contributes to oppressive relations, expresses contempt or violates autonomy, then there is a greater need to scrutinise the decision-maker's treatment as being necessary to achieve a legitimate aim. This means that institutional questions about the extent to which judges should defer to the primary decision-maker depend in part on the extent of harm to an individual's interests. Where the extent of violation of interests is small, then institutional considerations and deference towards the primary decision-maker should play a more prominent role. But when there is a clear and substantial violation of an individual's equality interests, this may outweigh concerns about institutional limitations of the judicial process. In such situations, the balance may be in favour of judicial intervention and strong scrutiny of the measures on the substantive principles.

## Stage 4: Is the Seriousness of the Interference with the Claimant's Interests Proportionate to the Benefits Gained in Pursuit of the Legitimate Aim?

To answer this, we must calculate the extent to which the measure violates one or more of the principles of the pluralist theory of age discrimination and calculate the extent to which the measure advances any of those principles. The court or tribunal must find the measure unlawful if it considers that the harm done to individuals outweighs the possible benefits of the impugned treatment.

However, a degree of deference may be appropriate at this stage if a democratic process or a democratically elected body is responsible for the decision.[29] Social policy decisions concerning the appropriate balance between the public benefit of age-differential treatment and its detrimental impact on individuals can be more

[28] *Council of Civil Service Unions v Minister for the Civil Service* [1983] UKHL 6, [1984] 3 All ER 935 [410].

[29] For detailed discussions on the importance of deference to democratic decisions, see Brady (n 6) 72; J Jowell, 'Judicial Deference and Human Rights: Question of Competence' in P Craig and R Rawlings (eds), *Law and Administration in Europe: Essays in Honour of Carol Harlow* (Oxford University Press, 2003) 80; J Jowell, 'Judicial Deference: Servility, Civility or Institutional Capacity?' [2003] *PL* 592.

appropriately decided by people who are directly elected to make decisions on behalf of the public.[30]

People making decisions in democratic institutions, including the institutions of Parliament, government departments and local authorities, hold power with the consent of the public, and the public can remove them from power if they disapprove of their decisions and policies. Courts and tribunals should therefore offer a degree of latitude to the decisions of these democratic institutions in balancing competing interests. There is more room for courts and tribunals to scrutinise the decisions of private employers, given that the decisions of the employer usually does not have democratic backing (but see the discussion below on collective bargaining).

The fact that a decision is made by a democratic institution should not, however, shield it entirely from scrutiny. The democratic process may disregard the interests of particular age groups and force through measures that discriminate against these groups. Groups with low voter turnout, such as young people, are particularly vulnerable to having their interests disregarded by democratic institutions. Courts and tribunals, therefore, should offer scrutiny of democratic institutions while also according weight to their decisions. This should be a contextual approach. The greater the degree a measure violates one or more of the principles of the pluralist theory of age discrimination, the greater the need for the courts and tribunals to offer intense scrutiny of the impugned measure. Where there is a clear and serious violation of a moral principle, the courts and tribunals should require a strong argument by the defendant that there is an appropriate balance between community interests and the discriminatory effect of the impugned measure.

Courts and tribunals should also consider offering deference in the final proportionality assessment when age discrimination claims concern polycentric issues.[31] A polycentric issue is 'one that comprises a large and complicated web of interdependent relationships, such that a change to one factor produces an incalculable series of changes to other factors'.[32] Resource allocation, such as changing the state pension age, is a classic polycentric issue because it directly affects spending in other areas of government that affect a wide range of people.[33]

The adjudicative process has difficulty addressing polycentric issues because adjudication is typically focused on addressing the arguments presented by the

[30] The case law adopts this position. For example, Lord Hoffmann held in *Secretary of State for the Home Department v Rehman* [2001] UKHL 47, [2003] 1 AC 153 that social policy should be decided by elected representatives because 'If people were to accept the consequences of such decisions, they must be made by persons whom the people have elected, and whom they can remove'.

[31] See the argument that polycentric disputes are unsuitable for adjudication in L Fuller, 'The Forms and Limits of Adjudication' (1978–79) 92 *Harvard Law Review* 353.

[32] ibid.

[33] The following papers argue that allocation of resources is a polycentric task that is unsuitable for adjudication: TRS Allan, *Constitutional Justice: A Liberal Theory of the Rule of Law* (Oxford University Press, 2001) 188–92; D Feldman, *Civil Liberties and Human Rights in England and Wales* (Oxford University Press, 2002) 229–30.

parties' representatives. Polycentric issues, however, affect an array of people not represented in the adjudication. This means that the decisions of judges on polycentric issues can lead to unintended consequences to these unrepresented groups.[34] Democratic institutions, in contrast, can tackle the complexity of the issues by considering the wide range of consequences a decision may have. Further, the democratic institutions can do this with an electoral mandate.

Age discrimination issues are often polycentric. For example, policies favouring particular age groups, such as the winter fuel allowance for older people, may have wide ramifications for a number of different groups that the courts will find difficult to address in adjudication. Removing the age-differential treatment, for example, by transferring the benefits to low income groups rather than to all people over 65 years of age, can lead to higher costs that result from having to means-test people for the benefits. This, in turn, can force cuts in other areas of state spending that can affect the income of large numbers of people in need. Only the state responsible for the budget is capable of calculating the consequences of removing age-linked benefits.

The fact that an issue is polycentric, however, should not automatically disqualify it from adjudication. As King has demonstrated, polycentricity is pervasive.[35] If courts and tribunals cannot intervene in polycentric issues at all, then the effectiveness of discrimination law in tackling ageism will be drastically reduced.

There are circumstances where justice clearly requires courts and tribunals to intervene in polycentric issues. For example, in the celebrated case *Brown v Board of Education*, the Supreme Court held that the policy of racial segregation in schools was unconstitutional because it violated the right to equal protection under the law.[36] Desegregating schools was a polycentric issue since it affected large groups of people beyond those represented in court, including schoolchildren across different states and people affected by the desegregation of other bodies, such as public beaches, golf courses, buses and parks. Despite the complexity of the consequences to the ruling, justice required judicial intervention to put an end to racist policies in resource allocation.

If there is a serious violation of the principles of the pluralist theory of age discrimination, then the courts can undertake an intense review of polycentric issues. For an impugned measure to be lawful under this intense review, the defendant should offer a strong argument that they struck an appropriate balance between community goals and the interest of individuals adversely affected by the measure. If there is a high degree of polycentricity but only a low or moderate violation of the principles of the pluralist theory of age discrimination, then the courts should offer lower levels of scrutiny.

[34] Brady (n 6) 401.
[35] See J King, 'The Pervasiveness of Polycentricity' [2008] *PL* 101.
[36] 347 US 483 (1954).

Deference is also appropriate for age distinctions that result from collective bargaining between employees and their employer. Collective bargaining is a type of democratic decision-making because it reflects decisions with the backing of the majority of the members of the negotiating union. However, certain interests may be ignored or disregarded in the process. A union may force through measures that benefit the majority of their members but discriminate against older people. Deferring in these circumstances would be failing to protect a disadvantaged older group. Courts and tribunals must consider whether there is a clear abuse of the interests of particular age groups.

Another factor that should determine whether deference is appropriate at this stage is whether the claimant agreed to the impugned measure. The principle of autonomy which forms one part of the pluralist theory of age discrimination means that people should have the ability to make decisions and exercise free will on negotiating terms. If a claimant has agreed to an age distinction, then there is a reason for the courts and tribunals to respect their exercise of autonomy and assume that the impugned measure is proportionate. Contractual terms, however, often do not reflect equal bargaining power. Even if the measure is part of an employment contract, an employee might not have had a realistic option to refuse to accept the terms of a contract. Courts must be wary in applying deference and must consider whether the parties to the agreement have equality of bargaining power.

If a decision-maker imposes an age distinction unilaterally rather than through consent or collective bargaining, then this provides support for the court or tribunal to offer a higher degree of scrutiny to ensure the original decision-maker made a proper balance between competing interests at stake.

If the deference factors do not apply at this stage of the proportionality test, then the court or tribunal should consider the extent to which the measure advances the principles of the pluralist theory of age discrimination (including equality of opportunity, social equality, autonomy and efficiency), and determine whether these advances exceed the harm to the claimant's interests.[37] The court or tribunal should consider the measure unjustified and therefore unlawful age discrimination when they consider that the harm to the applicant's equality and autonomy interests exceed the benefits of the measure advancing social equality, autonomy, equality of opportunity or efficiency.

[37] The respect principle will not be in play at this stage because disrespectful treatment should already be ruled out in stage 2.

## II. Visual Representation of the Four Stages of Settling Age Discrimination Claims

**Stage 1: Does the impugned treatment engage the direct or indirect discrimination provisions**

**Was the claimant treated less favourably than another person *because of* their age or the age they are thought to have, or because they associate with someone of a particular age? (Equality** Act 2010, section **13 – direct discrimination).**

**or**

**Was the claimant disadvantaged by a policy, criterion or practice that applies to everyone but particularly disadvantages people who share a particular age? (Equality Act 2010,** section **19 – indirect discrimination).**

Yes ↓

**The measure falls under the direct or indirect discrimination provisions of the EA 2010. Move to stage 2.**

No ↓

**No claim available under the EA 2010.**

**Stage 2: Proportionality**

Is the impugned treatment suitable for achieving the legitimate aim (the 'suitability' test)? – Equality Act 2010, sections 13(1) and 19(2)(d).

↓

**Does purported aim of the measure reflect age stereotyping, prejudice or convey the message that particular age groups have a diminished moral or social worth (the respect principle)?**

**Yes** →

**The aim is illegitimate and therefore the measure is unjustified age discrimination.**

No ↓

**Does the aim promote one of the following principles?**

- **Social integration of a disadvantage group (the social equality principle).**
- **Advancing the autonomy of members of a disadvantaged age group (autonomy principle).**
- **Distributing resources or opportunities equally (equality of opportunity principle).**
- **Efficiency (for direct discrimination claim only legitimate if promoting public policy goals).**

**No** →

**There is no demonstrated legitimate aim and therefore the measure is unjustified age discrimination.**

↓

Yes → **The measure is suitable to achieving a legitimate aim. Move to stage 3.**

**Stage 3: Proportionality**

Is the measure necessary to achieve the legitimate aim (the 'necessity' test)?

↓

**Is the original decision-maker in a better position than a court or tribunal to assess the necessity of the measure to achieving the legitimate aim?** Yes → **Consider deferring to original decision-**maker's **judgement. Move to stage 4.**

No

↓

**Are there other equally effective but less intrusive means to further the legitimate aim?** Yes → **The measure is unnecessary for achieving the legitimate aim and therefore is unjustified age discrimination.**

↓

**No** → **The measure is necessary for achieving the legitimate aim. Move to stage 4.**

**Stage 4: Proportionality**

Assessing whether the seriousness of the interference with the complainant's interests are proportionate to the benefits gained in pursuit of the legitimate aim ('proportionality in the *narrow sense*').

↓

**Weigh the harm to the complainant' interests.**

↓

**Does the measure perpetuate the oppression of age groups by, for example, diminishing their capacity to participate in social, economic and political life (the *social equality* principle)?**

↓

**Weigh the benefits of the measure.**

↓

**Does the measure integrate members of a disadvantage group into social and productive life (the *social equality* principle)?**

| | | |
|---|---|---|
| **Does the measure limit the complainant's ability to make decisions and plan their life (the *autonomy* principle)?**<br>**Is the measure likely to deny the complainant's interest in equal distribution of opportunities over a complete life (the *equality of opportunity* principle)?** | | **Does the measure advance the autonomy of members of a disadvantaged age group (the *autonomy* principle)?**<br>**Is the measure likely to distribute opportunities equally over people's complete lives (the *equality of opportunity* principle)?**<br>**Does the measure promote efficiency of a valuable undertaking?** |
| ↓ | ↙ | |
| **Did the complainant consent to the treatment and/or was the treatment negotiated fairly through collective bargaining?** | Yes<br>→ | **Consider deferring to the original decision-maker. The measure may be justified and therefore lawful.** |
| No<br>↓ | | |
| **Has the original decision-maker demonstrated they considered the range of interests and weighed them against each other in forming the impugned measure, and was the original decision-maker in a better or more appropriate position to weigh these interests than a court or tribunal?** | Yes<br>→ | **Consider deferring to the original decision-maker. The measure may be justified and therefore lawful.** |
| No<br>↓ | ↘ | |
| **If the harm to the complainant's equality and autonomy interests exceeds that of the benefits of the measure advancing social equality, autonomy, equality of opportunity or efficiency, then the measure is unjustified age discrimination.** | | **If the benefits of the measure in advancing social equality, autonomy, equality of opportunity and efficiency exceed the harm to the** applicant's **interests, then the measure is justified.** |

# III. Comparing and Contrasting the Approach of the Pluralist Theory of Age Discrimination to the Approach Adopted by the UK Cases

In chapter two, I briefly outlined the facts and reasoning of a number of age discrimination cases that are illustrative of a general failure to undertake the proportionality test in a way that ensures there is an open and transparent assessment of the competing interests and principles at stake. I now explain the findings and reasoning of the cases in more detail, and then compare this with the approach of the pluralist theory of age discrimination outlined in this chapter. I first discuss *Seldon*, which is the leading case for direct age discrimination, and explain how the pluralist theory of age discrimination would offer principles to explain the findings of the courts and tribunals, and how the theory would differ from the reasoning in the case.

## A. *Seldon v Clarkson Wright and Jakes*[38]

*Seldon* concerned a mandatory retirement age.[39] The claimant, a partner in a firm of solicitors, was compulsorily retired from his partnership at age 65 in accordance with the retirement age contained in the partnership deed. The law firm argued that the retirement age was lawful because it was a proportionate means of achieving a legitimate aim. They argued that the retirement age supported the following legitimate aims: (i) ensuring the law firm's associates have opportunities to reach partnership; (ii) facilitating planning of the partnership by opening vacancies; and (iii) limiting the need to undertake performance management reviews for older workers, thereby creating a congenial and supportive culture in the firm.

The Supreme Court offered guidance on how to undertake the proportionality test for direct age discrimination claims and remitted the issue of the proportionality of the retirement age to the ET. As I explained in chapter two, the Court held that only social policy aims are capable of justifying measures that engage

[38] There is a complex history to this case. The claimant complained that he had been discriminated against on the grounds of age, and there followed a hearing before the ET, judgment in which was given on 4 December 2007 ET1100275/07; an appeal to the EAT [2009] IRLR 267, judgment in which was given on 19 December 2008; a further appeal to the Court of Appeal [2011] ICR 60, where judgment was given on 28 July 2010; and then a hearing before the Supreme Court [2012] UKSC 16, where judgment was given on 25 April 2012. The matter returned, following the Supreme Court hearing, to the ET. The ET gave its decision for reasons delivered on 14 May 2013. It was appealed again to the EAT [2014] UKEAT/0434/13/RN, judgment delivered on 13 May 2014.

[39] In 2011, the government abolished the national default retirement age. However, employers may still adopt a retirement age if it is a proportionate means to achieving a legitimate aim and therefore falls under the exception of the Equality Act 2010, s 13(2).

the direct age discrimination provisions. Social policy aims include a wide variety of aims related to employment policy, the labour market or vocational training, and can be divided into two categories. The first category are aims that promote 'inter-generational fairness', and includes policies such as facilitating access to employment for young people, sharing work fairly between the generations and enabling older people to remain in the workforce.[40]

The second category are aims that protect 'dignity', and this includes aims to avoid placing older workers in capability assessments.[41] Increased monitoring and performance evaluation, the Court held, may lead to dismissals prior to the normal age of retirement, undermining the dignity of older workers.

Lady Hale argued that social policy can justify age distinctions but cannot justify distinctions on other protected grounds, such as race and sex, because

> age is different … not 'binary' in nature (man or woman, black or white, gay or straight) but a continuum which changes over time … younger people will eventually benefit from a provision which favours older employees, such as an incremental pay scale; but older employees will already have benefited from a provision which favours younger people, such as a mandatory retirement age.[42]

Lady Hale cited with approval *R (Carson and Reynolds) v Secretary of State for Work and Pensions*,[43] which held that age distinctions are different from other forms of discrimination because classifying people by age is not 'intrinsically demeaning' in the way that race or sex classifications are.[44]

The Supreme Court remitted the proportionality issue to the ET. The ET held that the retirement age was proportionate to achieving the legitimate aims of ensuring associates have opportunities to reach partnership and facilitating planning of the partnership by opening vacancies in the law firm. In finding the retirement age proportionate, the ET took into account the fact that the claimant signed the partnership agreement with equal bargaining power and at the time of signing did not question the retirement age. Further, the ET also took into account that, at the time, the government had introduced a default retirement age with the Employment Equality (Age) Regulations 2006, which permitted employers to dismiss employees over 65 without a reason.[45] At the time, the government considered 65 was an appropriate retirement age for employees.

The case was appealed again to the EAT. The appellant argued that the respondent law firm had not provided sufficient evidence to demonstrate that the particular choice of 65 years of age was necessary to achieve the legitimate aims. The EAT held that the ET was correct in reaching its conclusion on the evidence before it. It was acceptable, the EAT argued, for the ET to have relied on

[40] *Seldon* (n 1) [56].
[41] ibid [57].
[42] ibid [4].
[43] [2005] UKHL 37, [2005] 4 All ER 545.
[44] ibid [60].
[45] The government, in response to a public consultation, abolished the default retirement age in 2011.

> assumptions and estimates as to how people will act or react, not in general labour force terms such as might be the subject of expert evidence, though in part those are appropriate, but in relation in particular to the personalities and practice with which a firm is concerned.[46]

The EAT therefore deferred to the judgement of the witnesses for the law firm about 'what happened at that firm' and 'their own views as to the situation',[47] and held that the retirement age of 65 years was reasonably necessary to achieve the legitimate aims.

## *(i) Applying the Pluralist Theory of Age Discrimination to* Seldon

The pluralist theory of age discrimination would challenge the Supreme Court's comments concerning the nature of age discrimination. The court argued that age discrimination is a less serious ground for discrimination because older people once enjoyed the benefits and burdens of being young and the young will experience the benefits and burdens of being older as long as they live long enough. This line of reasoning suggests securing equality of opportunity reduces the harm of age distinctions.

The problem with this reasoning, however, is that, as I argued in chapter five, age distinctions do not necessarily contribute to equality of opportunity because age distinctions are unlikely to affect people in the same way. For example, it is unlikely that every worker in the law firm in *Seldon* will experience the retirement age. Some partners may leave the law firm before 65 years of age and may choose to work for an employer that does not have a retirement age. The retirement age, therefore, may affect the claimant while not affecting other workers in the law firm, and may not secure equality of opportunity since many may not experience the detriment of the retirement age.

Furthermore, contrary to the position of Lady Hale that 'age is different', the pluralist theory of age discrimination holds that unequal treatment on the grounds of age is not fundamentally 'different' to other forms of discrimination. Unequal treatment on the grounds of age can be wrong for the same reasons that unequal treatment on the grounds of race and sex can be wrong. Namely, it can perpetuate oppressive relations, stereotype people, express animosity and substantially reduce the autonomy of people. As I have argued in chapter five, unequal treatment on the grounds of age can express that particular age groups have a lesser or degraded moral worth in much the same way that race discrimination or sex discrimination can convey demeaning messages. We should not, therefore, assume (like the Supreme Court) that age discrimination is a less critical ground for discrimination.

[46] [2014] UKEAT/0434/13/RN [30].
[47] ibid.

Moreover, Lady Hale's distinction between the nature of age and the nature of other characteristics – that the latter tend to be binary while age is a continuum – is unsustainable. Gender/sex binary divisions are increasingly challenged. Many other protected characteristics are more malleable than once thought, including sexuality, which scholars argue can change over an individual's lifetime.[48] And some academics have argued that it ought to be possible for people to change their race.[49]

I now move on to outline how the pluralist theory of age discrimination assists in determining the proportionality and legality of the mandatory retirement age in *Seldon*. The first stage in this process is to determine whether the retirement age in *Seldon* engaged the direct or indirect age discrimination provisions. This is relatively simple. The treatment of the claimant engages the direct discrimination provisions because the retirement age had the effect of treating the claimant less favourably because of age by forcing them to retire. This treatment violates the principle of social equality by denying the claimant an opportunity to participate in society through productive work, thereby undermining the ability of the partner to equal participation in society with his younger peers.

The second stage of applying the theory of age discrimination is to assess whether the treatment was appropriate for achieving a legitimate aim. The pluralist theory of age discrimination holds that retirement ages should only be permitted if they promote one or more of the substantive principles identified in this book, including the principles of equality of opportunity, social equality, respect, autonomy and efficiency. Demeaning aims, however, are illegitimate.

The Supreme Court held that it was legitimate for the law firm to remove older workers in order to avoid capability assessments. However, the pluralist theory of age discrimination finds this aim to be illegitimate because it violates the respect principle of the pluralist theory of age discrimination. This form of age-differential treatment would constitute demeaning age discrimination because it conveys negative and insulting assumptions about age. The law firm's aim of using a retirement age for 'avoiding unseemly debates about capacity' is a form of demeaning stereotyping because it reflects a message that older workers should be removed from employment because they are less capable and may not be able to do their jobs effectively. There is no compelling empirical evidence to support the general claim that job performance declines with age (except at the extreme).[50] Even if we were to assume that older people have declining capability at a general level, it still

[48] M Rosario et al, 'Sexual Identity Development among Lesbian, Gay, and Bisexual Youths: Consistency and Change over Time' (2006) 43 *Journal of Sex Research* 46.

[49] Rebecca Tuvel argued that 'Society should accept such an individual's decision to change race the same way it should accept an individual's decision to change sex': R Tuvel, 'In Defense of Transracialism' (2017) 32 *Hypatia A Journal of Feminist Philosophy* 263.

[50] See G McEvoy and W Cascio, 'Cumulative Evidence of the Relationship between Employee Age and Job Performance' (1989) 74 *Journal of Applied Psychology* 11.

wrongs the claimant and is empirically unsound to make assumptions about their capability without assessing their actual capabilities as an individual. Furthermore, while capability assessments may cause embarrassment, they are less likely to be demeaning than dismissing workers on the assumption that older workers are bad workers. Contrary to the findings in *Seldon*, avoiding capability assessment should not be a strong enough reason to justify the imposition of a retirement age.

The other group of aims identified by the Supreme Court, namely 'inter-generational fairness' aims, are legitimate according to the pluralist theory of age discrimination. In chapter two, I explained that the Supreme Court failed to assess whether these inter-generational fairness aims have a sound theoretical basis for justifying unequal treatment on the grounds of age. The theory of age discrimination can fill this gap by explaining that inter-generational fairness can promote the principles of social equality and equality of opportunity. Unlike the dignity aims in *Seldon*, inter-generational fairness does not violate the respect principle by stereotyping people. Instead, inter-generational fairness aims to distribute opportunities to particular age groups by balancing the legitimate interests of different age groups. For example, the law firm in *Seldon* argued that the retirement age aimed to create job and promotion opportunities for younger age groups. This aims to promote equality of opportunity by requiring access to income and work to be withheld from those who have held employment for a considerable time (older workers) and given to age groups who experience relatively high unemployment (young people). While, as I have explained above, the retirement in *Seldon* is unlikely to create complete equality of opportunity for each worker in the law firm because some workers might leave before facing the detriment of the retirement age, the law firm's retirement age can work to create a wider equality of opportunity by granting opportunity to groups who may not have promotion opportunities if the older workers do not retire.

By distributing jobs and promotion opportunities from older workers to younger groups, a retirement age gives young people a chance to gain experience and develop their careers. In doing so, it can aim to provide a fair share of work opportunities across generations. This argument assumes that older workers have had a 'fair innings' in their careers and that young people have not.

Inter-generational fairness can also promote social equality by distributing opportunities to younger people who are disadvantaged because of lack of experience. Youth unemployment rates are much higher than unemployment in other age groups. The UK unemployment rate for 16- to 24-year-olds was 13.1% for August–October 2016, while the UK unemployment rate for people aged 16 and over was just 4.8%.[51] Social equality holds that it is legitimate to take measures to encourage young people into employment to ensure that they have a chance to participate productively in society as equals with other age groups. The high youth unemployment rate leads to social exclusion, undermining the ability of those age

[51] Data taken from ONS, Labour Market Statistical Releases.

groups to participate in society as equals with other age groups. Inter-generational fairness measures can legitimately aim to correct this by aiming to create employment for younger people.

However, for inter-generational fairness to constitute a legitimate aim, it should not convey that the interests of the young outweigh the old. As I have explained earlier in this chapter, demeaning age discrimination is unjustifiable. The retirement age can escape this finding if it is positive action in favour of disadvantaged young people.[52]

Some argue that positive action is wrong because it entails the transfer of opportunities away from people who may otherwise be in a position on an individual merit assessment of ability.[53] And some also argue that positive action is an illegitimate goal because it can reinforce stereotypes by conveying that 'certain groups are unable to achieve success without special protection based on a factor having no relationship to individual worth'.[54]

However, positive action should be legitimate because it does not have the effect of stigmatising older people or marking them as inferior. It has the intent to undo hierarchies of status on the grounds of age.[55] Positive action can be a means to remove the diminished standing of disadvantaged groups by integrating them into mainstream society. As Elizabeth Anderson has argued, a failure to do this means a 'failure [to] fully to realize civil society – extensive social spaces in which citizens from all origins exchange ideas and cooperate on terms of equality – which is an indispensable social condition of democracy itself'.[56] The positive action inherent in inter-generational fairness is a compelling interest in social equality and therefore legitimate.

Now that I have established that inter-generational fairness is a legitimate aim, I must evaluate whether the retirement age is rationally connected to this aim. Sandra Fredman has argued that retirement ages do not necessarily promote inter-generational fairness because they do not necessarily create more jobs and

[52] As noted in ch 2, ss 158 and 159 of the Equality Act 2010 provide exceptions from the age discrimination provisions for positive action measures. In the context of recruitment, s 159 only applies if the person benefiting from the positive action is as qualified as another candidate or candidates who are competing for the job or promotion and the recruiter does not have a policy of favouring people with the protected characteristic. However, it is possible that the proportionality test in the direct and indirect age discrimination provisions renders the positive action provisions redundant. *Seldon* recognised positive action in the form of inter-generational fairness aims as capable of justifying measures under the general proportionality test. As a result, decision-makers may bypass the stringent requirements in ss 158 and 159 and instead try to justify the measures as a proportionate means of achieving a legitimate aim.

[53] For this argument, see M Abram, 'Affirmative Action: Fair Shakers and Social Engineers' (1986) 99 *Harvard Law Review* 1312.

[54] *Regents of the University of California v Bakke* 438 US 265 (1978) [438].

[55] See Justice Brennan's argument in *Bakke* that positive action does not 'in any sense [stamp] as an inferior' the people who lose out [363].

[56] E Anderson, 'Integration, Affirmative Action, and Strict Scrutiny' (2002) 77 *New York University Law Review* 1195, 1270–71.

opportunities for young people at the macro level.[57] This is because the demand for labour is not fixed. Job opportunities do not arise simply because people are forced from their jobs.

However, Fredman also rightly notes that while jobs are not finite at a macro level, individual workplaces, including law firms, do offer a relatively fixed number of jobs.[58] For individual law firms, a retirement age can facilitate hiring and promotion opportunities. If the claimant in *Seldon* were not to retire, then the law firm's financial constraints may prevent it from creating additional opportunities for younger workers. Therefore, a retirement age can be rationally connected to the aim of creating job and promotion opportunities within the law firm.

The third stage of assessing the legality of the retirement age requires determining whether the retirement age is necessary to achieve the legitimate aim. This is a question of evidence to demonstrate whether a measure is, in fact, proportionate to the aim pursued and whether there are any other methods available to achieve the aims that are less harmful to the claimant's interests. For example, we should consider whether a retirement age set at 70 years (which will have permitted the appellant to work for another 5 years) would be able to achieve the legitimate aims as effectively.

I have explained above that deference at this stage is appropriate when the courts or tribunals do not have institutional competence to determine the necessity of the impugned treatment. In *Seldon*, the EAT rightly held that they were not well placed to assess whether the retirement age was necessary to create job and promotion opportunities within the firm. The EAT rightly noted that the possibility of job and promotion opportunities was dependent on knowledge of the personalities within the firm and their likely reactions to the retirement age rather than something that can be determined by expert reports. Deference to the law firm's view on necessity, therefore, was appropriate.

The fourth stage of assessing the legality of the retirement age requires determining whether the retirement age promotes the principles of the pluralist theory of age discrimination, including social equality and equality of opportunity, to the extent that justifies the seriousness of the interference with the claimant's interest in being free from the burden of the retirement age.

In chapter two, I explained that the ET and EAT did not engage in open reasoning on the burdens placed on the claimant in assessing proportionality. The pluralist theory of age discrimination recognises that while retirement ages can promote social equality by granting work opportunities to younger people, this compromises the ideal of social equality from the perspective of older workers since it hinders the claimant's capacity to participate in society through productive work. It treats the claimant as having had a 'fair innings' and that the claimant should

[57] S Fredman, 'The Age of Equality' in S Fredman and S Spencer (eds), *Age as an Equality Issue: Legal and Policy Perspectives* (Hart Publishing, 2003).

[58] ibid.

retreat from productive society to make way for younger workers. Consequently, the retirement age weakens the ability of the claimant to belong to the social group of working people and to pursue his work and social life through his job. A fair balance must be struck between the interests of young people and older workers.

The ET and EAT, however, were correct in finding the retirement age proportionate. The ET rightly held that there was a distinction between a retirement age unilaterally imposed on an employee and a partner who elects to enter into the partnership and agrees to be bound by a retirement age. The claimant in *Seldon* had an equal bargaining power and at the time of signing did not question the retirement age contained in the partnership agreement. This mitigates some of the deleterious effects of the retirement age by respecting the autonomy of the claimant, an important principle of the pluralist theory of age discrimination. In upholding the principle of autonomy, it was reasonable for the ET and EAT to find that the retirement age reflected the agreed mutual interests of the partners and younger workers. Furthermore, the claimant's consent to the retirement age also mitigated the harm to social equality since the claimant was able to negotiate his employment terms as an equal in his role as a partner. The retirement age, therefore, was not oppressive.

In applying the pluralist theory of age discrimination, the courts and tribunals could quite appropriately come to the decision that the retirement age was proportionate and lawful.

## B. *Lockwood v Department of Work and Pensions & Anor*

To reiterate the facts outlined in chapter two, the claimant began working at the Department for Work and Pensions (DWP) at 18 years of age. She continued working there for eight years, until she was 26 years old. The claimant then applied for redundancy and was accepted. The redundancy scheme entitled her to £10,849.04. However, the same scheme would have entitled her to significantly more money if she were over 30 years of age and had worked the same number of years at the DWP. The claimant argued this was direct age discrimination because it treated her less favourably because she was a young employee.

The ET held that there were differences between the different age groups that meant that those below the age of 30 were not treated less favourably than those above the age of 30.[59] The ET held that even if they were wrong about this, the treatment was a proportionate means of achieving a legitimate aim. The ET relied on the assumption that older people need more redundancy pay because they are more likely to have families than young people and this meant that they have greater financial obligations and have a harder time travelling to find work. It was

[59] [2011] ET/1808694/07, 101539/08, 115515/10.

a legitimate aim, the ET and the EAT upheld, to financially cushion older workers, who are in a more vulnerable position than younger workers.[60]

The ET also held that the measure was proportionate because the redundancy scheme was reasonably necessary to the aim of offering a financial cushion, and this legitimate aim outweighed the discriminatory effects of the scheme. The means were reasonably necessary because administrative workability required the use of clear bands so that everybody knew the pay they were entitled to. Levelling up younger workers' pay would achieve equality, but would be expensive. And levelling down older workers' pay to match younger workers would not adequately provide a financial cushion for older workers.

The EAT upheld the ET's decision, so the claimant appealed to the Court of Appeal.[61] The Court of Appeal held that the redundancy scheme engaged the direct age discrimination provisions. The claimant's comparator was an employee over 35 who had worked for the DWP for the same amount of time as the claimant. The comparator would receive at least twice what the claimant received, and it followed that she was treated less favourably and was so treated because of her age. However, the Court of Appeal found that the DWP had adopted a proportionate means to achieve the legitimate aim of producing a proportionate financial cushion for older workers. The Court applied *Seldon* by finding that the aim of offering a financial cushion for older workers was a legitimate social policy aim. This justified the redundancy scheme.

### *(i) Applying the Pluralist Theory of Age Discrimination to* Lockwood

The first stage is to determine whether the redundancy scheme engaged the direct age discrimination provisions. The Court of Appeal was correct in finding that the scheme did so. The claimant received less money than older workers received, and the reason for this was that she was younger. The DWP may have paid the claimant less because she would be in a position to find work more easily, but the reason the claimant was in this position was because of her age. Therefore, the reason for being treated less favourably was her age and so the treatment engaged the direct age discrimination provisions.

The second stage of applying the pluralist theory of age discrimination is to determine whether the redundancy scheme promoted a legitimate aim. The redundancy policy assumed that young people are less likely to be encumbered than older people because they are less likely to have dependants or to be married, and therefore, on average, will find it easier to obtain employment in a shorter amount of time than older people. People in their 30s will need more redundancy pay to cover what may be a longer period of unemployment or underemployment.

[60] [2013] UKEAT 0094/12/0402.
[61] [2013] EWCA Civ 1195.

Should this be a legitimate aim? The academic literature has cast doubt on the assumption that young people find it easier to obtain employment than older people, particularly because the evidence demonstrates that young people have a much higher unemployment rate than older workers.[62] In addition, the aim of financially cushioning older workers may violate the respect principle by offering less concern and respect for younger age groups. In chapter four, I explained that even accurate generalisations can be disrespectful when they can reinforce stereotypes that imply that particular groups have a lower moral and social worth. It follows that even if the generalisation in *Lockwood* that young people are more 'flexible' in finding work is an accurate categorisation, this treatment can still be wrong if it reinforces disrespectful ideas about young people. Is this harm present in the redundancy policy in *Lockwood*?

The redundancy policy does not necessarily represent animus or dislike for younger groups. However, the aim of the policy to cushion older workers in a period of unemployment relies on stereotypes about young people, namely, it reflects a generalisation that young people will react differently to unemployment than older people. The ET reasoned that

> Individuals in the younger categories and in their twenties can generally be expected to react more easily and more rapidly to the loss of their jobs and greater flexibility can, in general, be expected of them given their lesser family and financial obligations.[63]

The ET referred to 'the average date of marriage [being] 34 for women, and 38 years for men' as an explanation for why greater financial assistance was needed for people in their 30s compared to people in their 20s. This assumes that young people have an easier time finding employment and do not face the difficulties that older people face.

While this is not a stereotype that amounts to straightforward prejudice against young people, the stereotype does ignore people's individual circumstances and, as a result, can be unfair to young people, who do face significant disadvantages in finding employment. People under 30 years of age are less likely to be married with children, but many people of this age have family and financial obligations comparable to or exceeding those of older work colleagues. Although younger, they may have dependent parents, disabled siblings, cousins etc, as well as children, any of whom they may be supporting financially. They may face the difficulty of upending their family life by moving locations to find employment.

Also, as Blackham has argued, 'Just because young people do not have a mortgage or children does not mean that they lack onerous financial commitments or have less "need" for redundancy payments'.[64] Young people may have as much

[62] A Blackham, 'Falling on Their Feet: Young Workers, Employment and Age Discrimination' (2015) 44 *Industrial Law Journal* 246, 254.

[63] [2011] ET/1808694/07, 101539/08, 115515/10 [27].

[64] Blackham (n 62), 254.

difficulty paying rent in a period of unemployment as older people may face in paying a mortgage. By assuming that young people do not face the difficulties that people over 30 years of age face, the DWP were treating young people less favourably based on stereotypical assumptions about their private lives, and, in doing this, the impugned policy communicated that the interests of young people are of less concern and value. On this basis, the aim of financially cushioning older workers should not be capable of justifying the redundancy policy in *Lockwood*.

The ET argued that it was acceptable to use age generalisations because it was not practicable to assess severance payments on an individual basis.[65] This argument was upheld by the EAT and Court of Appeal. The argument is that it is more efficient to make use of age generalisations than to investigate individual circumstances of each employee who has applied for redundancy. However, the pluralist theory of age discrimination holds that efficiency cannot justify age stereotyping that reinforces the lower status of particular age groups. As I argued in chapter six, there are levels of sacrifice that should not be required of an individual, and this includes suffering treatment founded on ageist beliefs. The policy of the DWP conveys the message that young people deserve less financial assistance in times of unemployment and therefore do not deserve the same concern and respect as older workers. With the DWP offering no other aims for the scheme, the DWP's redundancy scheme should constitute unjustified and therefore unlawful age discrimination.

However, it is possible that the redundancy scheme could have been justified by an argument that it supports inter-generational fairness aims by creating employment opportunities for young people (which I have established as legitimate in this chapter). For example, the DWP could have argued that higher redundancy payments for older workers can encourage older workers to leave who might otherwise not have done so, which will create available space for more junior employees. This aim is legitimate for the reasons outlined in the discussion of *Seldon* above – young people are often disadvantaged in the employment market because of lack of experience, and it is legitimate to give young people a chance to gain experience and develop their careers.

A relevant consideration in determining whether the scheme was necessary to achieve the aim of inter-generational fairness is to consider that the aim could not be achieved as effectively if redundancy pay was equal for younger and older workers. Paying older workers more than younger workers is necessary to incentivise a greater proportion of older workers to vacate their places to leave room for younger workers. The alternative method of equal pay will not achieve this aim so effectively. The aim would therefore pass the necessity stage.

Moving to the final stage, we need to assess whether the benefits of the redundancy scheme justifies the seriousness of the interference with the claimant's

[65] *Lockwood* (n 2) [22].

interest. *Lockwood* is an example of a case where it would be appropriate for a court or tribunal to defer to the judgement of the people who negotiated the scheme. The scheme was an agreement between the trade union and the employer, and, in these circumstances, there is a democratic rationale for respecting the outcome of the democratic process of negotiation in balancing competing legitimate interests. The ET acknowledged the significance of the collective bargaining as a reason to find the redundancy scheme proportionate. However, even if union agreement to the scheme can bolster the argument of proportionality, the courts and tribunals must be alive to the risk of ageist stereotyping in motivating the scheme. The DWP based their aims for the scheme on age stereotyping, which should render the scheme unlawful. Because the DWP did not introduce the inter-generational aim of creating opportunities for young people, we are unable to assess the evidence of whether the scheme is likely to have the benefit of creating enough jobs for young people to justify its discriminatory effects on the claimant. Therefore, we cannot determine whether the scheme was proportionate to achieving this aim on this basis.

## C. *White v Ministry of Justice*[66]

In chapter two, I discussed this case as an example of the ET using age stereotypes to justify a retirement age without explaining why age stereotyping is acceptable in this context. The Ministry of Justice operates a compulsory retirement age for judges whereby they must retire when they reach 70 years of age. The claimant, a circuit judge who was retired, complained that the policy was directly discriminatory.

The ET applied *Seldon* in holding that the retirement age promoted the legitimate aims of inter-generational fairness by creating opportunities for younger people, preserving judges' dignity by avoiding capability assessments and maintaining public confidence by ensuring that the public do not form the belief that judges are undergoing age-based intellectual decline. The ET held that 'there can be no doubt that the aims which the [Ministry of Justice] is pursuing in having a retirement age of 70 are legitimate aims of social policy'.[67]

The ET acknowledged that the retirement age of 70 must be proportionate when balancing the importance of the legitimate aims pursued by the Ministry of Justice and the extent of the discriminatory effect it could have upon the claimant and other judges. The ET held that the claimant failed to show any significant harm of a retirement age of 70 as opposed to his suggested age of 75. The majority of judges retire before they reach the retirement age of 70. The claimant's suggestion that judges should be dismissed after individual assessments, the ET held,

[66] [2014] ET/2201298/2013.
[67] ibid [47].

would be damaging to the rule of law. The ET referred to an argument by the Lord Chancellor, who noted that a retirement age avoids the impression that judges are being removed because of the nature of their decisions. The ET also cited a statement by the Minister of Justice, who argued that a retirement age avoids any perception of unwarranted interference by the executive. The ET ruled that the retirement age of 70 was a proportionate means of achieving the aims.

### *(i) Applying the Pluralist Theory of Age Discrimination to* White

The first stage of applying the theory is straightforward. The claimant was retired when he did not wish to be and therefore was treated less favourably than other age groups. The retirement age engages the direct age discrimination provisions.

Moving on to the second stage, we must identify whether the retirement age promotes a legitimate aim by advancing one or more of the principles of the pluralist theory of age discrimination. As I have argued in the discussion of *Seldon*, it is a legitimate aim to use a retirement age to open vacancies that can be filled by younger workers. The nature of the tenure of judicial office ensures that the workforce is relatively inflexible. The methods available to remove workers in the private sector workforces are not available for the removal of judges. A retirement age offers a degree of flexibility to open vacancies to talented younger people who may not otherwise have the opportunity. The pluralist theory of age discrimination would accept this inter-generational fairness aim as legitimate because the retirement age promotes equality of opportunity and social equality by providing opportunities for younger people.

There is uncertainty about whether a retirement age can promote job opportunities. The creation of job opportunities depends on the demand for judges at a future date. Courts and tribunals cannot reliably predict whether the retirement age will create more job opportunities. As I have argued in this chapter, it is appropriate for courts and tribunals to accept the connection between the legitimate aim and the impugned measure where there is considerable uncertainty over the connection.

The pluralist theory of age discrimination would hold that preserving judges' dignity through a retirement age is an illegitimate aim because it reflects the stereotype that older judges must be expelled by a retirement age because they are likely to be undergoing age-based intellectual decline. The ET held that it was important to ensure that the public do not believe judges are undergoing this. While the public may believe that older judges have undergone intellectual decline, age stereotyping should not justify removing judges from their jobs. Age discrimination law should rule out prejudice and stereotypes.

Regarding the third stage of applying the pluralist theory of age discrimination, the ET could quite appropriately come to the decision that the retirement age of 70 was reasonably necessary to achieve the legitimate aim of creating opportunities for younger people. A retirement age set at 70 is more likely to achieve the goal of inter-generational fairness than a retirement age set at an older age or a policy of not having a retirement age. This is because it will prompt a higher turnover of judges, leading to a greater possibility of opening job opportunities for younger people.

In the final stage of the proportionality test, we must evaluate whether the possible benefits of the retirement age for judges are enough to justify its negative impact on individuals.[68] The retirement age harms the autonomy principle by forcing judges out of socially productive work and therefore prevents them from having control over their work lives. Further, the retirement age can harm social equality by denying older judges the opportunity to participate as equals with younger age groups. Despite these negatives, the claimant conceded that the retirement age has only a modest negative impact on autonomy because about two-thirds of judges choose to retire before their 69th birthday and roughly only one in ten judges choose to retire on their 70th birthday.[69] Very few judges are forced out of work.

There are also good reasons to defer to the defendant's judgement on the balance between promoting job opportunities and harming the interests of older judges. The government settled on a retirement age of 70 after consultations between the Lord Chancellor and senior members of the judiciary.[70] Given the limited adverse impact the retirement age has on judges, it would have been inappropriate for the ET to substitute its view for that of the democratically elected government acting in response to a consultation with the senior members of the judiciary.

## D. *Homer v Chief Constable of West Yorkshire*[71]

In chapter two, I explained that Homer is the leading case on the application of the indirect age discrimination provisions. The Supreme Court held that, unlike for measures engaging the direct discrimination provisions, private aims, including a real need on the part of the employer's business, can justify treatment that engages the indirect age discrimination provisions.

[68] The Constitution Committee have argued that the retirement age for senior members of the judiciary should be increased to 75 while the general retirement age for less senior judges should remain at 70. One of the arguments in support of this is that a retirement age of 70 for the senior judiciary makes it particularly hard for many women to reach this level. Reaching the senior judiciary typically requires a number of decades of experience in another career. Women who take career breaks to have children will have difficulty having enough career length to reach the senior judiciary. See Constitution Committee, *Twenty-Fifth Report – Judicial Appointments* (HL 2010–12, 272). Lord Neuberger has argued that the mandatory retirement age for judges should be increased to 75 in order to address the problem of judicial vacancies going unfilled because of a shortage of suitably qualified applicants. F Gibb, 'Let Judges Work Past 70 to Ease Recruitment Crisis, Peers Told' *The Times* (30 March 2017) accessed 16 June 2017.

[69] *White* [47].

[70] HL Deb 16 June 1992, col 122.

[71] [2012] UKSC 15, [2012] ICR 704.

Examples of aims that can justify indirect age discrimination include rewarding loyalty and business efficiency. The Supreme Court did not offer an explanation for why these sorts of aims can justify measures engaging the indirect age discrimination provisions when they cannot be used to justify measures that engage the direct age discrimination provisions. A theory of age discrimination may go some way to transparently revealing why direct and indirect age discrimination should be treated differently in this way.

## (i) *Applying the Pluralist Theory of Age Discrimination to* Homer

To determine whether the Supreme Court was correct to hold in *Homer* that private aims should be capable of justifying measures that engage the indirect discrimination provisions but not the direct discrimination provisions, we must evaluate whether the differences between direct and indirect discrimination warrant this different legal treatment. As I established in chapter two, direct discrimination involves a decision-maker treating someone less favourably because of a protected characteristic. Indirect discrimination, in contrast, concerns a policy, criterion or practice that has the effect of disadvantaging groups of people with a protected characteristic and this treatment is disproportionate. The crucial difference between the two concepts is that indirect discrimination is focused on the harmful effects of treatment whereas direct discrimination relates to a decision-maker targeting a person because of a protected characteristic.

There is moral similarity between direct and indirect discrimination. As I established in chapter four, indirect discrimination, like direct discrimination, can violate people's autonomy by foreclosing valuable options, violate social equality by reinforcing the subordination of vulnerable groups and violate equality of opportunity by disadvantaging people. I have also argued that both direct and indirect discrimination can send a disrespectful message to the discriminatee that their interests are unimportant and do not warrant accommodation.

However, there is a moral difference in the contrasting features of direct and indirect discrimination. Targeting a person's protected characteristic for less favourable treatment can demean people by sending the message that people who possess the protected characteristic have a diminished moral or social worth. Direct discrimination, in this way, is often associated with racism, sexism, ageism and other egregious attitudes. Indirect discrimination, in contrast, does not target particular social groups for poor treatment; the disadvantage caused by indirect discrimination is inadvertent. The deliberate targeting feature of direct discrimination means that it has the potential to offer greater expressive harms to the discriminatee.

Age is a key part of a person's identity that has social meaning connected to age norms. As I outlined in chapter five, age can be a criterion used to express animus and to stereotype people. Therefore, targeting age as a criterion for less favourable treatment has a much greater likelihood of being experienced as stigmatising and as an attack on personal identity than a decision that is age-neutral and is indirect discrimination. As Hellman has argued, it is often demeaning to use certain traits for classifying people when there has been a history of using the trait to convey that people have a diminished moral or social worth.[72]

Private interests should not be capable of justifying less favourable treatment on the grounds of age because such interests are consistent with selfish motives and are therefore unlikely to prevent the stigmatising effects of treatment that engages the direct discrimination provisions. Age discrimination law, therefore, should have no interest in legitimising private subjective gains from treatment that is stigmatising.

However, as explained in chapter five, age can be a useful proxy for promoting a number of important social goals. We accept using age as a category in education, healthcare and many other areas as a means to maximise the benefit of particular social goods. We accept these age-based structures as useful and non-demeaning when they serve clear public policy goals rather than merely private interests, such as maximising profit. Public policy aims should therefore be capable of justifying age distinctions if the decision-maker can demonstrate that it is proportionate to achieving important public policy aims.

The Supreme Court was correct to hold in *Homer* that a decision-maker can pursue private interests, including business efficiency, to justify indirect discrimination, given that these measures are unlikely to be experienced as demeaning. Indirect discrimination claims make distributive claims to resources to ensure that there is a level playing field. It ought to be legitimate for an employer to pursue private interests provided these promote one or more of the principles in the pluralist theory of age discrimination.

## E. *Woodcock v Cumbria Primary Care Trust*[73]

The North Cumbria Primary Care Trusts (PCT) made the claimant redundant and the claimant was unsuccessful in finding another position at the PCT. The PCT dismissed the claimant before the claimant reached 49 in order to avoid having to pay an enhanced early retirement pension. The claimant argued that this was direct discrimination and that it could not be justified by cost savings.

The Court of Appeal held that costs alone cannot justify measures that engage the direct age discrimination provisions. Cost savings combined with a legitimate aim, however, can be considered in determining proportionality. The dismissal was legitimate because it was not only aimed at cost saving, but was also the result of redundancy.

[72] D Hellman, *When Is Discrimination Wrong?* (Harvard University Press, 2008).
[73] [2012] EWCA Civ 330, [2012] ICR 1126.

## *(i) Applying the Pluralist Theory of Age Discrimination to* Woodcock

We would consider it wrong to use cost savings alone as a reason to treat women, racial groups etc less favourably. For example, it is wrong and unlawful for an employer to refuse to hire a woman on the grounds that they may cost more to hire due to the possibility of the applicant requiring career breaks to have children. This policy would place women at a severe disadvantage in the workplace and would also stereotype women as requiring career breaks. Similarly, using cost savings alone as a reason to disadvantage older people is wrong because of its equality and autonomy harms.

The Supreme Court was correct to find in *Woodcock* that costs alone should not be capable of justifying age-differential treatment. Treating people less favourably on the grounds of age solely in order to save costs can undermine a number of the principles of the pluralist theory of age discrimination. It can undermine social equality by casting older people out of work, thereby undermining their capacity to participate in society as equals with other age groups. It can also lead to autonomy costs by denying older people control over their working lives. And it can violate the respect principle by treating people as if they are disposable resources that can be thrown away after a certain time.

Dismissing workers on costs alone can also violate the respect principle by stereotyping particular age groups. For example, an employer may attempt to justify dismissing older workers because they cost more, but not all older workers are more expensive. As Michael Harper argues,

> An employer's rejection of a group of workers defined by age because the average member of the group will provide lower returns than the average worker outside the group means that all of the older workers in the age-defined group will be disadvantaged.[74]

This unfairly generalises about age groups, thereby ignoring people's individual characteristics.

Accepting costs alone as justifying age-differential treatment would undermine the effectiveness of age discrimination law in protecting people from harms to social equality, autonomy, and disrespectful and humiliating treatment.

Another reason why costs alone should not constitute a legitimate aim is that cost savings do not themselves vindicate any valuable principles. Cost savings can aim to maximise wealth, but, as I argued in chapter six, maximising wealth is not an intrinsically valuable goal because it is merely an instrument of creating value. Wealth maximisation is valuable only to the extent that it is 'useful so far as it enables someone to lead a more valuable, successful, happier, or more moral life'.[75] To justify age-differential treatment, a decision-maker must demonstrate that they

[74] M Harper, 'Reforming the Age Discrimination in Employment Act: Proposals and Prospects' (2012) 16 *Employment Rights & Employment Policy Journal* 13.

[75] R Dworkin, *A Matter of Principle* (Harvard University Press, 1985) 245–46.

are promoting an important value in addition to cost savings. For example, a business in financial difficulty might legitimately argue that cost savings from refusing to hire older (more expensive) applicants ensure that the business is financially secure and efficient, which, in turn, has the valuable goal of protecting employment by ensuring that the business does not face insolvency. The employer must also demonstrate that this age-differential treatment was necessary to achieve the aim, and that the benefits of the policy outweighs the harms to older employees.

## IV. Conclusion

Unequal treatment on the grounds of age can result in significant harms, such as expressions of disrespect, stereotyping, prejudice and the creation of oppressive social relations, and significant violations of liberty and practical and utilitarian harms, such as a poor use of talent and ability. In assessing whether the age-differential treatment is justified or not, we should consider whether and to what extent the treatment causes these harms.

In this chapter, I have reviewed a number of age discrimination cases and have sought to illustrate how the principles of the pluralist theory of age discrimination can approach the issues in the cases. I have explained that much of the courts' reasoning, particularly with regard to identifying legitimate aims, fails to properly identify the harms done by age-differential treatment. Applying my framework of principles better scrutinises these aims and offers a more comprehensive, coherent and open assessment of the key conflicting interests and principles at stake in the cases.

# 8

# Healthcare Rationing and the Pluralist Theory of Age Discrimination

This book has now outlined and defended a pluralist theory of age discrimination. In the previous chapter, I demonstrated how this theory improves the transparency of legal reasoning in age discrimination cases. This chapter applies the pluralist theory of age discrimination against the method of healthcare rationing in the UK – the Quality-Adjusted Life Year (QALY) – to determine if that method can constitute unjustified age discrimination. This chapter works as a case study to illustrate how the pluralist theory of age discrimination can settle complex age discrimination cases.

The QALY method calculates the cost-effectiveness of treatment, and therefore determines which treatments should be offered by the National Health Service (NHS), by considering three things: the cost of a treatment; the resulting quality of life; and the number of years gained by the use of that treatment. John Harris has argued that the use of the QALY method by the National Institute for Health and Care Excellence (NICE) is discriminatory against older people because they are more likely to generate a low QALY score due to, on average, having fewer life years that can be gained by medical treatment and by being more likely to have conditions that can prevent a large gain in quality of life that can result from treatment.[1] As part of this case study, I consider a hypothetical judicial review claim against NICE, which is the institution responsible for using the QALY method to issue guidance on the cost-effectiveness of treatments. I apply the pluralist theory of age discrimination to examine whether NICE's guidance can constitute unlawful age discrimination.[2]

I have selected the QALY method as a case study because it implicates each principle of the pluralist theory of discrimination, including efficiency, equality of opportunity, social equality, autonomy and respect, and therefore it is a useful

[1] J Harris, 'It's Not NICE to Discriminate' (2005) 31 *Journal of Medical Ethics* 373.

[2] My analysis will focus on the lawfulness of NICE's use of the QALY method, but other issues of age discrimination can arise in healthcare allocation. For example, claimants can bring judicial review claims against the Department of Health and health authorities if the decisions of these bodies disadvantage particular age groups. I will focus on NICE as a means to undertake a philosophical analysis. I am not attempting to provide a complete overview of age discrimination in UK healthcare.

topic to illustrate how the pluralist theory of age discrimination can navigate the complex moral issues. For example, the central rationale of the QALY method is the *efficient* allocation of health resources. It attaches higher scores to treatments that maximise quality of life and extends life. However, some argue that this efficiency violates the *respect* principle by communicating that older people's lives are worth less than those of younger people.[3] The QALY method also engages the *social equality* principle because it can exclude older people from valuable health resources that ensure people are able to continue to actively participate in society. Autonomy is implicated because the QALY method offers a lower QALY score for treatments for conditions that largely or exclusively affect older people, including Alzheimer's disease, osteoarthritis and osteoporosis, which are conditions that can have a devastating effect on autonomy. Also, equality of opportunity can be implicated if a treatment previously denied funding on the NHS becomes cheaper, which can lead to the NHS offering the treatment for young people when such treatment was not available to older people at an equivalent age. I will use the pluralist theory of age discrimination to examine whether NICE, in using the QALY method, acts proportionately in balancing each of these moral considerations.

Further to this, I argue that NICE's use of the QALY method can engage the indirect age discrimination provisions, but NICE will be able to justify using QALY on the grounds that the method is a proportionate means of achieving a legitimate aim under section 19(2) of the Equality Act 2010.[4] In support of this argument, I use the principles of the pluralist theory of age discrimination at different stages of the proportionality test and introduce considerations about the institutional limitations of courts to evaluate health allocation decisions. Importantly, NICE has taken measures to ensure that the method does not disproportionately harm the interests of older people, including calculating QALY in a way that avoids denying treatments to particular age groups and considering age as a factor in equality impact assessments for every item of guidance. NICE has also adopted democratic procedures to inform its decision-making, and is accountable to Parliament and the Department of Health. It follows that it is appropriate to hold that NICE's use of QALY is proportionate and therefore lawful.

The application of the pluralist theory of age discrimination against the QALY method in this chapter demonstrates the theory's capacity to produce just outcomes and reasoning in real-life dilemmas and therefore demonstrates the value and plausibility of the theory as a guide to age discrimination law.

The structure of this chapter is as follows: section I explains NICE's legal duty not to do anything that amounts to discrimination on the grounds of age; section II explains that the QALY method used by NICE can engage the discrimination provisions of the Equality Act 2010; and section III argues that the QALY method can be justified as a proportionate means of achieving a legitimate aim.

[3] Harris (n 1).
[4] NICE's use of the method is lawful under Equality Act 2010, s 19(2)(d).

# I. NICE's Anti-discrimination Duties under the Equality Act 2010

NICE's role is 'to improve outcomes for people using the NHS and other public health and social care services' by 'producing evidence-based guidance and advice for health, public health and social care practitioners … Developing quality standards and performance metrics for those providing and commissioning health, public health and social care services' and 'Providing a range of information services for commissioners, practitioners and managers across the spectrum of health and social care'.[5] NICE provides guidance for 'technology appraisals' that 'assess the clinical and cost-effectiveness of health technologies, such as new pharmaceutical and biopharmaceutical products, but also include procedures, devices and diagnostic agents'. 'This is to ensure that all NHS patients have equitable access to the most clinically- and cost-effective treatments that are viable.'[6] The NHS uses NICE's guidance to determine the cost-effectiveness of treatments.

In issuing its guidance, NICE is performing a public function and is therefore under a duty under section 29(6) of the Equality Act 2010 to ensure that its guidance does not constitute discrimination.[7] It follows that NICE's guidance must be compliant with the section 13 duty not to directly discriminate on the grounds of age and the section 19 duty not to indirectly discriminate on the grounds of age. Under these provisions, NICE may recommend age-stratified treatment or adopt methodology that disadvantages particular age groups, but only if this is a proportionate means of achieving a legitimate aim.[8] As a public authority, NICE is also subject to the public sector equality duty under section 149 of the Equality Act 2010 to have due regard to the need to eliminate unlawful age discrimination and advance equality for people of different ages.

It is possible to bring a legal claim against a decision by NICE to recommend that a particular treatment should not be funded by the NHS. To bring a claim, a complainant must apply to the High Court for a judicial review claim that this rationing decision is unlawful. For a judicial review claim to proceed, the High Court must grant permission and the applicant must have standing.[9] Standing is granted when the applicant has a 'sufficient interest' in the matter, and this includes anyone directly affected by the decisions of NICE, including those denied treatment as a result of NICE's recommendations and drug manufacturers that are

[5] NICE, 'What We Do' www.nice.org.uk/about/what-we-do.

[6] ibid.

[7] The Equality Act 2010, s 29(6) provides that 'A person must not, in the exercise of a public function that is not the provision of a service to the public or a section of the public, do anything that constitutes discrimination, harassment or victimisation'. As a statutory non-departmental public body accountable to the Department of Health, NICE is performing a public function when it issues guidance to NHS practitioners rather than the public.

[8] Equality Act 2010, ss 13(2) and 19(2)(d).

[9] Supreme Court Act 1981, s 31(3).

denied the opportunity to provide a service to offer drugs for use via the NHS.[10] An elderly person, for example, who has been denied treatment may apply to the High Court to bring a judicial review claim on the grounds that NICE's use of the QALY method has disadvantaged older people and therefore violated the duty not to discriminate under section 29(6) of the Equality Act 2010. Groups not directly affected by NICE's decision are likely to have standing provided they can demonstrate that they are a prominent campaign group with expertise in the subject area.[11]

Once a court grants standing and permission, the High Court can evaluate whether NICE's guidance is discriminatory. If the Court finds that an age group was in fact disadvantaged as a result of the use of the QALY method, then NICE's guidance would only be lawful if NICE could demonstrate that the QALY assessment was a proportionate means of achieving a legitimate aim.

It is also possible to judicially review decisions by NHS institutions, including health authorities and primary care trusts, if these bodies have been responsible for a decision to deny treatments that has the effect of disadvantaging particular age groups.[12] The NHS is providing a service directly to the public and is therefore under a duty from section 29(1) of the Equality Act 2010 to perform this service in a way that does not constitute discrimination. It is also possible to bring a judicial review application to make a claim against decisions made by the Secretary of State for Health to deny funding for treatments.[13]

It is worth noting, however, that it is difficult to succeed in a discrimination claim against NICE.[14] As I explain in section III, NICE has greater institutional

[10] ibid.

[11] See *R v Secretary of State for Foreign and Commonwealth Affairs ex parte World Development Movement* [1994], EWHC Admin, [1995] 1 WLR 386. The High Court accepted that campaign groups can have standing to challenge decisions that do not directly affect the group. The Court held that one should consider the following to determine when a campaign litigant should have standing: (i) the importance for vindicating the rule of law; (ii) the importance of the issue; (iii) the likely absence of any other responsible challenger; (iv) the nature of the breach of duty; and (v) the prominent role of these applicants in the field.

[12] An example of a successful judicial review claim against an NHS health authority is *R v North West Lancashire Health Authority Ex Parte A, D and G* [2000] EWCA Civ 2022, [2000] 1 WLR 977. The Court of Appeal held that it was unlawful for the health authority to refuse to offer gender reassignment surgery. The health authority adopted a 'blanket policy' to determine the availability of gender reassignment surgery. The Court of Appeal held that the proper approach should have been to consider each case on its own merit. An example of a successful judicial review against a primary care trust is *R (Rogers) v Swindon NHS Primary Care Trust and another* [2006] EWCA Civ 392, [2006] 1 WLR 2649, where the Court of Appeal held that it was unlawful for the primary care trust to deny the applicant the cancer drug Herceptin.

[13] An example of a successful judicial review claim against the Department of Health is *R v Secretary of State for Health, ex parte Pfizer Ltd* [2002] EWCA Civ 1566, [2003] 1 CMLR 19. Pfizer successfully argued that the government acted unlawfully when it issued guidance to doctors advising them to refrain from prescribing the drug Viagra.

[14] To date, there has been one successful discrimination claim made against NICE – the case of *R (Eisai Ltd) (Alzheimer's Society & Shire Ltd, Interested Parties) v the National Institute for Health and Clinical Excellence* [2007] EWHC 1941 (Admin), (2007) 10 CCL Rep 638. The applicant, the manufacturer of the drug Donepezil (brand name Aricept), and the interested third party, the Alzheimer's

competence and democratic legitimacy than the courts to determine the justifiability of its healthcare recommendations. In undertaking the proportionality assessment of NICE's guidance, it is therefore appropriate that a court would offer a degree of deference to NICE's judgement on the justifiability of its guidance. Only in examples where NICE has disregarded the interests of particular age groups would it be appropriate to find its guidance disproportionate and therefore unlawful. This chapter argues that NICE does take steps to appropriately balance the interests of young and older people in its recommendations for funding treatments by the NHS.

## II. NICE's Use of the QALY Method can Engage the Indirect Age Discrimination Provisions

QALY is a measure used to calculate the cost-effectiveness of a particular treatment or medical intervention. As explained in the introduction to this chapter, the QALY method determines the value of treatment by considering three things: the cost of a treatment; the resulting quality of life; and the number of years gained by the use of that treatment.[15] QALY assigns a value to each treatment corresponding to the number of quality life years a patient can look forward to with the treatment minus the number of QALYs the patient would have if left untreated. We then must calculate the cost of each QALY gained. NICE considers that interventions costing the NHS less than £20,000 per QALY gained are cost-effective, whereas treatment above £30,000 per QALY will not be recommended for funding unless there is a very strong case for supporting the treatment as an effective use of NHS resources.[16] Williams, one of the originators of the approach, writes that

> The general idea is that a beneficial healthcare activity is one that generates a positive amount of QALY, and that an efficient healthcare activity is one where the cost of QALY is low, and a low priority activity is one where cost per QALY is high.[17]

Society, claimed that it was discriminatory for NICE to recommend that Donepezil should not be funded for those with the early stage of Alzheimer's disease. The Court held that NICE is a public body and is therefore bound by duties under s 19B of the Race Relations Act 1972 and s 21B/D of the Disability Discrimination Act. The Alzheimer's Society and Eisai successfully argued that the guidance would result in discrimination against 'atypical groups', such as those from a non-English-speaking background and those with learning disabilities. NICE failed to give due regard to the need to eliminate race and disability discrimination, and the Court held that it was unlawful to overlook that responsibility under the discrimination legislation.

[15] NICE, 'Judging whether Public Health Interventions Offer Value for Money' (September 2013) www.nice.org.uk/advice/lgb10/chapter/introduction.

[16] ibid.

[17] A Williams, 'The Value of QALYs' in S Holland (ed), *Arguing about Bioethics* (Routledge, 2012) 423.

QALY can be used at the macro or micro level. At the macro level, QALY calculates the cost-effectiveness of a treatment for a health service as a whole. At the micro level, QALY calculates whether a treatment is cost-effective for a particular patient.

When NICE uses QALY to inform decisions about which interventions to fund for the NHS, and what the access criteria for interventions should be, the method has the potential to disadvantage older patients and therefore to engage the indirect discrimination provisions of the Equality Act 2010.[18] QALY can disadvantage older people because the calculation of QALY uses remaining life expectancy to determine the number of years gained by the use of that treatment. Since young people are more likely to have a higher QALY score because there are likely to be greater gains for a younger person in receipt of a life-saving treatment than for an older person, young people will be more likely to receive access to treatment under the QALY method. For example, while a 20-year-old can expect to live for another 55 years, a 70-year-old could only expect to live another five years. Saving the life of a 20-year-old creates more QALYs than saving the life of a 70-year-old. Therefore, the QALY method is more likely to recommend saving the life of the 20-year-old.[19]

It is important to note, however, that a younger patient will not always generate more QALYs than an older patient. A particular younger patient may have a lower life expectancy than a particular older patient and the quality of life of a particular younger patient may be less improved by a medical treatment than that of a particular older patient. In these circumstances, the younger patient will produce fewer QALYs overall. But where two patients have normal life expectancy, and a treatment will produce the same improvement in quality of life in these patients, treating the younger patient will produce more QALYs.

For these reasons, the use of the QALY method in determining healthcare distribution can engage the indirect age discrimination provisions when the NHS denies older people treatment that is available for younger people. This will be unlawful unless the distribution is a proportionate means of achieving a legitimate aim.[20]

However, NICE's use of QALYs usually avoids age discrimination in practice. This is because NICE calculates QALYs by averaging results across the QALY

[18] For an account of the discriminatory effects of QALY, see Harris (n 1).

[19] This argument was supported by the Royal College of Physicians of Edinburgh, who presented to the Joint Committee on Human Rights the argument that NICE's use of the QALY method has a discriminatory impact on older people because it can result in the denial of beneficial treatment to older people. Joint Committee on Human Rights, *The Human Rights of Older People in Healthcare* (HL 2006–07, 156-I; HC 2006–07, 278-I).

[20] Measures that engage the indirect discrimination provisions but do not fit into an exception to the age discrimination provisions are only lawful if they are a proportionate means of achieving a legitimate aim. See Equality Act 2010, s 19(2)(d).

scores from patients of different ages.[21] NICE therefore assumes treatments will have an equal benefit for different age groups by 'assum[ing] that what applies to one age group within a particular appraisal will apply inter alia to others'.[22] This prevents the majority of calculations and recommendations of NICE from engaging the indirect discrimination provisions.[23] Some treatments, however, are restricted to particular age groups, including access to in vitro fertilisation,[24] flu vaccinations[25] and cervical screening;[26] they therefore engage the age discrimination provisions and will only be lawful if the measures are a proportionate means of achieving a legitimate aim.

Issues of indirect discrimination do arise when NICE uses the QALY method to assess the cost-effectiveness of treatments that are only or mainly of benefit to older people compared to treatments that benefit a range of age groups. This is because 'The benefits to older people will still be lower and so treatments that mostly impact on an older population will still be affected by a generally lower ability to produce QALYs'.[27] Therefore, NICE's use of the QALY method to assess the cost-effectiveness of treatments will disadvantage patients who can benefit from treatments for conditions such as Alzheimer's disease, osteoarthritis and

[21] See I Dey and N Fraser, 'Age-Based Rationing in the Allocation of Health Care' (2000) 12 *Journal of Aging and Health* 511: 'The influence of age on QALY league table estimates is normally quite small because the estimates derive from averaging results from patients of different ages. Where a treatment is predominantly for older patients, the estimate would be affected by the lower life expectancy of the elderly …'.

[22] A Stevens et al, 'National Institute for Health and Clinical Excellence Appraisal and Ageism' (2012) 38 *Journal of Medical Ethics* 258.

[23] While this macro approach to scoring QALY tends to offer greater support for the social equality principle of the pluralist theory of age discrimination by ensuring that different age groups tend to have equal access to healthcare, this comes at a cost to the efficiency principle because it establishes equal access to treatment for different age groups even though older age groups may only have a small health gain due to having a shorter life expectancy. Attaching QALY scores to particular age groups is more efficient because it will lead to high QALY scores (and therefore priority for treatments) to groups that are most likely to benefit from treatment.

[24] Guidance from NICE recommends that up to three IVF cycles should be available on the NHS if the woman is aged between 23 and 39 years at the time of treatment, and has been diagnosed with a fertility problem or the partner has a fertility problem, or if they been infertile for more than three years. NICE recommends women aged 40–42 years only in more restricted circumstances.

[25] Those over 18 years of age do have access to free flu vaccination, but only if they have an underlying health condition (particularly long-term heart or respiratory disease) or weakened immune systems.

[26] For example, the Department of Health invites women aged 25–49 years for a cervical screening test every three years, whereas women aged 50–64 years are invited every five years. This is because statistics show that the younger group are more susceptible to the disease than the older group. In this example, the health service is likely to be able to justify offering more regular screening to the younger age group, as this can be understood as a proportionate response to statistical evidence that this group is at the greatest risk of developing cervical cancer.

[27] R Edlin et al, 'Cost-Effectiveness Analysis and Ageism: A Review of the Theoretical Literature [Prepared for the Department of Health]' (Leeds Institute of Health Sciences, 2008).

osteoporosis, which largely or solely affect older people.[28] It follows that when an older patient has been denied treatment for such a condition, then that patient (or a prominent interest group acting on their behalf) may apply to the High Court to bring a judicial review claim against NICE. If the court grants permission for a judicial review claim and standing is established, then NICE must demonstrate that the use of the QALY method is a proportionate means of achieving a legitimate aim.

## III. The Proportionality of the QALY Method

NICE's use of the QALY method for conditions that largely or solely affect older people will only be proportionate and lawful if it is rationally connected to a legitimate aim, necessary to achieve that legitimate aim and does not impose burdens or cause harms to other legitimate interests that outweigh the objectives achieved. As I outlined in detail in chapter seven, the pluralist theory of discrimination can assist in each of these stages of the proportionality test to determine legality. For each stage of the proportionality test, we should consider each of the five principles of the theory.

To determine whether the QALY method is rationally connected to a legitimate aim, we should consider whether the method is supporting one or more of the five substantive principles of the pluralist theory of age discrimination, including equality of opportunity, social equality, autonomy, respect or efficiency. Importantly, as explained in chapters six and seven, the respect principle acts as a deontological constraint at this stage. Aims cannot be legitimate if they convey the message that a particular age group has a diminished social or moral worth.

In the necessity stage, the pluralist theory of age discrimination comes into play by considering whether the original decision-maker is in a better position than a court to determine whether the treatment is necessary to advance the moral principles of the pluralist theory of age discrimination. If they are, then a court or tribunal should consider deferring to the original decision-maker's judgement that the method is necessary.

In the final stage of the proportionality test, we should consider which principles of the pluralist theory of age discrimination are promoted or violated by the QALY method and then consider whether NICE have struck an appropriate balance between these principles. Deference can also come into play if the original decision-maker is in a better position to determine where the best balance between the competing principles lies.

[28] Centre for Policy on Ageing, 'A Review of Age Discrimination in Primary and Community Health Care, Secondary Health Care, Mental Health Care and Social Care Services in the United Kingdom' (January 2010).

## Stage 1: Does the QALY Method Pursue a Legitimate Aim?

The QALY method promotes efficiency by aiming to distribute scarce health-care resources in such a way as to maximise the aggregate health benefit. Promoting efficiency is a principle of the pluralist theory of age discrimination and can therefore constitute a legitimate aim, but only if the efficiency promotes a valuable end and does not amount to treating individuals as if they have a diminished social or moral worth. The QALY method does promote valuable ends by maximising life expectancy and quality of life. We can defend this from a utilitarian perspective:

> Health care is a limited resource. It must be allocated in the way which achieves the greatest good for the greatest number. If all lives are of equal value more is effected by saving the one with more years left. Utilitarianism is necessary if not sufficient for ethical rationing decisions.[29]

From this perspective, the QALY method efficiently rations health resources and, in doing so, aims to maximise quality of life and to extend life. This, in turn, maximises welfare.

However, the respect principle acts as a deontological constraint, which means that we must then consider whether QALY violates the respect principle. John Harris argues that the QALY method places more weight on younger people's desire to go on living than an older person's desire to go on living. The QALY method does this by prioritising patients for treatment who have more life expectancy and this happens to be disproportionately young people. Harris argues that, contrary to the QALY method, we should treat every person's desire to go on living with equal force because the desire to live 'the rest of our lives' is of equal value whether we are young or old.[30] Because we do not know the date of our deaths, the 'the rest of our lives' is an indefinite duration, and we each, according to Harris, suffer the same injustice if our desire to go on living is cut short as a result of someone else's decision.[31]

Quigley has also argued that the use of QALY is a way of expressing that some lives are worth more than others:

> When we engage in the sort of evaluations inherent in QALYs, we make value judgments about the kind of people that we think are worth the expenditure of public resources. Specifically, we are saying that we think those people who belong to a particular category have more worthwhile lives. By using the QALY we are implicitly (or perhaps explicitly) accepting that those patients with a better quality of life and who live longer have more worthwhile lives. Although it may be acceptable to hold a private

[29] AB Shaw, 'In Defence of Ageism' (1994) 20 *Journal of Medical Ethics* 188.

[30] This argument is made in J Harris, 'The Age-Indifference Principle and Equality' (2005) 14 *Cambridge Quarterly of Healthcare Ethics* 93.

[31] ibid 89.

> opinion regarding this, we ought not permit these personal conclusions to creep into public policy.[32]

Contrary to Quigley and Harris's argument, however, the QALY method does not imply that people with longer life expectancies have more worthwhile lives. The QALY method evaluates the worth of treatments and their benefits. This is not the same as evaluating the worth of individuals.[33] QALY requires that we prioritise treatments that are likely to produce the greatest health benefits for the population. In this way, QALY values effective treatments over ineffective ones rather than valuing some lives more than others. Further, this does not imply older people are less worthy of concern and respect. QALY stipulates that it is better to choose the most effective treatment whoever may benefit from that treatment, whether young or old. The QALY calculation simply recognises that treatment that has greater health benefits produces more welfare and should be preferred for this reason.

Part of the error in Quigley and Harris's argument is suggesting that people are equally wronged if their lives are cut short. The respect principle requires weighting equal interests equally, but not all individuals have an equal interest in life-saving treatment. Some people suffer a greater loss if their wish to live is frustrated and suffer a greater misfortune. An example of this is that each of us has an equal interest in living from youth to old age. The young, because they have not had the opportunity to live to old age, have a stronger claim towards life-saving treatment than people who have reached old age. We can respect people as equals by distributing health resources to ensure people have a chance to have a full life.

It is also possible to doubt Quigley and Harris's assertion that older people, subjectively, have the same desire to live the rest of their lives as younger people. It is plausible that the older people are, the less they may feel that they need to live out the remainder of their life; partly because what is left is shorter and partly because they have already had a 'good innings'. Moreover, even if older people do have as strong a desire as younger people to live the remainder of their lives, we might argue that, objectively, they have less basis for the same degree of desire given that they have experienced a long life while young people have not.

Also, crucially, NICE in practice uses QALY in a way that is acutely sensitive to the interests of older people and their need to access healthcare. For example, NICE has created end-of-life rules that accord additional value, largely overlooked by the QALY method, to the last few months of life in situations where treatment can extend the life of those with a short life expectancy.[34] This reveals that their

[32] M Quigley, 'A Nice Fallacy' (2007) 33 *Journal of Medical Ethics* 465.
[33] C Claxton, 'Wickedness or Folly? The Ethics of NICE's Decisions' (2006) 32 *Journal of Medical Ethics* 373.
[34] NICE, 'Appraising Life-Extending, End of Life Treatments' (2009) https://www.nice.org.uk/guidance/gid-tag387/documents/appraising-life-extending-end-of-life-treatments-paper2.

use of QALY does operate to respect older people's lives, which goes some way to addressing the concern that the QALY method does not attribute enough value to older people's desire to go on living.[35]

## Stage 2: Is the QALY Method Necessary to Achieve the Legitimate Aim?

The necessity stage of the proportionality test requires one to determine whether there are methods of healthcare rationing that can secure the same level of efficiency as the QALY method but do so in a way that is less disadvantageous to older people. If we can answer this in the affirmative, then the QALY method is unnecessary to achieve the legitimate aim of efficiency and therefore can be unjustified age discrimination under section 19 of the Equality Act 2010 when older people are denied treatments.

There are many methods of healthcare rationing advocated in the academic literature, but most of these methods are at least as disadvantaging to older people as the QALY method and are less likely to be as efficient. For example, an alternative to the QALY method is the 'fair innings' method of healthcare rationing. There are two ways of approaching the fair innings argument. First, we can understand it as a duty-based argument inviting older people to say of themselves that they have had a fair innings, and to deprioritise their own requests for medical treatment. This version is not about denying services to older people, but rather encouraging people to exercise restraint in demanding healthcare.

The second version of the fair innings argument requires prioritising lifesaving treatment for younger people because younger people have not had a fair innings in life.[36] This position incorporates fairness arguments into healthcare rationing. The fair innings argument is an equality of opportunity argument that health provision should ensure that each person has an equal opportunity for a complete life.

[35] This distinguishes NICE's use of generalisations in the QALY method to the generalisations operating in the redundancy scheme in the *Lockwood* case discussed in chapter seven. The QALY method in practice is sensitive to the unique experiences of older people. In *Lockwood*, the redundancy scheme violates the respect principle because it was insensitive to the challenges young people face on unemployment.

[36] For a defence of this, see Shaw (n 29). An interesting example of balancing efficiency with fairness is Williams's QALY method adjusted for equality weighting. His method represents a balance between working towards efficiency and the goal of ensuring as many people as possible reach old age. Williams explains a method for weighting QALY to account for the fair innings argument. The fair innings weight applied to health gains of each individual is defined as a function of their present expected lifetime QALY and the fair innings, so that if their expected lifetime QALY at present age falls short of the fair innings, the weights are larger than 1. A Williams, 'Intergenerational Equity: An Exploration of the "Fair Innings" Argument' (1997) 6 *Health Economics* 117.

However, the first version of the fair innings argument is not actually a healthcare distribution method because it is not about determining who should receive services. It therefore is not an alternative to the QALY method of healthcare distribution. The second version of the fair innings argument disadvantages older people because it uses a person's age as a reason to determine whether they should be granted treatment. Further, it is unlikely to promote the efficiency as effectively as the QALY method because it sacrifices total health benefits to minimise the unfairness of younger people dying before they reach old age. The fair innings argument will prioritise the young in extending their life even if to do so produces fewer QALY and therefore fewer health benefits overall. The fair innings method does not render the QALY method unnecessary because the fair innings method will not achieve the level of efficiency that the QALY method can secure and will disadvantage older people to at least the extent that the QALY method will.

There are methods of healthcare rationing that do not disadvantage older people, but these methods are less likely to maximise quality and quantity of life to the extent that the QALY method does. Harris, for example, argues for an 'age-indifference' method of healthcare rationing, where health resources are allocated in a way that does not disadvantage any particular age group in accessing treatment.[37] The age-indifference method, Harris argues, values lives equally by assigning equal weight to what remains of a person's life regardless of the person's life expectancy so long as the person desires to go on living. This avoids the disadvantaging impact on older people that may result from QALY calculations, but the age-indifference method fails to advance the legitimate aim of efficiency to the extent that the QALY method does. The age-indifference method is less efficient because it assigns an equal weight to treatments that produce a small amount of health benefit to older people as to treatments that provide a large gain for young people. This will result in diminished aggregate healthcare benefits compared to the QALY method unless there are large increases in spending on healthcare. The QALY method, therefore, is likely to be necessary to achieve the legitimate aim of efficient rationing of healthcare.

## Stage 3: Is the Gain in Efficiency Secured by the QALY Method Enough to Justify the Disadvantaging Impact of the QALY Method on Older People?

This final stage of the proportionality test requires an assessment of whether there is an acceptable balance between the competing interests at stake in the use of QALYs to ration healthcare. This requires a cost–benefit analysis of QALY,

[37] Harris (n 30) acknowledges that a younger person should be given treatment in preference to an older person when the older person has already had a fair innings, and it was impossible to save both.

including an assessment of whether the likely gain in efficiency resulting from the QALY method outweighs its potential detrimental impact on older people accessing treatments. If the costs to older people exceed the gain offered by the QALY method, then the use of QALY is disproportionate and therefore unlawful.

At this stage, we must identify which principles of the pluralist theory of age discrimination are implicated. I have explained that the QALY method promotes efficiency and does not violate the respect principle. The use of the QALY method, however, will disadvantage older people in accessing treatments. This violates the social equality principle when it leads to the denial of treatment for conditions that largely or exclusively affect older people. The problem with QALY, on the social equality account, is that it is not strictly based on medical need, but may benefit those who are younger at the expense of the old. According to social equality, no subgroup of society should dominate access to particular valuable resources.

The QALY method also violates the autonomy principle by providing a lower QALY score to treatments that can enhance the autonomy of older people. Conditions that largely or exclusively affect older people, including Alzheimer's disease, osteoarthritis and osteoporosis, can have a devastating effect on the autonomy of older people. The failure to offer adequate treatment for these conditions can make it harder for older people to retain their autonomy as they age.

The QALY method can be consistent with equality of opportunity to access healthcare, but only if NICE's guidance is stable and consistent over time thereby ensuring that people will face the same benefits and disadvantages over their complete lives. However, NICE's guidance may not be stable and consistent over time as the cost of treatments may change. If a treatment previously denied funding by the NHS becomes cheaper, NICE may start to recommend that treatment for funding. This will mean that as young people age they may not face the same disadvantages as older people in accessing treatment. NICE's future activities are uncertain, however, and therefore it is uncertain whether different age cohorts will have equal access to healthcare over time.

Despite the fact that the QALY method has the potential to violate social equality, the autonomy principle and equality of opportunity, the courts should find that NICE has struck an appropriate balance between efficiency and these principles. NICE has incorporated a model of participative democracy into its procedures with the establishment of the Citizens Council, and it is appropriate for a democratic body to determine a proper balance between competing principles in the allocation of resources without interference from a court.[38] There are 30 members of the public on the Council, and that group of people reflects the general demographic proportions of the UK. This group of people offers a public view on the principles that NICE ought to consider when making decisions on guidance. The Council's recommendations to NICE are then incorporated into a document

[38] NICE, 'Citizens Council' www.nice.org.uk/get-involved/citizens-council.

called Social Value Judgements, and NICE take this into account in its method of healthcare allocation. The Council considers the views of experts on a topic under consideration and discusses and debates the issues by letting them put their view on a particular distributive issue.

The Council has published a report relating to the use of age in healthcare.[39] In this report, the Council concluded that age should be used as a consideration in healthcare allocation where age is an indicator of either benefit or risk. This recommendation reflects the QALY approach of distributing health resources to maximise the total health benefits even if this has the effect of disadvantaging particular age groups.

In using the values identified by the Council to inform healthcare rationing, NICE ensures that its appraisals are receptive to principles held by a wide range of people in society. This democratic procedure promotes social equality by providing that a cross-section of society has a say on health rationing and that this makes a difference to how NICE operates. This democratic process for deciding an appropriate balance between competing interests is a more ideal form of decision-making on healthcare allocation than the legal process is able to offer. It follows that the courts should defer to NICE's judgement on the balance between competing interests unless there is evidence that the use of the QALY method disregards the interests of older people.

Furthermore, the polycentric nature of healthcare rationing offers another reason to respect the decisions of NICE on their balancing the competing principles of efficiency against social equality and the diminished autonomy of older people. A decision to offer treatment is a public expenditure and can limit spending in other areas, including education, social security etc. A court only has the competence to look at healthcare resource allocation in isolation since it does not have access to and control over the national budget.[40] NICE, in contrast, can deliberate upon polycentric matters and, as a non-departmental public body, is accountable to the Department of Health, which is responsible for the NHS budget. NICE is also accountable to Parliament, in that it is responsible for producing annual reports to Parliament on its activities. This provides a further reason to show a somewhat deferential approach towards NICE. Again, so long

[39] NICE, 'NICE Citizens' Council Report on Age' (November 2003) www.nice.org.uk/pdf/Citizenscouncilreport_age.pdf.

[40] Lord Hoffmann, 'The COMBAR Lecture 2001: The Separation of Powers' (2002) 7 *Judicial Review* 137 comments on the appropriateness of deference in these circumstances: 'A court deciding a case which will affect one form of public expenditure – for example, impose a burden on education authorities – has no way of being able to decide whether such expenditure should or should not have a prior claim over other forms of expenditure. It may consider that, viewed in isolation, it is fair and reasonable that children in schools should receive certain benefits or financial compensation for not having received other benefits. But because it can only view the matter in isolation, it has no way of knowing whether this means that other people dependent upon social security, police protection and so on will have to make sacrifices because there is less money for them. The only people who can make such decisions are the democratically elected bodies who are in charge of the budget as a whole.'

as the QALY method is not operating in an oppressive way towards older people, then it is appropriate for the court to defer to NICE on its view of the appropriate balance of interests.

There is evidence that NICE does not act in an oppressive way towards older people. NICE has adopted procedures to ensure that its recommendations on medical treatments have limited disadvantaging effects on older people and therefore a limited impact on the social equality and autonomy principles. For example, NICE deliberately operates the QALY method at the macro level – determining which from a range of possible treatments or interventions are most cost-effective for society as a whole, rather than for individuals – in order to 'assume that what applies to one age group within a particular appraisal will apply inter alia to others'.[41] The result is that age is rarely used as a reason to recommend medical interventions and NICE's guidance rarely disadvantages particular age groups. Further, as I explained earlier, NICE has created end-of-life rules that accord additional value to the last few months of life in situations where treatment can extend the life of those with a short life expectancy.[42]

Other safeguards to protect the interests of older people and to minimise harmful consequences for these groups include consultation exercises and considering age issues in equality impact assessments for every item NICE is giving guidance on. All of this points towards NICE's use of the QALY method as proportionate and therefore lawful under the Equality Act 2010.

## IV. Conclusion

The QALY method is not intrinsically ageist because it does not necessarily involve direct expressions that older patients are less worthy of concern and respect. The QALY method is useful for maximising health gains and therefore welfare in society. The downside is that QALYs have the effect, in theory, of disproportionately benefiting younger people in accessing resources (since treatments that largely or solely benefit older people generate lower QALY than treatments than benefit younger people or a range of age groups), thus violating the prescription of social equality that people should be able to access resources as equals. Further, it also harms the autonomy principle that requires doing as much as possible to ensure that people can live autonomously as they age.

Nonetheless, I have argued that the QALY method is a proportionate means of achieving a legitimate aim. The method pursues the legitimate aim of efficiently allocating health resources to maximise health benefits. It is also necessary to achieve this aim since suggested alternative methods lack the efficiency of QALY

[41] Stevens et al (n 22).
[42] NICE (n 34).

and some are at least as disadvantaging to older people as QALY. Further, NICE has medical expertise that can inform on the efficacy of different methods of healthcare rationing. As a result, the courts should defer to NICE on the necessity of the QALY method.

NICE has also made an appropriate balance between the efficiency of QALY and the impact this has on older people. It has adopted procedures, including the method of placing additional value on the last few months of life and ensuring that age is almost never a reason for recommending treatment, that minimise the disadvantaging effects of QALY on older people. NICE has also adopted democratic procedures to inform its decision-making, and it is accountable to a democratic government department – the Department of Health. This points to a democratic reason for deferring to NICE's approach to balancing the competing interests at stake in healthcare rationing. Courts and tribunals should hold that NICE's use of the QALY method is proportionate, justified and legal under the age discrimination provisions of the Equality Act 2010.

The pluralist theory of age discrimination has assisted in determining that NICE's use of the QALY method is indeed proportionate and therefore lawful under the Equality Act 2010. Applying the pluralist theory of age discrimination to a hypothetical judicial review claim ensures that the rationalisation behind NICE's allocative decisions is transparent and subject to scrutiny. This scrutiny also aids the legitimacy of NICE's decisions by

> structuring decision-making and ensuring that the policy choice made, even if reasonable, is explained and justified … [and ensuring] not only that all relevant factors are taken into account but also that they are subjected to a rigorous and open analysis before a conclusion is reached.[43]

[43] R James and D Longley, 'Judicial Review and Tragic Choices' (1995) 3 *PL* 367, 373.

# 9

# Conclusion

This book has outlined and defended a pluralist theory of age discrimination that offers a framework for identifying unlawful age discrimination. In this conclusion, I summarise the main features of this theory, the value and limitation of my research method, and the possible implications of the theory beyond the scope of the book, including the implications of the theory for understanding discrimination law more generally, the usefulness of the theory in relation to systems other than the UK and the possible value of the theory for identifying which grounds should be protected under discrimination law.

## I. Summary of the Pluralist Theory of Age Discrimination

The Equality Act 2010 holds that unequal treatment on the grounds of age and age-neutral treatment that disadvantages particular age groups is lawful only if is a proportionate means of achieving a legitimate aim or fits into a specifically prescribed exception.[1] This proportionality test requires that we distinguish justified from unjustified treatment in order to determine legality. I have argued that to determine proportionality, we must identify a number of principles to explain when and why age-differential treatment wrongs people and when and why this treatment can be justified.

These principles include the following: equality of opportunity, social equality, respect, autonomy and efficiency. I constructed this theory by identifying anti-discrimination and equality principles that both fit and justify our moral intuitions about different forms of wrongful discrimination and applied these norms to issues of age discrimination.

Equality of opportunity requires an equal distribution of benefits and detriments over people's complete lives except insofar as inequality is caused by individual choices. This principle serves to justify those age-based distinctions, for example, in job recruitment, promotion and other terms of employment, which are based on stable policies that apply uniformly to all people.

[1] Equality Act 2010, ss 13 and 19.

Social equality requires conditions that offer people opportunities to participate equally in social, economic and political life. Age discrimination can violate the principle of social equality by contributing to social exclusion, marginalisation and oppression. Social equality can also work to justify some age distinctions. I have argued that positive age discrimination can promote social equality by integrating people from age groups that typically suffer from social exclusion.

The principle of autonomy requires that people have control over their lives. Age discrimination can undermine this principle by diminishing choice over a person's lifetime. Age discrimination can also undermine autonomy if the messages conveyed by age discrimination become internalised. For example, older people may internalise the stereotype that they are less productive and therefore leave the labour force. Like social equality, the principle of autonomy can work to justify some forms of age distinctions which work in favour of age groups who typically suffer from lower levels of autonomy.

The principle of respect recognises the harm of denying access to goods when that denial expresses the message that some age groups have a diminished moral and social worth. On this account, age-differential treatment wrongs people when based on prejudice, stereotyping or other demeaning attitudes. The respect principle acts as a deontological restraint on particular actions. It holds that aims that reflect age stereotyping and prejudice are illegitimate and should not justify age-differential treatment even if these aims promote efficiency or other collective goals.

The principle of efficiency recognises that we can justify age-differential treatment if it efficiently promotes valuable social goods. Age is linked to certain attributes – physical and intellectual. Using age as a proxy for these traits can be less costly than assessing each person individually. Age distinctions can also force people to sequence and order their lives chronologically, and this sequence ensures people undertake certain tasks at a time of life when there is the greatest benefit to the individual and society.

## II. How the Pluralist Theory Assists in Age Discrimination Claims

Identifying unlawful age discrimination is a four-stage test. The first stage requires determining whether a measure engages the direct or indirect discrimination provisions of the Equality Act 2010. A measure engages the direct age discrimination provisions when an individual is treated less favourably than another person because of their age or the age they are thought to have, or because they associate with someone of a particular age.[2] A measure will engage the indirect age

[2] Equality Act 2010, s 13.

discrimination provisions when that measure disadvantages people of a particular age.[3] The principles of the pluralist theory of age discrimination can identify when an impugned measure engages these provisions by determining when a measure treats an individual less favourably because of their age and when it disadvantages particular age groups.

If the measure engages the direct or indirect age discrimination provisions, we must move on to the second stage, which is to consider whether the treatment is a proportionate means of achieving a legitimate aim.[4] Stage 2 requires addressing the first consideration of the proportionality assessment, namely, determining whether the measure is rationally connected to achieving a legitimate aim. I have argued that we should hold that all aims reflecting age stereotyping or prejudice are illegitimate in accordance with the respect principle and therefore incapable of justifying age-differential treatment. This acts as a deontological constraint on pursuing aims that communicate demeaning messages. Unless there are other aims that do not reflect age stereotyping and prejudice, we should hold the impugned measure unjustified and unlawful because it is not connected to a legitimate aim.

If the aim does not reflect age stereotyping or prejudice, then we must assess whether the purported aims of the measure relate to one of the remaining principles of the pluralist theory of age discrimination, including assessing whether the aims promote social integration of a disadvantaged group (the social equality principle), advances the autonomy of members of a disadvantaged age group (the autonomy principle), distributes resources or opportunities equally (the equality of opportunity principle) or promotes efficiency. If the aims do not relate to one or more of these principles, then the measure is unjustified age discrimination in accordance with either section 13 (for measures engaging the direct discrimination provisions) or section 19 (for measures engaging the indirect discrimination provisions) of the Equality Act 2010.

If the aims promote one or more of these principles, then we move to stage 3, which requires assessing whether the measure is necessary to achieve its purported aims. This is an empirical calculation of whether there are any alternative methods for pursuing the aims that are less harmful to the claimant's interests. It is appropriate to defer to the original decision-maker on this question if the original decision-maker is in a better position than a court or tribunal to assess the necessity of the measure. If this is the case, then we should move to stage 4. If the original decision-maker is not in a better position to assess the necessity of the measure, then the measure will be unjustified age discrimination if the court or tribunal calculates that there are plausible alternatives to the measure that are less harmful to the claimant. If the court or tribunal considers there are no equally plausible alternatives, then we move to stage 4.

[3] Equality Act 2010, s 19.
[4] Equality Act 2010, ss 13(2) and 19(2)(d).

Stage 4 requires assessing whether the seriousness of the interference with the claimant's interests are proportionate to the benefits gained in pursuit of the legitimate aims. To make this assessment, we should consider which of the principles of the pluralist theory of age discrimination are advanced and which are violated.

Judges should consider deferring to the original decision-maker where the impugned measure is the outcome of a democratic process or concerns a polycentric issue that has multiple complex outcomes that judges may not be equipped to determine. Judges should consider deferring in these circumstances because they may lack democratic accountability for deciding on the appropriate balance of principles at stake. Further, judges should also consider deferring if the claimant consented to the impugned measure. Respect for autonomy means that a court or tribunal should generally assume that voluntary agreements to age distinctions match an appropriate balance of competing principles. In these circumstances, courts and tribunals should hold the measure justified and therefore lawful.

If the courts or tribunals do not, ultimately, consider it appropriate to defer at this stage, then the court or tribunal should hold the measure justified and lawful only when the benefits of the measure in advancing social equality, autonomy, equality of opportunity and efficiency exceed the harm to the claimant's interests. The court or tribunal should consider the measure unjustified and therefore unlawful age discrimination when the harm to the claimant's interests exceeds the possible benefits of the measure advancing equality of opportunity, social equality, autonomy or efficiency.

## III. The Role of Moral Reasoning in Adjudication

This book has argued that judges should engage with moral reasoning in age discrimination cases by applying the principles of the pluralist theory of age discrimination to determine the proportionality of measures that engage the direct and indirect age discrimination provisions. The proportionality test directs judges to the complex task of grappling with all the relevant moral reasons in an age discrimination claim.[5] The pluralist theory of age discrimination is valuable in assisting judges to identify all the relevant principles at stake.

Even though I have argued that courts and tribunals must consider deferring where the original decision-maker is better placed to make a decision on proportionality, this deference does not mean courts and tribunals should completely forgo making moral judgements in these circumstances. Judges must be alive to the fact that these processes may have the effect of sidelining the interests of particular age groups. Where this is the case, judges should undertake a strict scrutiny of the impugned measure.

[5] F Urbina, '"Balancing as Reasoning" and the Problems of Legally Unaided Adjudication: A Reply to Kai Möller' (2014) 12 *International Journal of Constitutional Law* 1214.

# IV. How I Arrived at the Pluralist Theory of Age Discrimination

In chapter one, I explained that I would be adopting the reflective equilibrium method, which requires that we start from our intuition about the morality of a situation and, on reflecting on its plausibility in light of other beliefs that we hold, we consider revising the belief to form a coherent and stable set of principles that can explain our intuitions about a range of scenarios. The reflection process requires taking everything relevant into account about age discrimination (all the relevant principles that can explain why it is a moral problem and all theories relating to the phenomena of age and ageing).

This method requires subjecting our moral beliefs to detailed reflection, consideration and coherence building. Further to this, I have compared the approaches to age discrimination proposed by academics, governments, courts and tribunals with our intuitions about particular scenarios and adjusted these suggested approaches to account for our intuitions about age discrimination.

Before engaging in the reflective equilibrium process, I outlined the structure of age discrimination law. In chapter two, I explained that age discrimination law requires distinguishing justified from unjustified treatment that engages the direct and indirect age discrimination provisions. I argued that the leading UK age discrimination cases indicate a general problem of courts and tribunals failing to offer principles justifying their decisions. A theory of age discrimination, developed from the reflective equilibrium method, I argued, can work to present the important moral principles at stake in any age discrimination claim and therefore ensure age discrimination cases can be decided fairly and appropriately.

In chapter three, I started the process of identifying principles that can assist in distinguishing justified from unjustified age-differential treatment. In this chapter, I identified norms that cohere with our intuitions about when and why it is wrong when some are worse off than others. Age discrimination creates inequality because it treats some people 'less favourably' than others on the grounds of age.[6] It follows that a plausible theory of age discrimination must address what is wrong with inequality to determine what is wrong with discrimination. Further to this, I argued that inequality is wrong when someone is worse off than others due to circumstances outside their control (the equality of opportunity principle). However, I found that equality of opportunity fails to account for many of our intuitions about the wrongness of inequality. I argued that we should revise the equality of opportunity principle to incorporate the idea that inequality is wrong when it creates conditions where people are unable to interact as equals (the social equality principle).

[6] Equality Act 2010, ss 13 and 19.

In chapter four, I verified whether these equality principles can explain the wrongness of discrimination. I argued that the equality principles can explain many forms of discrimination, but not all. A theory of discrimination must incorporate non-equality principles, including the principles of autonomy and respect.

In chapter five, I verified whether the principles identified in chapters three and four can explain the problem of age discrimination and can therefore form a theory of age discrimination. Equality of opportunity, social equality, autonomy and respect all play a role in explaining our intuitions about when and why age-differential treatment can be wrong and also when and why age-differential treatment can be justified. Each of these principles can therefore work to guide age discrimination law. These principles should form a theory of age discrimination. Furthermore, a background theory of age and ageing reveals that age-differential treatment is especially well suited to structuring society to maximise the gain of a number of important social goals, including education and health. From this, I argued that a theory of age discrimination should incorporate an efficiency principle that can justify age-differential treatment.

In chapter six, I considered theories of age discrimination proposed by government consultation documents on the introduction of age discrimination law and Hansard statements relating to age discrimination law. These documents explained the rationales for age discrimination law, including the rationales of promoting fairness and promoting business efficiency. I argued that courts and tribunals should not defer to the approach to age discrimination found in these sources. I rejected the governments' view that age discrimination is wrong when it inhibits business efficiency. The efficiency account of the wrongness of age discrimination is problematic because it can lead to the position that age discrimination is justified so long as it does not harm efficiency. On the contrary, efficiency should not be capable of justifying certain types of age-differential treatment. I argued that we should revise the pluralist theory of age discrimination to incorporate the idea that efficiency or other principles should not be capable of justifying age-differential treatment that communicates the message that particular age groups have a diminished moral or social worth.

In chapter seven, I demonstrated how the pluralist theory of age discrimination can assist in deciding age discrimination cases. I compared and contrasted the approach in the UK case law with the pluralist theory of age discrimination outlined in this book. I argued that the pluralist theory of age discrimination offers much greater transparency on the relevant principles at stake.

In chapter eight, I tested the pluralist theory of age discrimination by using it to evaluate the quality-adjusted life year (QALY) method of healthcare rationing. I argued that the pluralist theory of age discrimination finds that the QALY method is not inherently ageist because QALY does not communicate the message that particular age groups have a diminished moral or social worth. Further, we should find the method proportionate to achieving the legitimate aim of efficiently promoting healthcare resources to the UK population. The courts should defer to NICE in its judgement of the necessity of the QALY method to achieve efficient healthcare allocation. The courts lack the expertise to determine whether the QALY method is the most effective method to maximise healthcare outcomes, whereas NICE is staffed by medical professionals with the expertise to make this judgement. The courts should also defer to NICE's judgement that QALY has an appropriate balance between competing principles. Healthcare rationing is a polycentric issue which NICE can address more satisfactorily than a court. Further, NICE follows democratic procedures in making this judgement and is accountable to both the Department of Health and Parliament. I conclude that the QALY should not be held to violate the age discrimination provisions of the Equality Act 2010.

## V. The Value and Limitations of Reflective Equilibrium as a Method for Investigating Legal Issues

Reflective equilibrium requires formulating abstract moral theories and testing these theories against our intuitions about particular scenarios. This feature of reflective equilibrium has enabled this book to engage with rigorous philosophical analysis on the one hand and doctrinal analysis on the other. Using reflective equilibrium in this way challenges the common intellectual approach to understanding the concept of discrimination. The philosophical literature on discrimination has tended to engage in philosophical enquiry separately from doctrinal analysis, and the doctrinal analysis of discrimination law has tended to be undertaken separately from philosophical analysis. In this book, in contrast, philosophical reasoning and doctrinal analysis have informed the principles that should guide age discrimination law.

Reflective equilibrium has proven useful for investigating age discrimination, but it is not limited to this area of the law. When a legal source, such as the Equality Act 2010, requires open-ended moral reasoning, judges have to draw on their moral convictions to decide cases. The reflective equilibrium process is an effective method for identifying the principles they should use in making these sorts of judgements.[7] Nor is this limited to courts and tribunals. Academics, practitioners, organisations and laypeople can equally use reflective equilibrium to identify the appropriate principles that assist in identifying unjustified and therefore unlawful age discrimination.

Reflective equilibrium is likely to prove useful for any area of law that ties the legality of an action to the moral justifiability of that action. There are swathes of the law that require judges to use their moral judgement to decide cases and reflective equilibrium can identify the principles that are relevant. For example,

[7] For a discussion on reflective equilibrium in legal disputes, see Z Bankowski and J MacLean (eds), *The Universal and the Particular in Legal Reasoning* (Ashgate Publishing, 2006).

reflective equilibrium can identify principles that relate to laws that require judges to determine whether a defendant behaved reasonably, fairly or proportionately. The method may prove useful for finding principles to guide judges in determining whether an employer has unfairly dismissed an employee or to determine the principles that assist in identifying a fair divorce settlement. In administrative law, reflective equilibrium can identify the principles that determine when the executive has created a legitimate expectation that fairness requires they should be bound to fulfil.[8] It is also likely to prove useful in hard cases where judges must decide which principles should prevail.[9] This includes any area of law that requires judges to engage in a proportionality assessment, including human rights and discrimination cases.

The limitation of reflective equilibrium, however, is that it cannot help judges in legal cases when there is clear legal direction. In these circumstances, judges must decide cases according to the legal direction and there is little room for moral reasoning through the reflective equilibrium process. Nor does reflective equilibrium help direct which outcome a judge should choose when there are competing incommensurable values at stake. This is because there is no principle that can determine which outcome should prevail in any given case. Instead, judges must assess which principles are satisfied and which are violated, and they must determine, as best they can, which among various arguments they find most compelling. In many cases, moral intuition might provide direction on the principle that should prevail in a particular case.

On a connected point, the reflective equilibrium method is limited in its capacity to build coherence. While the method assists in building coherence between our intuitions and more general moral theories, the method has difficulties in building coherence between different plausible principles. As I have argued throughout this book, adopting pluralism as a moral theory is the best way to account for our intuitions, but pluralism comes at the cost of different principles pulling in different directions. This means that I have had to temper the coherence building of the reflective equilibrium method to account for our intuitions.

## VI. The Implications for the Pluralist Theory of Age Discrimination for Understanding the Concept of Discrimination More Generally

In chapter five, I argued that moral pluralism is necessary for grasping the complexity of age discrimination as a phenomenon. If I am right about unitary accounts

[8] For an argument that judges do in fact engage in reflective equilibrium when applying the law, see L Alexander, 'Banality of Legal Reasoning' (1997) 73 *Notre Dame Law Review* 517.

[9] See C Sunstein, *Legal Reasoning and Political Conflict* (Oxford University Press, 1998) ch 1.

of discrimination not working in the highly contextual area of age discrimination, then it is unlikely that unitary theories of discrimination can work as general theories of discrimination. The implications for this are that we should also adopt a pluralist theory when trying to understand other forms of discrimination, such as race or sex discrimination.

## VII. The Usefulness of the Pluralist Theory of Age Discrimination in Relation to Systems Other than the UK

I have made no claims about whether the pluralist theory of age discrimination can assist in systems other than the UK. However, the findings in this book are likely to work in a number of jurisdictions that have discrimination laws that are structured in a similar way to the UK. For example, section 9 of the South African Constitution provides that 'The state may not unfairly discriminate directly or indirectly against anyone on one or more grounds, including … age' and 'National legislation must be enacted to prevent or prohibit unfair discrimination'.[10] Like UK law, the South African Constitution requires a moral theory to distinguish justified from unjustified treatment, although it emphasises fairness rather than proportionality. In applying these provisions of the South African Constitution, we would need a set of principles to determine when and why age-differential treatment is unfair.

The principles of the pluralist theory of age discrimination could be helpful in doing this. Indeed, the South African courts have grappled with the task of identifying principles to identify unfair discrimination. We could use the pluralist theory of age discrimination to critique the approach in the South African courts and perhaps offer a more satisfactory account of discrimination than the courts are currently offering.

In *Harksen v Lane*, the South African Supreme Court held that courts should consider the following principles in identifying unfair discrimination: (i) the position of the complainants in society and whether they have suffered from past patterns of discrimination; (ii) the nature of the provision or power and the purpose sought to be achieved by it; and (iii) any other relevant factors, including the extent to which the discrimination has affected the rights or interests of the complainants and whether it has led to an impairment of their fundamental human dignity.[11]

This approach bears some similarity to the pluralist theory of age discrimination. For example, the first principle identified in *Harksen* is similar to the equality

[10] The Constitution of the Republic of South Africa, 1996, s 9.

[11] [2000] ZACC 29, 2000 (2) SA 825 (CC), 2000 (1) SACR 300, 2000 (5) BCLR 478 (30 March 2000).

of opportunity and social equality principles outlined in this book. The second principle recognises that equality of opportunity and social equality can, in some circumstances, justify differential treatment. The third principle, which refers to dignity, bears a resemblance to the respect principle of the pluralist theory of age discrimination that rules out demeaning treatment.

The pluralist theory of age discrimination may be useful for pinning down when differential treatment violates the principles identified in *Harksen*. It can explain that someone's dignity is impaired when a discriminator is motivated by prejudice or stereotyping, or conveys demeaning ideas about particular age groups. It can also explain that 'patterns of past discrimination' can amount to conditions that undermine equality of opportunity to welfare, resources or capabilities, and conditions that undermine the equality of status of different age groups.

We can also apply the pluralist theory of age discrimination to Canadian discrimination law. Section 15(1) of the Canadian Charter of Rights and Freedoms provides that

> Every individual is equal before and under the law and has the right to the equal protection and equal benefit of the law without discrimination and, in particular, without discrimination based on race, national or ethnic origin, colour, religion, sex, age or mental or physical disability.

The pluralist theory of age discrimination can offer principles to assist in determining when age-differential treatment means people are not equal before and under the law. The theory can also assist in critiquing the approach in the case law. For example, in *Law v Canada (Minister of Employment and Immigration)*, the Supreme Court of Canada held that wrongful discrimination is

> where the differential treatment reflects the stereotypical application of presumed group or personal characteristics, or otherwise has the effect of perpetuating or promoting the view that the individual is less capable, or less worthy of recognition or value as a human being or as a member of Canadian society.[12]

In *R v Kapp*, the Supreme Court of Canada adopted a different test that identified wrongful discrimination as that which perpetuates group disadvantage and prejudice, or imposes disadvantage on the basis of stereotyping.[13] These cases adopt the respect and equality of opportunity principles. The pluralist theory of discrimination may add that the courts should also identify wrongful discrimination as differential treatment that undermines the social equality principle by undermining equality of status and also differential treatment that undermines autonomy of vulnerable groups.

The theory can also offer a critique of the courts' approach to age discrimination in the USA. The US Supreme Court held in *Massachusetts Board of*

[12] [1999] 1 SCR 497 [51].
[13] [2008] 2 SCR 483, 2008 SCC 41.

*Retirement v Murgia* that age-differential treatment by state bodies is constitutional provided the treatment is rationally related to a legitimate state interest.[14] The Court explained that, in evaluating the constitutionality of age-differential treatment, the courts should adopt a low level of scrutiny because older age groups have not experienced a 'history of purposeful unequal treatment' or been 'subjected to unique disabilities on the basis of stereotyped characteristics not truly indicative of their abilities'.[15]

The pluralist theory of age discrimination can provide a strong argument that the case law had taken a wrong turn in its understanding of age discrimination. Contrary to the position in the US case law, age discrimination can be wrong for the same reasons that race or sex discrimination can be wrong, namely, it can express animosity, convey demeaning ideas about people and undermine autonomy. *Murgia* should be overturned so that age-differential treatment is not always subject to a low form of scrutiny.

## VIII. The Value of the Pluralist Theory of Age Discrimination for Identifying which Grounds should be Protected under Discrimination Law

The pluralist theory of age discrimination is also likely to be useful for determining which characteristics anti-discrimination law should protect from discrimination. For example, we may use the theory to determine whether the law should protect hitherto unprotected characteristics, including appearance, weight and/or low socio-economic status.[16] If we find that other forms of discrimination that are not currently subject to legal prohibition violate the principles of the theory in a similar way to the protected grounds, then this may offer a good reason for legal protection for the currently unprotected grounds.

For example, consider lookism. Imagine two people apply for a role to work in a clothing store and the employer chooses one of those candidates because, in the employer's view, that person is more physically attractive than the other candidate.[17] We can use the principles of the theory of age discrimination to

[14] 427 US 307 (1976), 312.

[15] ibid 427.

[16] For arguments in favour of looks being a protected characteristic in anti-discrimination law, see K Zakrzewski, 'The Prevalence of "Look"ism in Hiring Decisions: How Federal Law should be Amended to Prevent Appearance Discrimination in the Workplace' (2004) 7 *University of Pennsylvania Journal of Labor and Employment Law* 431. For an argument that weight should be a protected characteristic, see K Horner, 'A Growing Problem: Why the Federal Government Needs to Shoulder the Burden in Protecting Workers from Weight Discrimination' (2004) 54 *Catholic University Law Review* 589.

[17] A famous example of lookism is the clothing company Abercrombie & Fitch adopting a policy of hiring physically attractive employees. In an infamous article, the company's CEO said 'We go after

consider whether the law should prohibit this type of lookism in hiring practices. The practice certainly seems to send a demeaning message to the rejected applicant, thereby violating the respect principle. Lookism also undermines equality of opportunity because less conventionally attractive people have fewer opportunities in many areas of life.[18] There is evidence, for example, that children perceived to be unattractive have more experience with rejection and, as a result, have fewer opportunities for social-skills development that can enable them to access valuable opportunities.[19] This can also have the effect of damaging autonomy by foreclosing valuable options. We might then conclude that lookism is wrong for similar reasons that racism and sexism are wrong and therefore should be unlawful in the way that denial of opportunity on the grounds of race or sex is unlawful.

## IX. The Pluralist Theory of Age Discrimination and Political Debate

The principles of the pluralist theory of age discrimination may also contribute to political debate, for example the grammar school controversy. Theresa May's Conservative government mooted the idea of developing new grammar schools that will only admit pupils who pass an 11-plus examination. The government defended the policy on the grounds of the belief in social mobility. The pluralist theory of age discrimination can challenge such a policy on the grounds that evidence reveals that grammar schools disproportionately benefit wealthier pupils at the expense of the poor, thereby undermining equality of opportunity.[20] Grammar schools undermine social equality by creating hierarchies, with grammar schools having higher status, which will bestow higher status on their pupils.

the attractive all-American kid with a great attitude and a lot of friends. A lot of people don't belong [in our clothes], and they can't belong. Are we exclusionary? Absolutely … That's why we hire good-looking people in our stores … Because good-looking people attract other good-looking people, and we want to market to cool, good-looking people. We don't market to anyone other than that.' B Denizet-Lewis, 'The Man Behind Abercrombie & Fitch' (*Salon*, 24 January 2006) www.salon.com/2006/01/24/jeffries/.

[18] There is a great deal of research confirming that lookism influences hiring decisions. Busetta et al sent fake CVs to a number of employers, with the fake applicants having equal skills and qualifications but with different photographs attached. The photographs were judged by a group of people and assigned into 'attractive' or 'unattractive' categories. The study found that attractiveness played a big part in the likelihood of making the second stage of the recruitment process. See G Busetta et al, 'Searching for a Job is a Beauty Contest' (2013) https://mpra.ub.uni-muenchen.de/49392/2/.

[19] G Jarvie et al, 'Childhood Obesity and Social Stigma: What We Know and What We Don't Know' (1983) 3 *Developmental Review* 237.

[20] S Gorard and N Siddique, 'Grammar Schools in England: a New Analysis of Social Segregation and Academic Outcomes' (2018) 39 *British Journal of Sociology of Education* 909.

On the other hand, we would need to weigh these negatives against any promotion of efficiency in educational attainment, assuming this can be demonstrated.

The pluralist theory of age discrimination has usefulness beyond the application of age discrimination law in the UK. Further research can reveal its use for discrimination law beyond the UK, for identifying the grounds that should be protected in discrimination law, for understanding the general concept of discrimination and for its contribution to different political debates.

# BIBLIOGRAPHY


Abram, M, 'Affirmative Action: Fair Shakers and Social Engineers' (1986) 99 *Harvard Law Review* 1312.

Alexander, L, 'What Makes Wrongful Discrimination Wrong? Biases, Preferences, Stereotypes and Proxies' (1992) 141 *University of Pennsylvania Law Review* 149.

Alexander, L, 'Banality of Legal Reasoning' (1997) 73 *Notre Dame Law Review* 517.

Alexy, R, 'Constitutional Rights and Proportionality' (2014) 16 *Ratio Juris* 131.

Allan, TRS, *Constitutional Justice: A Liberal Theory of the Rule of Law* (Oxford University Press, 2001) 188.

Allport, G, *The Nature of Prejudice* (Addison Wesley, 1954).

Altman, A, 'Discrimination' in E Zalta (ed), *The Stanford Encyclopedia of Philosophy*, Winter 2016 edn https://plato.stanford.edu/archives/win2016/entries/discrimination/.

Anderson, E, 'Integration, Affirmative Action, and Strict Scrutiny' (2002) 77 *New York University Law Review* 1195.

Anderson, E, 'What is the Point of Equality?' (1999) 109 *Ethics* 287.

Arneson, R, 'Equality and Equal Opportunity for Welfare' (1989) 56 *Philosophical Studies* 77.

Arneson, R, 'What is Wrongful Discrimination' (2006) 43 *San Diego Law Review* 775.

Arneson, R, 'Luck Egalitarianism: A Primer' (2011) in Carl Knight and Zofia Stemplowska (eds), *Responsibility and Distributive Justice* (Oxford University Press, 2011).

Arneson, R, 'Equality of Opportunity' in E Zalta (ed), *The Stanford Encyclopedia of Philosophy*, Summer 2015 edn https://plato.stanford.edu/archives/sum2015/entries/equal-opportunity/.

Bagenstos, S, 'Rational Discrimination Accommodation, and the Politics of (Disability) Civil Rights' (2003) 89 *Virginia Law Review* 825.

Bamforth, N, 'Conceptions of Anti-discrimination Law' (2004) 24 *OJLS* 693.

Bankowski, Z, and MacLean, J (eds), *The Universal and the Particular in Legal Reasoning* (Ashgate Publishing, 2006).

Bateman, T, Criminalising Children for No Good Purpose: The Age of Criminal Responsibility in England and Wales (2012) Report, National Association for Youth Justice Campaign http://thenayj.org.uk/wp-content/files_mf/criminalisingchildrennov12.pdf.

Berlin, I, *Four Essays on Liberty* (Oxford University Press, 1969).

Bernardi, B, *Age Class Systems, Social Institutions and Politics Based on Age* (Cambridge University Press, 1985).

Blackham, A, 'Falling on Their Feet: Young Workers, Employment and Age Discrimination' (2015) 44 *Industrial Law Journal* 246.

Bloom, D, Canning, D and Fink, G, 'Implications of Population Ageing for Economic Growth' (2010) 26 *Oxford Review of Economic Policy* 583.

Blum, L, *'I'm Not a Racist, but …': The Moral Quandary of Race* (Cornell University Press, 2002).

Boghossian, P, 'What Is Social Construction?' [2001] *Times Literary Supplement*.

Bond, J, Coleman, P and Coleman, S (eds), *Ageing in Society: An Introduction to Social Gerontology* (SAGE Publications, 1993).

Boxill, B, *Blacks and Social Justice*, revised edn (Rowman & Littlefield, 1992).

Brady, A, *Proportionality and Deference under the UK Human Rights Act: An Institutionally Sensitive Approach* (Cambridge University Press, 2012).

Brandt, R, *A Theory of the Good and the Right* (Oxford University Press, 1979).

Brandt, R, 'The Science of Man and Wide Reflective Equilibrium' (1990) 100 *Ethics* 259.

Brest, P, 'In Defense of the Antidiscrimination Principle' (1976) 90 *Harvard Law Review* 1.
Brown A, *Personal Responsibility: Why It Matters* (Bloomsbury Publishing, 2009).
Brudney, J, 'Below the Surface: Comparing Legislative History Usage by the House of Lords and the Supreme Court' (2007) 85 *Washington University Law Review* 1.
Busetta, G et al, 'Searching for a Job is a Beauty Contest' (2013) https://mpra.ub.uni-muenchen.de/49392/2/.
Casal, P, 'Why Sufficiency Is Not Enough' (2007) 117 *Ethics* 296.
Cavanagh, M, *Against Equality of Opportunity* (Clarendon Press, 2002).
Centre for Policy on Ageing, 'The Likely Costs and Benefits of Legislation to Prohibit Age Discrimination in Health, Social Care and Mental Health Services and Definitions of Age Discrimination that might be Operationalised for Measurement' (2007) www.cpa.org.uk/information/reviews/CPA-age_discrimination_costs_report.pdf.
Centre for Policy on Ageing, 'Ageism and Age Discrimination in Primary and Community Health Care in the United Kingdom' (2009) www.cpa.org.uk/information/reviews/CPA-ageism_and_age_discrimination_in_primary_and_community_health_care-report.pdf.
Centre for Policy on Ageing, 'Ageism and Age Discrimination in Secondary Health Care in the United Kingdom' (2009) www.cpa.org.uk/information/reviews/CPAageism_and_age_discrimination_in_secondary_health_care-report.pdf.
Centre for Policy on Ageing, 'Ageism and Age Discrimination in Mental Health Care in the United Kingdom' (2009) www.cpa.org.uk/information/reviews/CPA-ageism_and_age_discrimination_in_mental_health_care-report.pdf.
Centre for Policy on Ageing, 'Ageism and Age Discrimination in Social Care in the United Kingdom' (2009) www.cpa.org.uk/information/reviews/CPA%20ageism_and_age_discrimination_in_social_care-report.pdf www.cpa.org.uk/information/reviews/CPA-age_discrimination.
Centre for Policy on Ageing, 'A Review of Age Discrimination in Primary and Community Health Care, Secondary Health Care, Mental Health Care and Social Care Services in the United Kingdom' (January 2010).
Chiu, W et al, 'Age Stereotypes and Discriminatory Attitudes towards Older Workers: An East–West Comparison' (2001) 54 *Human Relations* 629.
Cinneide, C, 'Age Discrimination and the European Court of Justice: EU Equality Law Comes of Age' (2009) 2 *Revue des Affaires Europeennes* 253.
Cinneide, C and Liu, K, 'Defining the Limits of Discrimination Law in the UK – Principle and Pragmatism in Tension' (2014) 14 *International Journal of Discrimination and the Law* 2.
Claxton, C, 'Wickedness or Folly? The Ethics of NICE's Decisions' (2006) 32 *Journal of Medical Ethics* 373.
Cohen, G, 'On the Currency of Egalitarian Justice' (1989) 99 *Ethics* 906.
Coleman, J, 'Efficiency, Utility, and Wealth Maximization' (1979) 8 *Hofstra Law Review* 509.
Collins, H, 'Discrimination, Equality and Social Inclusion' (2003) 66 *MLR* 16.
Constitution Committee, *Twenty-Fifth Report – Judicial Appointments* (HL 2010–12, 272).
Cupit, G, 'Justice, Age, and Veneration' (1998) 108 *Ethics* 702.
D'Agostino, F, 'Relativism and Reflective Equilibrium' (1998) 71 *The Monist* 420.
Daneker, M, 'Moral Reasoning and the Quest for Legitimacy' (1993) 43 *American University Law Review* 49.
Daniels, N, 'Wide Reflective Equilibrium and Theory Acceptance in Ethics' (1979) 76 *Journal of Philosophy* 256.
Daniels, N, *Am I My Parents' Keeper?* (Oxford University Press, 1998).
Daniels, N, 'Is There a Right to Health Care and, if so, What Does It Encompass? in H Kuhse and P Singer (eds), *A Companion to Bioethics*, 2nd edn (Wiley-Blackwell, 1998) 81.
Daniels, N, 'Justice between the Young and the Old' (1999) 30 *Philosophy and Public Affairs* 152.
Davies, A, 'Judicial Self-Restraint in Labour Law' (2009) 38 *Industrial Law Journal* (2009) 278.
Denizet-Lewis, B, 'The Man behind Abercrombie & Fitch' (*Salon*, 24 January 2006) www.salon.com/2006/01/24/jeffries/.

Dennett, D, *Elbow Room: The Varieties of Free Will Worth Wanting* (MIT Press, 1984).
Department for Trade and Industry, *Towards Equality and Diversity* (2001).
Department for Trade and Industry, *Age Matters. Age Consultation 2003: Summary of Responses* (2005).
Department for Trade and Industry, *Equality and Diversity: Coming of Age* (2005).
Department for Work and Pensions, *Workforce Management without a Fixed Retirement Age* (2011).
Dey, I and Fraser, N, 'Age-Based Rationing in the Allocation of Health Care' (2000) 12 *Journal of Aging and Health* 511.
Discrimination Law Review, *A Framework for Fairness: Proposals for a Single Equality Bill for Great Britain* (2007).
Dunn, C, 'The Effects of Ageing on Autonomy' in H Lesser (ed), *Ageing, Autonomy and Resources* (Ashgate, 1999) 7.
Dworkin, D, *Taking Rights Seriously* (Harvard University Press, 1977).
Dworkin, D, 'Is Wealth a Value?' (1980) 9 *Journal of Legal Studies* 191.
Dworkin, D, 'What is Equality? Part 1: Equality of Welfare' (1981) 10 *Philosophy and Public Affairs* 185.
Dworkin, D, 'What is Equality? Part 2: Equality of Resources' (1981) 10 *Philosophy and Public Affairs* 283.
Dworkin, D, 'Rights as Trumps' in J Waldron (ed), *Theories of Rights* (Oxford University Press, 1984) 153.
Dworkin, D, *A Matter of Principle* (Harvard University Press, 1985).
Dworkin, D, 'Affirming Affirmative Action' (1998) 45 *New York Review of Books* 1.
Dworkin, D, 'Affirmative Action: Is It Fair?' (2000) 28 *Journal of Blacks in Higher Education* 79.
Dworkin, D, *Sovereign Virtue: The Theory and Practice of Equality* (Harvard University Press, 2002).
Edlin, R et al, 'Cost-Effectiveness Analysis and Ageism: A Review of the Theoretical Literature [Prepared for the Department of Health]' (Leeds Institute of Health Sciences, 2008).
Eidelson, B, *Discrimination and Disrespect* (Oxford University Press, 2015).
Elder, G, 'Age Differentiation and the Life Course' (1975) 1 *Annual Review of Sociology* 165.
Elliot, M, 'Proportionality and Deference: The Importance of a Structured Approach' (2013) University of Cambridge Faculty of Law Research Paper No 32.
Ely, J, *Democracy and Distrust* (Harvard University Press, 1980).
Epstein, R, *Forbidden Grounds: The Case against Employment Discrimination Laws* (Harvard University Press, 1992).
European Commission, *Towards a Europe for All Ages – Promoting Prosperity and Intergenerational Solidarity* (Com No 221, 1999).
Evans, G, 'Age Discrimination: Implications of the Ageing Process' in S Fredman and S Spencer (eds), *Age as an Equality Issue* (Hart Publishing, 2003) 20.
Feldman, D, *Civil Liberties and Human Rights in England and Wales* (Oxford University Press, 2002) 229.
Fingarette, H, *The Meaning of Criminal Insanity* (University of California Press, 1972).
Finnis, J, *Natural Law and Natural Rights* (Clarendon Press, 1980).
Finnis, J, *Fundamentals of Ethics* (Georgetown University Press, 1983) 66–67.
Fiss, O, 'A Theory of Fair Employment Laws' (1971) 38 *University of Chicago Law Review* 235.
Fiss, O, 'The Fate of an Idea Whose Time Has Come: Anti-discrimination Law in the Second Decade after Brown v Board of Education' (1974) 41 *University of Chicago Law Review* 742.
Fiss, O, 'Groups and the Equal Protection Clause' (1976) 5 *Philosophy and Public Affairs* 157.
Fleurbaey, M, 'Equal Opportunity or Equal Social Outcome?' (1995) 11 *Economics and Philosophy* 25.
Flew, A, 'Three Concepts of Racism' (1990) 75 *Encounter* 63.
Frankfurt, H, 'Alternate Possibilities and Moral Responsibility' (1969) 66 *Journal of Philosophy* 829.
Frankfurt, H, *Necessity, Volition, and Love* (Cambridge University Press, 1999).
Fredman, S, 'What Do We Mean by Age Equality' (2001) Paper presented to the IPPR Seminar on Age as an Equality Issue, 30.
Fredman, S, 'The Age of Equality' in S Fredman and S Spencer (eds), *Age as an Equality Issue: Legal and Policy Perspectives* (Hart Publishing, 2003).

Fredman, S, 'Transformation or Dilution: Fundamental Rights in the EU Social Space' (2006) 12 *European Law Journal* 41.
Fredman, S, *Discrimination Law*, 2nd edn (Oxford University Press, 2011).
Fuller, L, 'The Forms and Limits of Adjudication' (1978–79) 92 *Harvard Law Review* 353.
Gardner, J, 'On the Ground of Her Sex(uality)' (1998) 18 *OJLS* 167.
Gibb, F, 'Let Judges Work Past 70 to Ease Recruitment Crisis, Peers Told' *The Times* (30 March 2017) www.thetimes.co.uk/edition/news/let-judges-work-past-70-to-ease-recruitment-crisis-peers-told-fdvj9ddpd.
Giddens, A, *The Third Way: The Renewal of Social Democracy* (John Wiley & Sons, 2013).
Goffman, E, 'The Interaction Order' (1983) 48 *American Sociological Review* 1.
Goldson, B, 'Counterblast: "Difficult to Understand or Defend: A Reasoned Case for Raising the Age of Criminal Responsibility"' (2009) 48 *The Howard Journal* 514.
Goosey, S, 'Is Age Discrimination a Less Serious Form of Discrimination?' (2019) 39 *Legal Studies* 533.
Gorard, S and Siddique, N, 'Grammar Schools in England: a New Analysis of Social Segregation and Academic Outcomes' (2018) 39 *British Journal of Sociology of Education* 909.
Gosseries, A, and Hungerbühler, M, 'Rule Change and Intergenerational Justice' in J Tremmel (ed), *Handbook of Intergenerational Justice* (Edward Elgar Publishing, 2006) 106.
Gosseries, A, and Hungerbühler, M, 'What Makes Age Discrimination Special? A Philosophical Look at the ECJ Case Law' (2014) 43 *Netherlands Journal of Legal Philosophy* 59.
Government Equalities Office, *Equality Bill: Making it Work. Policy Proposals for Specific Duties* (2010).
Government Equalities Office, *The Equality Act 2010: Banning Age Discrimination in Services* (2011).
Greenawalt, K, 'How Empty Is the Idea of Equality?' (1983) 83 *Columbia Law Review* 1167.
Haidt, J, 'The New Synthesis in Moral Psychology' (2007) 316 *Science* 998.
Harper, R, Reforming the Age Discrimination in Employment Act: Proposals and Prospects 16 (2012) *Employment Rights & Employment Policy Journal* 13.
J Harris, 'The Age-Indifference Principle and Equality' (2005) 14 *Cambridge Quarterly of Healthcare Ethics* 93.
Harris, J, 'It's Not NICE to Discriminate' (2005) 31 *Journal of Medical Ethics* 373.
Hart, HLA, *The Concept of Law*, 2nd edn (Clarendon Press, 1994).
Hayek, F, *The Constitution of Liberty* (Routledge, 1960).
Hayek, F, *The Road to Serfdom* (Routledge, 2014).
Hellman, D and Moreau, S (eds), *Philosophical Foundations of Discrimination Law* (Oxford University Press, 2013).
Hellman, D and Moreau, S, *When Is Discrimination Wrong?* (Harvard University Press, 2008).
Hoffmann, L, 'The Separation of Powers' (2002) 7 *Judicial Review* 137.
Holmes, E, 'Anti-discrimination Rights without Equality' (2005) 68 *MLR* 175.
Hooker, B, *Ideal Code, Real World: A Rule-Consequentialist Theory of Morality* (Oxford University Press, 2000).
Horner, K, 'A Growing Problem: Why the Federal Government Needs to Shoulder the Burden in Protecting Workers from Weight Discrimination' (2004) 54 *Catholic University Law Review* 589.
Hume, D, *An Enquiry Concerning Human Understanding*, P Nidditch, ed (Clarendon Press, 1978).
Hutton, J, Horowitz-Kraus, T, Mendelsohn, A, DeWitt, T, Holland, S and the C-MIND Authorship Consortium, 'Home Reading Environment and Brain Activation in Preschool Children Listening to Stories' (2015) 136 *Pediatrics* 466.
Intergenerational Fairness and Provision Committee, *Tackling Intergenerational Unfairness* (HL, 2017–19).
Issacharoff, S and Harris, E, 'Is Age Discrimination Really Age Discrimination: The ADEA's Unnatural Solution' (1997) 72 *New York University Law Review* 780.
Jarvie, G et al, 'Childhood Obesity and Social Stigma: What We Know and What We Don't Know' (1983) 3 *Developmental Review* 237.
John, B, 'Patterns of Ageism in Different Age Groups' (2013) 4 *Journal of European Psychology Students* 16.

Joint Committee on Human Rights, *The Human Rights of Older People in Healthcare* (HL 2006–07, 156-I; HC 2006–07, 278-I).
Jowell, J, 'Judicial Deference: Servility, Civility or Institutional Capacity?' [2003] (Winter) *PL* 592.
Jowell, J, 'Judicial Deference and Human Rights: Question of Competence' in P Craig and R Rawlings (eds), *Law and Administration in Europe: Essays in Honour of Carol Harlow* (Oxford University Press, 2003) 80.
Joyce, R, *The Evolution of Morality* (MIT Press, 2006).
Kant, I, *Groundwork of the Metaphysics of Morals*, Mary Gregor tr, ed (Cambridge University Press, 1998).
Katz, S and Marshall, B, 'New Sex for Old: Lifestyle, Consumerism, and the Ethics of Ageing Well' (2003) 17 *Journal of Ageing Studies* 3.
Kavanagh, A, 'Original Intention, Enacted Text, and Constitutional Interpretation' (2002) 47 *American Journal of Jurisprudence* 255.
Kavanagh, A, 'Judicial Restraint in the Pursuit of Justice' (2010) 60 *University of Toronto Law Journal* 23.
Khaitan, T, *A Theory of Discrimination Law* (Oxford University Press, 2015).
King, J, 'The Pervasiveness of Polycentricity' [2008] *PL* 101.
King, J, 'Institutional Approaches to Judicial Restraint' (2008) 28 *OJLS* 425.
Knight, C, 'The Injustice of Discrimination' (2013) 32 *South African Journal of Philosophy* 55.
Kronman, A, 'Wealth Maximization as a Normative Principle' (1980) 9 *Journal of Legal Studies* 227.
Krugman, P, *The Return of Depression Economics and the Crisis of 2008* (WW Norton & Company, 2009).
Kumm, M, 'The Idea of Socratic Contestation and the Right to Justification: The Point of Rights Based Proportionality Review' (2010) 4 *Law & Ethics of Human Rights* 140.
Kutner, L, 'How Children Develop Empathy' http://psychcentral.com/lib/how-children-develop-empathy/0001234.
Lacey, N, 'Legislation against Sex Discrimination: Questions from a Feminist Perspective' (1987) 14 *Journal of Law and Society* 411.
Lazear, E, 'Why Is There Mandatory Retirement?' (1979) 87 *Journal of Political Economy* 1261.
Levy, B et al, 'A Culture–Brain Link: Negative Age Stereotypes Predict Alzheimer's Disease Biomarkers' (2016) 31 *Psychology and Aging* 82.
Lippert-Rasmussen, K, 'Equality, Option Luck, and Responsibility' (2001) 111 *Ethics* 548.
Lippert-Rasmussen, K, 'Discrimination and Equality' in A Marmor (ed), *Routledge Companion to Philosophy of Law* (Routledge, 2012) 569.
Lippert-Rasmussen, K, *Born Free and Equal? A Philosophical Inquiry into the Nature of Discrimination* (Oxford University Press, 2014).
Lippert-Rasmussen, K, 'Justice and Bad Luck' in E Zalta (ed), *The Stanford Encyclopedia of Philosophy*, Summer 2014 edn https://plato.stanford.edu/archives/sum2014/entries/justice-bad-luck/.
Lowe, R, 'Childhood through the Ages' in T Maynard and N Thomas (eds), *An Introduction to Early Childhood Studies* (SAGE Publications, 2004) 65.
MacIntyre, A, 'Determinism' (1957) 66 *Mind* 28.
Macrae, N, Stangor, C and Hewstone, M (eds), *Stereotypes and Stereotyping* (Guilford Press, 1996).
Marino, P, 'Moral Coherence and Value Pluralism' (2013) 43 *Canadian Journal of Philosophy* 117.
Marshall, W and Tanner, J, 'Variations in Pattern of Pubertal Changes in Girls' (1969) 44 *Archives of Disease in Childhood* 291.
Marshall, W and Tanner, J, 'Variations in the Pattern of Pubertal Changes in Boys' (1970) 45 *Archives of Disease in Childhood* 13.
Mason, A, 'XI – Equality, Personal Responsibility, and Gender Socialisation' (2000) 100 *Proceedings of the Aristotelian Society* 227.
Mason, A, *Levelling the Playing Field: The Idea of Equality of Opportunity and Its Place in Egalitarian Thought* (Oxford University Press, 2006).
McCrudden, C, 'Theorising European Equality Law' in C Costello and E Barry (eds), *Equality in Diversity: The New Equality Directives* (Irish Centre for European Law, 2003).

McDiarmid, C, 'An Age of Complexity: Children and Criminal Responsibility in Law' (2013) 13 *Youth Justice* 145.
McEvoy, G and Cascio, W, 'Cumulative Evidence of the Relationship between Employee Age and Job Performance' (1989) 74 *Journal of Applied Psychology* 11.
McKerlie, D, 'Equality and Time' (1989) 99 *Ethics* 475.
McKerlie, D, 'Equality between Age-Groups' (1992) 21 *Philosophy & Public Affairs* 275.
Mill, JS, 'Utilitarianism' in R Shafer-Landau (ed), *Ethical Theory: An Anthology* (John Wiley & Sons, 2012).
Miller, D, 'Equality and Justice' (1997) 10 *Ratio* 222.
Miller, D, 'What Kind of Equality Should the Left Pursue' in J Franklin (ed), *Equality* (Institute for Public Policy Research, 1997).
Miller, D, *Principles of Social Justice* (Harvard University Press, 1999).
Möller, K, 'Proportionality: Challenging the Critics' (2012) 10 *International Journal of Constitutional Law* 709.
Moreau, S, 'The Wrongs of Unequal Treatment' (2004) 54 *University of Toronto Law Journal* 291.
Moreau, S, 'What Is Discrimination?' (2010) 38 *Philosophy and Public Affairs* 143.
Nagel, T, *Mortal Questions* (Cambridge University Press, 1979).
Nagel, T, *The View from Nowhere* (Oxford University Press, 1986).
Nagel, T, *Equality and Priority* (Oxford University Press, 1991).
National Institute for Care and Health Excellence, 'Judging Whether Public Health Interventions Offer Value for Money' (September 2013) www.nice.org.uk/advice/lgb10/chapter/introduction.
National Institute for Care and Health Excellence, 'What We Do' www.nice.org.uk/about/what-we-do.
National Institute for Care and Health Excellence, 'Fertility Problems: Assessment and Treatment' (2013) www.nice.org.uk/guidance/cg156.
National Institute for Care and Health Excellence, 'Citizens Council' www.nice.org.uk/get-involved/citizens-council.
Neugarten, B, Moore, J and Lowe, J, 'Age Norms, Age Constraints, and Adult Socialization' (1965) 70 *American Journal of Sociology* 710.
Neugarten, D (ed), *The Meanings of Age: Selected Papers of Bernice L Neugarten* (University of Chicago Press, 1996).
Nozick, R, *Anarchy, State and Utopia* (Basic Books, 1974).
Nozick, R, Philosophical Explanations (Harvard University Press, 1981).
Otsuka, M, 'Luck, Insurance, and Equality' (2002) 113 *Ethics* 40.
Parsons, T, 'Age and Sex in the Social Structure of the United States' (1942) 7 *American Sociological Review* 604.
Phillips, A, 'Defending Equality of Outcome' (2004) 12 *Journal of Political Philosophy* 1.
Posner, R, 'The Ethical and Political Basis of the Efficiency Norm in Common Law Adjudication' (1979) 8 *Hofstra Law Review* 487.
Posner, R, 'Utilitarianism, Economics, and Legal Theory' (1979) 8 *Journal of Legal Studies* 103.
Posner, R, 'An Economic Analysis of Sex Discrimination Laws' (1989) 56 *University of Chicago Law Review* 1311.
Posner, R, *Aging and Old Age* (University of Chicago Press, 1995).
Posner, R, *The Problematics of Moral and Legal Theory* (Harvard University Press, 2009).
Pritchard-Jones, L, 'Ageism and Autonomy in Health Care: Explorations through a Relational Lens' (2014) 25 *Health Care Analysis* 72.
Puhl, R and Brownell, K, 'Bias, Discrimination, and Obesity' (2001) 9 *Obesity* 788.
Puhl, R, Andreyeva, T and Brownell, K, 'Perceptions of Weight Discrimination: Prevalence and Comparison to Race and Gender Discrimination in America' (2008) 32 *International Journal of Obesity* 992.
Pust, J, 'Intuition' in E Zalta (ed), *The Stanford Encyclopedia of Philosophy*, Spring 2016 edn https://plato.stanford.edu/archives/spr2016/entries/intuition/.
Quigley, M, 'A Nice Fallacy' (2007) 33 *Journal of Medical Ethics* 465.

Rawlins, M, 'Pharmacopolitics and Deliberative Democracy' (2005) 5 *Clinical Medicine* 471.
Rawls, J, *A Theory of Justice* (Harvard University Press, 2009).
Raz, J, *The Morality of Freedom* (Clarendon Press, 1986).
Réaume, D, 'Discrimination and Dignity' (2003) 63 *Louisiana Law Review* 645.
Reinharz, S, 'The Embeddedness of Age: Toward a Social Control Perspective' (1987) 1 *Journal of Aging Studies* 77.
Rivers, J, 'Proportionality and Variable Intensity of Review' (2006) 65 *CLJ* 174.
Roemer, J, 'A Pragmatic Theory of Responsibility for the Egalitarian Planner' (1993) 22 *Philosophy & Public Affairs* 146.
Roemer, J, *Equality of Opportunity* (Cambridge University Press, 1998).
Rosario, M et al, 'Sexual Identity Development among Lesbian, Gay, and Bisexual Youths: Consistency and Change Over Time' (2006) 43 *Journal of Sex Research* 46.
Ross, D and Ross, WD, *The Right and the Good* (Oxford University Press, 2002).
Royal College of Psychiatrists, 'A Collective Responsibility to Act Now on Ageing and Mental Health: A Consensus Statement' (Mental Health and Older People Forum, 2008).
Royal College of Psychiatrists, 'The Need to Tackle Age Discrimination in Mental Health – A Compendium of Evidence' (2009).
Sangiovanni, A, 'Global Justice, Reciprocity, and the State' (2007) 35 *Philosophy & Public Affairs* (2007) 3.
Sargeant, M, *Age Discrimination in Employment* (Routledge, 2016).
Scanlon, T, 'The Significance of Choice' (1998) 8 *The Tanner Lectures on Human Values* 149.
Scheffler, S, 'Responsibility, Reactive Attitudes, and Liberalism in Philosophy and Politics' (1992) 21 *Philosophy and Public Affairs* 299.
Scheffler, S, 'What Is Egalitarianism?' (2003) 31 *Philosophy and Public Affairs* 5.
Schroeter, F, 'Reflective Equilibrium and Anti-theory' (2004) 38 *Noûs* 110.
Segall, S, 'What's so Bad about Discrimination?' (2012) 24 *Utilitas* 82.
Segall, S, *Equality and Opportunity* (Oxford University Press, 2013)
Segev, R, 'Making Sense of Discrimination' (2014) 27 *Ratio Juris* 47.
Sen, A, 'Equality of What?' (1979) *The Tanner Lectures on Human Values* 197.
Sen, A, *Inequality Reexamined* (Clarendon Press, 1992).
Shapiro, D, 'In Defense of Judicial Candor' (1987) 100 *Harvard Law Review* 731.
Sherwin, S, *No Longer Patient: Feminist Ethics and Health Care Philadelphia* (Temple University Press, 1992).
Singer, P, 'Ethics and Intuitions' (2005) 9 *Journal of Ethics* 331.
Smedley, A and Smedley, B, 'Race as Biology Is Fiction, Racism as a Social Problem Is Real: Anthropological and Historical Perspectives on the Social Construction of Race' (2005) 60 *American Psychologist* 16.
Smilansky, S, 'Egalitarian Justice and the Importance of the Free Will Problem' (1997) 25 *Philosophia* 153.
Smith, M, 'Review Lectures on Senescence. I. The Causes of Ageing' (1962) 157 *Proceedings of the Royal Society of London B: Biological Sciences* 115.
Smith, P and Morton, G, 'New Labour's Reform of Britain's Employment Law: The Devil is Not Only in the Detail but in the Values and Policy too' (2001) 39 *British Journal of Industrial Relations* 119.
Solanke, I, *Discrimination as Stigma: A Theory of Anti-discrimination Law* (Bloomsbury, 2017).
Stemplowska, Z, 'Making Justice Sensitive to Responsibility' (2009) 57 *Political Studies* 237.
Stevens, A et al, 'National Institute for Health and Clinical Excellence Appraisal and Ageism' (2012) 38 *Journal of Medical Ethics* 258.
Strawson, P, 'Freedom and Resentment' (1962) 48 *Proceedings of the British Academy* 1.
Sunstein, C, 'The Anticaste Principle' (1994) 92 *Michigan Law Review* 2410.
Sunstein, C, *Legal Reasoning and Political Conflict* (Oxford University Press, 1998).
Syrett, K, 'NICE and Judicial Review: Enforcing "Accountability for Reasonableness" through the Courts?' (2008) 16 *Medical Law Review* 127.

Temkin, L, 'Equality, Priority, and the Levelling Down Objection' in M Clayton and A Williams (eds), *The Ideal of Equality* (Macmillan, 2000) 126.
Temkin, L, 'Egalitarianism Defended' (2003) 113 *Ethics* 63.
Thomas, WH and Feldman, D, 'The Relationship of Age to Ten Dimensions of Job Performance' (2008) 93 *Journal Applied Psychology* 392.
Tsakyrakis, S, 'Proportionality: An Assault on Human Rights?' (2009) 7 *International Journal of Constitutional Law* 468.
Tuvel, R, 'In Defense of Transracialism' (2017) 32 *Hypatia: A Journal of Feminist Philosophy* 263.
Urbina, F, '"Balancing as Reasoning" and the Problems of Legally Unaided Adjudication: A Reply to Kai Möller' (2014) 12 *International Journal of Constitutional Law* 1214.
Vallentyne, P, 'Brute Luck, Option Luck, and Equality of Initial Opportunities' (2002) 112 *Ethics* 529.
Vallentyne, P, 'Brute Luck and Responsibility' (2008) 7 *Politics, Philosophy & Economics* 57.
van Parijs, P, *Arguing for Basic Income* (Verso Books, 1992).
van Thiel, G and van Delden, J, 'Reflective Equilibrium as a Normative Empirical Model' (2010) 17 *Ethical Perspectives-Katholieke Universiteit Leuven* 183.
van der Burg, W and van Willigenburg, T (eds), *Reflective Equilibrium: Essays in Honour of Robert Heeger*, vol 2 (Springer Science & Business Media, 2012) 5.
Waldron, J, 'Judges as Moral Reasoners' (2009) 7 *International Journal of Constitutional Law* 2.
Warren, K, 'The Power and Promise of Ecological Feminism' (1990) *Environmental Ethics* 125.
Watson, G, 'Reason and Responsibility' (2001) 111 *Ethics* 374.
Westen, P, 'The Empty Idea of Equality' (1982) 95 *Harvard Law Review* 537.
Willetts, D, *The Pinch: How the Baby Boomers Took Their Children's Future – and Why They Should Give It Back* (Atlantic Books, 2011).
Williams, A, 'Intergenerational Equity: An Exploration of the "Fair Innings" Argument' (1997) 6 *Health Economics* 117.
Williams, A, 'The Value of QALYs' in S Holland (ed), *Arguing About Bioethics* (Routledge, 2012) 423.
Williams, B, *Moral Luck* (Cambridge University Press, 1981).
Wolff, J, 'Fairness, Respect, and the Egalitarian Ethos' (1998) 27 *Philosophy & Public Affairs* 97.
Young, I, *Justice and the Politics of Difference* (Princeton University Press, 2011).
Young, M, *The Metronomic Society: Natural Rhythms and Human Timetables* (Thames and Hudson, 1988).
Zakrzewski, K, 'The Prevalence of "Look"ism in Hiring Decisions: How Federal Law should be Amended to Prevent Appearance Discrimination in the Workplace' (2004) 7 *University of Pennsylvania Journal of Labor and Employment Law* 431.

# INDEX

www.ingramcontent.com/pod-product-compliance
Ingram Content Group UK Ltd.
Pitfield, Milton Keynes, MK11 3LW, UK
UKHW020815290926
15470UKWH00003B/1165